JUST A GUY

An Autobiography by the Quiet Founder of ESPN
DON RASMUSSEN

Copyright © 2013 Don Rasmussen
All rights reserved.
ISBN: 1482742020
ISBN 13: 9781482742022
Library of Congress Control Number: 2013904915
CreateSpace Independent Publishing Platform
North Charleston, South Carolina

TABLE OF CONTENTS

PROLOGUE v

FAMILY
- Chapter 1   The Family Through Young Don 1
- Chapter 2   A Rough Ride 17
- Chapter 3   Coping With Irrational Behavior 29
- Chapter 4   The Anatomy of a Dysfunctional Family 41
- Chapter 5   Beth 47
- Chapter 6   My Growing Family 55

SCHOOLING:
- Chapter 7   Early Strides in Education 83
- Chapter 8   High School and a Taste of Normalcy 93
- Chapter 9   High School: Education beyond the Classroom .. 109
- Chapter 10 Transition: The Hard, Cold Facts of Life 125
- Chapter 11 College On My Own 133
- Chapter 12 I Did It My Way 143

WORKING:
- Chapter 13 Jobs 159
- Chapter 14 The Air Force Years 169
- Chapter 15 Substitute Teaching and The New Jersey Fiasco .. 193
- Chapter 16 New and Different Careers 209
- Chapter 17 Experimentation – A New Business and My Final Job in Education 225
- Chapter 18 Ownership of ESPN 233

Chapter 19	ESPN Job	247
Chapter 20	Enterprise Radio & Group W	263
Chapter 21	Texas : ESPN Ownership Conclusion and MER Properties	273
Chapter 22	Tearoom and Diner	291
Chapter 23	The Telephone Call: Analysis and Conclusion	309

THE WRAP UP

Chapter 24	My Roller Coaster Health	323
Chapter 25	Sports: Yeah I was an Athlete	341
Chapter 26	Building a Personal Philosophy	365
Chapter 27	Retirement: The Adventure of Aging	369

EPILOGUE 377

ACKNOWLEDGEMENTS 381

BIBLIOGRAPHY 383

PROLOGUE

My life has been a bumpy ride emotionally, mentally, and physically.

Depression, anxiety, and fear of not belonging have lurked in the shadows and leaped out from time to time to paralyze me, only to be confronted and beaten back.

From feelings of inadequacy and frustration to the elation of accomplishment and success and back again, and I wonder, "Why am I afraid of roller coasters?" and I realize that I have been on one most of my life.

The family you are born into is forever, and knowledge of your grandparents and the way they lived with their families also have an impact on your life.

Unfortunately, most people do not have an awareness of their grandparents. I was not one of those. Due to my wife's research, I learned of my grandfathers life, and that knowledge unlocked doors to my emotional instabilities and allowed me to reach the point that I am at today—almost normal, whatever that is, or at least, comfortable with who I am.

It is hoped that my children, grandchildren, as well as students of family life interrelationships will enjoy this personal history.

FAMILY

Chapter I

THE FAMILY THROUGH YOUNG DON

During the last two decades of the nineteenth century, immigration to the United States was burgeoning, primarily from Europe. The Danish were no exception to this movement. Thousands of Danes came to America seeking a better life, and Chicago became an inviting destination. Chicago was to become the densest population for Danish immigrants in America.

Among those was Peter Arnold Christian Rasmussen, who arrived in Chicago in 1892 and immediately started plying his trade, which was as a glazier. He was an expert at making leaded stain glass windows. Many of Chicago's finest buildings constructed in the last decade of the nineteenth century have examples of his work.

His wife, Emma Margrethe Frederikke Christiansen, and the couple's four daughters immigrated to the United States approximately a year later. The birth of the fourth daughter is speculated to be the reason the family couldn't travel together in 1892.

Once in this country, Emma Margrethe dropped her first name and became known as Margrethe. She also made sure that everyone who became familiar with the family knew they were now Americans, and she committed herself to learn English.

When the girls started school and began to learn the language, Margrethe required them to teach her and not to speak Danish in the home.

Carl Johannes Thorvold Rasmussen followed his brother to America in 1906. Since he also was a glazier, he went to work with his brother.

Carl was known to the family in Denmark and America as Thorvold. Everyone else that he met and knew would call him Carl.

The reason Carl didn't bring his family with him was strictly because he could not afford to get them to the United States. Working with Arnold, he would save part of his earnings each week to put toward the day his family could travel to Chicago. To better assure Carl that his money would be saved in a proper fashion, Arnold advised Carl to give him the money he was saving and he would see to it that Carl would not be able to spend any money that he was saving inadvertently. Carl, knowing that his big brother would look after his money properly, turned his funds over to his brother.

Later, when Carl knew that he had saved up enough to go and get his family, he asked Arnold for his money. Arnold didn't have the money anymore. What he might have spent the money on is open to conjecture; however, it was well known about town that Arnold was a "Dandy."

More than disappointed in his brother, Carl returned to Denmark to reunite his family and earn the funds to travel across the ocean again, this time with his family in tow.

He had left Chicago a year and a half after arriving, and it took him until 1913 to be able to return to what he knew was truly the land of opportunity. He lived and worked in the Windy City until 1918 when he was part of an exodus of Danes to Wisconsin.

Before he left, he witnessed the bankruptcy of his older brother in 1915.

Arnold had accumulated a large number of properties in the Chicago area, leveraging one piece of land against another. Some of the land was in prime locations, such as Sixty-Third and Halsted that housed The Englewood Glass Company, which was to outlast Arnold and as of this writing, still exists today. This old corporation is now located in Oak Lawn, a southwest Chicago suburb that has annexed Columbus Manor, where I was raised. The business that did Arnold in was The Hamlet Inn, which he owned in partnership with a man named Victor C. Anderson.

Within six months of taking over this business, both men had declared bankruptcy and the Englewood Glass Company was lost in the process.

As a teenager, I played baseball across the street from the Englewood Glass Company on sixty-second and Damen and I knew of my Grandfather's connection with the company, as his picture still hung on the wall when I walked into the building during the fifties.

With my lifelong love affair with baseball, I found it interesting that the head judge in the bankruptcy case of Arnold Rasmussen, was Kenesaw Mountain Landis of the Northern Federal District of Illinois. Within five years Landis would become the first commissioner of baseball, charged with cleaning up baseball and ridding the sport of gamblers. In the move to do this, he established a severe penalty for associating with gamblers and signaled his stern intent by suspending the eight members of the Chicago White Sox for their suspected mingling with gamblers. The suspensions were permanent.

When Carl arrived in Hayward, he began building a home on farmland that he had acquired. The home would house him, his wife, and their four children.

As he was building his home, Arnold showed up to help, but did little to no work on the home, preferring to spend his time carousing with the ladies in town.

The two brothers were opposite in their lifestyles. Arnold chose to be a risk taker and live his life in the fast lane, while Carl was hard working, responsible, and steadfast.

Arnold moved on to Detroit and later to Greenwich Village, where he spent most of his life until his death at the age of seventy-nine. It was said by family members that he had returned to see his wife in Chicago one time. When he died, two of his sons, Arnold and my dad, went out east to fetch his body and return him to Chicago for burial. There never was a divorce, and when his wife died, she was laid to rest next to her husband.

On my mother's side of the family, my grandpa Franklin Newton O'Connor was an absolute favorite of mine, and the only grandparent that I knew. He worked for the United States Post Office and was a totally committed baseball fan.

I probably remember farther back than anything else in my life, sitting on Grandpa O'Connor's lap, as he went over the 1906 World Series between the Cubs and White Sox, game by game. This was supposed to be a wipe out of a series in favor of the Cubs, the greatest team in the history of the game. The Cubs had won 116 games that year, and the Sox came into the World Series as "The Hitless Wonders."

The Sox won the World Series four games to two. This was undoubtedly the greatest thing that ever happened in Grandpa's life, as he related it to me every chance he got for year after year.

Grandpa gave each of us kids a brand new wristwatch when we graduated from grade school. What a cool thing that was. He also gave Dad $250 for my college education. I assume he also had done the same for Bill and Bob.

With this versatile background of my grandparents, my parents were born into different levels of society. Arnold, the businessman, Carl, the laborer, and Franklin, the middle-class government worker as a postman for the post office.

Dad came into this world on January 11, 1908, the eleventh child of Arnold and Margrethe. He had four brothers and six sisters. Mom was born on December 19, 1910. She was a somewhat spoiled child and when she wanted a baby sister, her parents accommodated her by adopting a sister for her. At this time Mom was about sixteen years old. What a choice they made. My Aunt Florence has been, throughout my life, my favorite aunt. Dad has told me that it was Florence that taught me how to walk. I was kind of slow developing, and Aunt Florence would have me put my feet on hers and she would walk backward for more than an hour at a time.

As a young adult, I would occasionally have this dream where I was standing on someone's feet and be walking. The craziness of the dream was that I was five foot ten, and I came up to the waist of the person whose feet I was walking on. There is probably a case of some kind that can be made by a psychologist over that dream. Mom also had an older brother. His name was Robert, so I assume that my brother was named after him.

When Dad was young, his mother baked and sold confectioneries, and the older girls worked in vaudeville as pianists to support the younger children. As each child became old enough to work, the life of those remaining became somewhat easier.

The family lived in a small house on the southwest side of Chicago in the area known as West Englewood. A Quonset hut was built in the backyard for the boys to sleep in. That was a workable way to survive and maintain a modicum of family structure and sanity. The family remained very close for years. My earliest remembrance of the family was frequent gatherings in the basement, where it appears the family lived most of the time. I was in my teens before I ever saw the upstairs area of the house. I was escorted by my Aunt Jeff when I asked about the rest of the house.

The family was secretive about much of their life. An example of this secrecy I learned about as an adult was that my Aunt Alma was a concert pianist. According to all that I asked about her piano playing, she was the most accomplished of all the girls. When I asked, "Why did she stop playing?" The subject was always changed. Finally, when Aunt Jeff realized that I would not stop asking until my curiosity was satisfied, she sat me down and told me about the argument that Aunt Alma had with her husband, in what was a stormy marriage. He concluded the disagreement by stabbing her with a large knife. Alma put her hand up in front of her face to protect herself and the blade caught her flush in the middle of her palm, severing several tendons. She lost use of a couple of her fingers for the rest of her life.

As the youngest son of the youngest brother, I didn't really know my aunts very well, except for Aunt Jeff. When I heard of this sad story, it upset me deeply and I couldn't think of much else for close to a week, and when I think of Aunt Alma today, it is always with a heavy heart.

The prime area of secrecy was the split between Arnold and his brother, Carl. I didn't learn of the existence of Carl and his family until Beth established the unequivocal fact of their existence through the work she had been doing on genealogy. She then set out to find what she could about the family.

Through her genealogy network, she found a gentleman by the name of Gilbert Rasmussen (no relation) who had moved to Hayward, Wisconsin, from Chicago with Carl, my great uncle. Gilbert called me, and we had a long talk on the phone. This led to me learning that Carl's daughter was celebrating her ninety-ninth birthday in about a week. We were so excited about the discovery that I drove from Texas to Hayward to participate in the celebration. It was an extremely broadening experience for me. Not only did I meet family that I didn't know existed, but I learned that Johanna, the object of my journey, had a son who lived just down the street from me in East Peoria, Illinois, when I was the junior high school principal in District Fifty, just east of East Peoria. All of the daughters of Carl had driven past my home on the way to see Alan Thannum, my cousin, whose children had gone to high school with my daughters.

This family background is probably more or less than normal of most families of the era.

Dad dropped out of high school as a sophomore and went to work. He was initially a bank messenger, being led into this area of endeavor by his older brother Arnold. His father had given his name, as a middle name to four of the sons, but Arnold had no middle name. From this humble beginning, Dad worked himself up to being a clerk and then a cashier. His primary non-working activities revolved around sports, particularly in his late teens, playing football for the Boyle's Black Devils along with brothers Arnold and Elmer. The team was owned, sponsored, and coached by John Boyle, a federal judge occupying the same position that Kenesaw Mountain Landis had.

My Aunt Jeff was the "Mother Hen" of the team, sewing uniforms, tending minor injuries, etc. I didn't learn much about the team, as the only thing Dad would ever talk about was the time the Black Devils played a game against the Chicago Cardinals, and Jim Counselman, the Cardinals coach, commented to John Boyle that although his boys were generally smaller than the Cards, they acquitted themselves well.

This bit of information was emphasized at my Aunt Jeff's eightieth birthday party, which included the surviving members of the team. It was June 6, 1971, and I was in the area, so I decided to swing by and see Aunt Jeff, not an unusual thing for me to do. I did not know that a party was in progress, but for the cars in the area, I knew something was going on, and if Jeff caught wind of the fact that I might have been seen and didn't come in to see her, I would have been in her doghouse. So, being totally ignorant of her birthday, I rang the bell.

I was yelled in, and when Dad saw me, he came over and asked about my invitation. Of course, I didn't have one. That led to a quiet, lengthy discussion about courtesy. Eventually that wound down, and he told me that there was someone there that he wanted me to meet.

He took me over to a corner and introduced me to Pete Spoo, a member of the team. I was pleased to meet him, since I played briefly with his son, Bob, in 1955 when he played a few games with the JC Colts at Sherman Park. Bob caught for us, and I remembered him as having the strongest throwing arm of any catcher I ever played with.

In general discussion with him, I learned that he was heading to Purdue, where he would earn his bachelor's degree and play football for the Boilermakers. He would later become the longtime football coach at Eastern Illinois University, from which I earned my master's degree, prior to his arrival.

I just think it was pretty cool that our fathers played football on the same team, and coincidentally, for a short time we played on the same baseball team.

Mom dropped out of high school and went to work. She never talked about her life before she and Dad married, so the only information we have was provided by her sister. I got the idea from Aunt Florence that, although she was adopted because Mom wanted a sister, the two never did form any kind of sibling togetherness. Aunt Florence did tell me, that, generally, Mom liked to party and never missed a dance.

Mom went to work in a bank. It was at the bank that she met my dad. Although Mom would not talk to her kids about her life, she did tell Bob's widow, Marlene, that she had met Dad at the drinking fountain in the bank. She did provide another tidbit of information that will be covered later in its proper context.

That meeting led to a courtship and marriage between William A. Rasmussen and Gertrude A. O'Connor on November 12, 1930, as the two eloped to Crown Pointe, Indiana. Dad was twenty-two years old and Mom was nineteen. A little over six months later, on May 26, 1931, a baby girl was stillborn. She was not given a name and was buried in the Rasmussen family plot at Oakhill Cemetery.

Due to the knowledge they had that Mom was pregnant, they announced to the families that they were married on September 12. Based on the time they thought she might have become pregnant, they were sure that the date would be close. They did well; the baby was born eight and a half months after that September date.

Judging from the Mom and Dad that I knew, they never recovered from the trauma of this time in their lives. Every September 12 for the rest of their married life, they had to have been reminded of that horrible time in their relationship and the fact that they had to get married.

If ever a couple had as difficult an early marriage as Mom and Dad, I can't imagine what it could be. Unfortunately, this early difficulty cast a dark shadow over their entire lives.

Once the story had been developed, it couldn't be changed, . Mom and Dad never showed any kind of love or affection toward each other or toward any of their children. As their family began to develop on October 15, 1932 with the birth of William Franklin, the mixture of joy and anxiety that Mom felt at that time must have been intense. Bill entered this world as the perfect baby that became the perfect son, who could do no wrong. And so it would be for the rest of our parents' lives.

Four years after Bill was born, along came Robert Edward on September 15, 1936. Bob was born at home and from the very beginning, was quiet and non-demanding. Bill was enough older than Bob that Bob was no threat to Bill's place at the top of the mountain and as the years would pass, Bob, in his quiet way, would follow Dad's advice, as well as he could, to be like Bill.

THE FAMILY THROUGH YOUNG DON

I came screaming into the world eleven and a half months after Bob on September 2, 1937. With no knowledge or understanding of the past, I would develop into the problem child. I guess that the protestations from Dad, to be like Bill, from my earliest days were not accepted well. I was me, and I wanted attention. I was different, and I demanded to be treated differently. Now, understand, at the time, I didn't know why I did anything; my attitudes and behavior were just something inside of me that made me who I was.

I was born sickly and did not overcome the problems attributed to the conditions until I was in third grade. Apparently I had a weak immune system that enabled me to catch every childhood illness known to mankind.

In those days, doctors made house calls, and our doctor was a frequent visitor. The story told often was that on one occasion, when he came by to give me a shot for something or another, I disappeared. Everyone in the family was looking for me, but I was nowhere to be found. The general anger toward me, in time, turned to concern of my well-being. They hunted and hunted. I had been lying in Mom and Dad's bed, so they started there. Looking under the bed to no avail. After searching the rest of the house, the search went back to its origin of Mom and Dad's bedroom. No luck. It was after the second time through that the concern found its genesis.

Each time someone came near the bedroom door, I, hiding under the bed, would put my feet up in the bedsprings, and using my arms, pull my body up tight against those bedsprings.

After several pull-ups, I decided it was time to make a break for it. I stealthily slipped out of the house and made a run for it. After I made it outside, I headed for the street in front of our house. Before I made it to the street, I was spotted, run down, and captured. Hauled back in the house, my punishment was Dr. Schusler giving me a shot. Needless to say, I screamed my head off as if I were getting an amputation.

It was only after the doctor left that the interrogation began. Mom and Dad were not going to let me get away with all the trouble I caused. Finally, I cracked.

Under intense pressure, which no amount of tears could ease, I confessed that I was hiding under their bed. Not believing me, I was forced to demonstrate my technique. Afterward, everyone looked at each other and broke out in laughter. I was off the hook, but I could never again use that ruse.

That event should have made everyone aware that I must have some intelligence to come up with such a daring scheme, but alas, I remained not very bright, just sneaky.

The feeling that I was different at an early time in my life easily led to the determination that I just didn't fit—I didn't belong!

I learned years later that Bob was not expected to be a boy. When I came along less than a year later, and was sickly at that, Mom became even more depressed. I truly believe that Mom lived most of her life in a deep depression.

Well, two years and four months later, Vivien was born on January 9, 1940. Mom finally had her baby girl, just short of nine years from the birth of her first, stillborn daughter.

For Mom, there was a lot going on within her depression. It was extremely emotional, with attitudes, behavioral adjustments, and expectations all in need of changing. Looking at Mom's situation since she was nineteen years old would be like standing on the side of a road and watching a roller coaster being constructed in the distance. From a happy teenager on top of the world, down to the depths of the valley with an unwanted pregnancy, marriage, and stillbirth of a baby girl, up again two years later with the birth of her son, that in her eyes was perfect. Downhill again four years later when Bob was born a boy, and not the girl she desperately wanted, driven further down to the utter depths of that depression less than a year later when I came charging onto the scene. That low point would last until Vivien was born, when the roller coaster would once again be on the upswing. Sadly, the roller coaster of highs and lows would remain a part of her life through all of her days.

Life has taught me that Mom was not alone regarding her emotional problems. Too many ladies throughout history suffered the same type of experiences. Although she was not alone, she suffered alone, and she was the only Mom I had.

At the time, it was too much for a child to understand or comprehend. Bill carried the burden of expectation well and was never a problem or concern for our parents. Bob withdrew into himself, but tried to emulate Bill in all things. I was just lost and didn't know if I belonged or not. I never tried to emulate or be like anyone. Vivien adored Bill almost to the point of worship.

My earliest memories all seem to revolve around sickness and a definite feeling that I didn't belong. Being sick most of my preschool life, which caused me to be smaller and weaker than most of the kids my age, also led to feelings of inadequacy.

There were incidences where Bob and I would do something that would stand out and create a family story for the ages. The earliest one was, "The Great Oil Spill."

On a beautiful spring day, Dad was cleaning out the furnace and the coal bin so it would be ready for the next winter. This was always his practice before starting ground preparation for the spring planting of his garden. It was his way of self-discipline as well as relaxation. The garden wouldn't be very big, but it would provide fresh produce for part of the year.

In the midst of his work, Bob came in and was looking for something. Bob was busy looking in cabinet doors and various shelves. After watching his futile search for a minute or so, Dad asked, "What are you looking for?"

Bob said, "A rag."

"What do you need a rag for?"

"Don spilled some oil, and I want to wipe it up."

"Where did you find oil that needs to be wiped up?"

"Next to the house." Bob was beginning to act nervous. "Don and I were playing, and he spilled the oil—and I want to wipe it up."

In addition to being quiet, Bob was the neat one in the family, so it was not out of character for him to be the one to clean up the mess. I, on the other hand, would be more inclined to either walk off and leave it, or just as likely be found playing in the mess, regardless of what it might be. In this case, I was riding my tricycle through the small lake of oil.

Dad stopped what he was doing and decided to investigate. He was puzzled as to where the oil could come from and how Bob planned to wipe it up with a rag. The only oil he was aware of was that fifty-five-gallon drum of oil that he bought to change his own oil in the car. He knew it was too heavy for a little kid to turn on its side.

When he and Bob reached the side of the house, all of his thoughts about the source of the spill were answered. Unfortunately, he learned that two little kids could put a fifty-five-gallon drum of oil on its side.

Although I was riding my tricycle through the oil when Dad arrived, it was obvious that I had gotten off at least once to feel the silky smooth oil with my hands, clothes, and face. In other words, I was oil from head to foot. Dad didn't know whether to laugh or cry. We had just destroyed his plan to save some much-needed money, but the sight of me, riding through that black goo, completely covered by it was hilariously funny.

Nevertheless, he snatched me from my tricycle, took me inside the house, and stripped me naked as he yelled for Mom. Poor Mom had no idea what had happened, but Dad gave me to her and directed her to "clean up this mess"—meaning me. She took me in and gave me a bath. I protested; it was not Saturday night. Bob was clean as a whistle and didn't need a bath. That was Bob, he could walk through a mud puddle and look like he just stepped out of the shower, and all I had to do was think dirt and I would look like I had been rolling in it.

The oil eventually soaked into the ground, but that area would not grow grass and eventually became as hard as concrete. As we grew older, we would bounce the ball against the wall and it would rebound through the oil slick as we practiced throwing and catching. The hardened oil slick would cause the ball to skid when it hit that area. I noticed that the skidding tennis ball coming off the oil slick would speed up, making it harder to catch, like the baseball would hit and speed up when Bob would hit me ground balls on wet grass. Both situations required faster reactions to be able to catch the ball. Bob and I knew that we needed baseball gloves if we were going to continue to play.

Even with the primitive reasoning skills we had, we knew that this was not the time to ask Dad to buy us baseball gloves. That hard, black area remained until Dad and I built a garage next to the house in 1954. The two-car garage that we built really made the house look so much smaller than I always imagined it to be. Digging through that old oil slick became my job, the reasoning being that I created the mess, so it was only right that I get rid of it

The intervening years had exonerated Bob from any guilt in creating the "Great Oil Spill."

Back in 1943 Bob and I decided that it was time we had baseball gloves and started to play with a baseball rather than a softball that was used at our elementary school. We found what we wanted in the Sears, Roebuck Catalog, so we showed Dad the pictures and asked if we could get them. Although he had bought Bill a glove a few years earlier, he told us that "of course you can get baseball gloves, as soon as you earn the money to buy them."

We asked, "How can we make that much money?"

He responded, "Get a job or start a business."

We needed about ten dollars for the two left hander's gloves, so we decided we could mow lawns, as we were way too young to even think about real jobs. We would charge fifty cents for a normal size yard and a dollar for larger yards. We couldn't get anyone to hire us so we decided to ask the old witch that lived up the street.

All of the boys avoided that area because of the stories passed down, so shaking in our boots (so to speak), we knocked on her door—hoping that she wouldn't answer the door so that we could tell ourselves that we tried. Well, she answered the door and asked, "What do you kids want?"

I told her who we were and that we wanted to mow her lawn because we needed to earn money to buy baseball gloves. "How much money am I going to have to give to you to do the front and backyards?"

I said to her, "We would do the whole yard, front and back, for fifty cents each."

To our amazement, she agreed.

We went home and got the lawn mower and got started—or I should say—tried to get started. The weeds were so high that we couldn't begin to push the mower through those weeds. We decided that we weren't too smart, but this was the only job we had, so we went home and got a couple of sickles and started hacking and whacking. It took us three days until we got the yards (front and back) ready to mow, but every day the lady would yell out at us to come up and join her for some milk and cookies, or water, or lemonade. She was fun to talk with, and she wanted to know all about us. After almost a week, we had the job done.

When we finished we went up and told her that we were through with the job. We were concerned about asking her for money, but we needn't have been. She handed us a ten-dollar bill and complimented us on the job. I told her, "We don't have any change."

She laughed and said, "I didn't expect you to. You two boys have worked hard and did a good job, and I want to pay you ten dollars."

I told her, "We had an agreement for fifty cents each, and we had to live up to our agreement or our Dad would kill us."

She reluctantly gave us a dollar and asked us if we would mow her lawn once a week. We agreed and left. Unbeknownst to us, she called Dad and told him what occurred and asked if he would approve of her paying us that ten-dollar bill. He told her that it would be okay and he would send us back to talk with her, but he would not tell us why.

We went back up to Mrs. Mueller's house to see what she wanted to talk with us about. We couldn't think of any good reason for her to want to see us again.

"Would she want her dollar back?" When we arrived, she invited us in and told us of her conversation with Dad and that he had agreed that we earned the ten dollars and could accept the money. After she gave us the money, we tried to give the dollar she paid us back to her, but she refused to take it and instead said that that dollar was in advance for next week, to make sure that we would come back.

Although we visited with her during the week, when we went back a week later, she paid us again, and when I said, "You have already paid us for this week," she responded that she was paying us in advance for each week.

When the summer ended and we mowed her lawn for the last time, she gave us another dollar, which she said was just because she wanted to, and we better not say no or she would put a spell on us. She knew that all the boys thought she was a witch. We all had a good laugh and Bob told her that we were trying to tell them that she was a nice lady.

At the end of summer, Dad presented us with a bill for ten percent of what he determined we had earned, for rental of equipment. He said that we needed to learn that there is a cost of running a business and there is no time like the present to begin learning. We gave him the money and still had plenty left over to buy our gloves.

I bought a first baseman's glove because I knew that was what I was going to be. Bob figured that he would be an outfielder, so he bought a regular fielder's glove. We would be ready for next summer.

When we got our gloves, the first thing we did was hustle up to Mrs. Mueller's house to show them off.

We continued to mow her lawn for a couple of summers after that. At some point during our high school years, we learned from Dad that she had died from the cancer she had suffered from for years.

I didn't know what cancer was, but I know that every time we went up to her door, she greeted us with a smile.

**Don on second birthday
September 2, 1939**

Chapter 2

A ROUGH RIDE

It was a rough ride being sickly with a negative attitude developing and a Super Brother, whose mere presence made me feel even more inferior. Bob was my equalizer.

He didn't have the personality, determination, or skills to stand up to our situation. I say *ours* because he was always in Bill's shadow. His way of coping was to be silent, agree, and get along.

Where Bob could follow in that manner, I couldn't. I had to be me and that just didn't fit, even though I didn't know who *me* was. I was compliant, rebellious, a clown, disrespectful, and mostly confused.

Earning the money to buy our baseball gloves really brought Bob and I together for a good period of time. We both spent so much time playing catch and throwing each other grounders that summer that the days flew by. As we got into the fall and school, he wanted to spend more time studying.

Why studying was so important was pretty much lost on me. When I did get to go to school, for the first couple of years, it was about half the time. If I wasn't coming down with something, I either had it or was getting over it. When I was feeling well, the last thing I wanted to do was study, or even pretend to study.

Whenever I could, I was playing "baseball," I could play a game by myself, using a tennis ball and a bat. When you flip a tennis ball in the air and hit it with an undersized bat, it just doesn't go very far. I would play the top of the first for three or four batters and then play the bottom of the inning. I always played low-scoring games and never got tired.

The truth of the matter was that after first or second grade, I should have been held back a year. I understand that it was discussed between the school and my parents, but since Dad was the president of the school board, it just wouldn't look good for his son to be held back. That was amazing since I had barely attended one year out of the first two years combined, according to the family story that I had heard over and over again.

Bob wanted to do things other than baseball the second summer after we had bought our gloves. That is all I wanted to do. It was a conflict that would break out in violence between us.

One day Bob didn't want to share our bike. Bill had a new bike, and Bob and I had his old one. This was a bad mistake. After some yelling at each other, Bob pushed me down. I fell right next to a hammer that had been left out. As Bob rushed me, I hit him in the head. He screamed, and I got blood all over me.

Mom and Dad heard him and came running out into the front yard. He really was bleeding a lot, so while Mom called the doctor, Dad was trying to stem the flow of blood. There was no hospital in the area, and if there was, no one could have afforded a trip there anyway, so they took Bob to Dr. Schusler's office and he stopped the bleeding.

Once that happened, everything began to settle down and the doctor studied the wound. He pointed out the location and the depth of the wound and assured my parents he would be all right.

With everything really quieted down, Dr. Schusler told them that if the strike to the head had been a quarter of an inch left or right, it likely could have been fatal. I didn't know what that meant, but it sure brought a lot of glares in my direction.

Bob had to spend some time in bed and then additional time being inactive, so I got to do a lot of bike riding. My parents probably thought it was better for me to be out riding around the neighborhood than being home. Bob became more quiet than usual after that. We still had to share one bike.

Although I always seemed to be getting into trouble for one thing or another, I had a strong support system built in that I wasn't even aware of. On a weekly basis, the clan would gather at Gramma Kayo's basement. My Aunt Jeff was always there, and quietly, she always had something nice to say to me. That always made me feel better, no matter what. The other influence was my Aunt Florence.

Aunt Florence was the most beautiful lady I have ever seen. She had stature in my eyes. That and a fantastic smile, which I saw every time she looked at me. We didn't see Aunt Florence very often over the years, but when we would visit with her, I always seemed to be the focus of her attention. She would find time to be alone with me and talk about my interests and get me thinking about dreaming big dreams. As I got older and she began to realize that my real goal in life was to be a baseball player, she encouraged me.

The two of them would be my ladies for the remainder of their lives.

Then there was Uncle Elmer, who was Dad's brother that worked on the streetcars with Dad and came over to our house on his way home from work about every day. It was always good to see him because he was always happy and had a good word for me. This went on for a long time until Dad left the streetcars for a different kind of job.

I didn't see as much of him after that until just before he moved his family to Texas. We were on our annual one-week vacation at Lake Ripley, near Cambridge, Wisconsin, when Uncle Elmer drove up to see Dad. He spent the night with us and the following morning woke me up early to go fishing. We quietly left the house with everyone else still sleeping. The sun was just beginning to come up as we shoved off from the shore and rowed to the middle of the lake.

After we settled in with our fishing lines and bait seeking fish in the lake, he began to talk with me about school and encouraging me to do well. From there he discussed many other subjects as he praised me and let me know that I was smart and talented. This went on all day until the sun began to go down. He finally said that we needed to get back and he had to get on with moving to Texas. He obviously didn't want to go. After he left, Dad questioned me about what we had talked about all day. I told him that we talked about everything and nothing important. He seemed to want to just spend time with me.

Dad didn't like my answers, and I just quietly reveled in the knowledge that I had received so much support from Uncle Elmer. I didn't see my uncle for what seemed forever until the fall of my first year in high school when I visited him in the hospital.

We talked a long time, and he and I laughed a lot. He encouraged me to keep playing baseball as well as other sports. I was really feeling good when I left the hospital without realizing that he had cancer. Uncle Elmer died in June of 1952. I missed him and his cheerful outlook for many years, as he was the third member of my support group that I desperately needed.

After I nailed Bob in the head, I should have known that payback would rear its ugly head at some point.

Bob and I were constantly trying to establish a pecking order between us; we didn't know it, but that's what we were doing. One day when we were about seven and eight years old, fairly late in the afternoon, we were playing on the side of the house and sometimes in the alley behind the house. While in the alley, Bob decided that we needed to fight.

He picked up a Coke bottle and using the telephone pole, swung the bottle and broke the bottom off. Now he held the bottle by the neck and began swinging it back and forth in front of me.

We must have recently seen a Western movie that Bob was emulating because when I looked at him, he was trying to portray this mean look with a squinting eye and a curled lip. I'm sure I was playing the part of a guy that didn't want to get chopped up by a Coke bottle.

As Bob got closer, I ducked, weaved, and put my hands in front of my face to protect myself. And, as they say, "And then it happened," he got too close. With one lunge, I saw the sharp edges of that bottle coming closer and closer. Without any feeling of pain, I was surprised to see blood squirting out of the two center fingers of my right hand. Not so much the ring finger, but the finger to the left of the ring finger; or, if you prefer, two fingers over from the little finger. That finger was shooting blood out about six inches.

I yelled, because now I was scared. Bob yelled for Mom, "Don cut himself, bad!" Mom came out and when she saw the blood, I became real scared because I could see that she was really scared. She hustled me into the bathroom and started running cold water on the open wounds. The bleeding didn't even slow down. She then wrapped a towel around them and told me to hold the towel as tightly as I could to stop the bleeding. I was put to bed with orders to keep squeezing the ends of the fingers and keep my hands over my head until Dad got home.

Before Dad got home, they were really hurting. It was kind of like a constant pounding with little relief in between. Dad took the towel off and cleaned the wounds with alcohol and began squeezing the tips of the finger to put a bandage on the cuts. Now, you really learn the true meaning of the word pain when you mix alcohol with an open wound—particularly—when you are seven years old.

With blood oozing from under the bandage, I suggested that a trip to the hospital for a couple of stitches might be a good idea. As Dad continued to work on my fingers, he explained to me that hospitals cost money that we don't have.

I was puzzled and stated that the Sterns went to the hospital all the time for every little scratch. Dad answered with an agitated voice: "The Sterns (our neighbors about a block away down the alley) have this newfangled thing called 'hospital insurance.'" He followed that with a little tidbit that has stayed with me from the moment I heard it and has actually become a foundation of my personal philosophy.

He said, "If someone else pays your 'bills,' you don't care what it costs. If that 'hospital insurance' ever catches on, it will destroy our country." (Think about that)

He got the bleeding stopped and the fingers healed. Dad advised me to avoid Bob when he has a broken bottle in his hand.

I don't know what he said to Bob, but I never saw Bob with a broken bottle in his hand after that. As a matter of fact, I had never seen Bob with a broken bottle in his hand before that. Now if he could just talk to Bob about throwing things at me—like blocks and knives.

What I learned about paying your own "bills" (even though at that time I only made the connection to money, not really knowing what bills were) made the whole experience worthwhile and less I forget, all I have to do is look at the scars on my fingers.

That ranks right up there with: "If someone hires you for a job, you owe him the right to make a profit from your labor. If you don't make money for your boss, he doesn't need you."

When I began working for money, I always put in extra effort to make sure that my boss needed me.

I was sent back to bed with instructions to stay there until the thumping stopped. I should have been more concerned about the bleeding because within ten minutes or so, I could feel my hand getting wet all over again.

I called for Dad, and he saw the blood before he could say anything. We went through the whole process again.

I didn't sleep much that night. The thumping never did really go away. It seemed to ease off as the sun began to rise. Dad came in to check on me before he headed off to work and seemed pleased to see that my face was no longer the same color as the sheet. That was the first time I thought I saw something in his being, that maybe I might belong after all.

By the time he came home from work, I was outside experimenting on ways to get my hand in my first baseman's glove. I was impatient to get back to doing what I was really wanting to do.

I think Dad saw something in me that day that I didn't comprehend, even as I began to see the ramifications developing. If there were any way possible, I would push myself physically to force my body to do what I wanted it to do. Mentally, not so much. I still bought the notion that I was not too bright.

★ ★ ★ ★

It was an historic day, the day of my eighth birthday. On September 2, 1945 on the deck of the USS Missouri anchored in Tokyo Bay, the Japanese signed the unconditional surrender that brought WWII to an end.

Now, I can assure you that on that day I began the day without a clue of what was happening half way around the world. I woke up that morning thinking about the Wisconsin Dells.

Our family was about to wrap up our annual summer vacation with a trip to the Wisconsin Dells, seventy-five miles from our cottage in Cambridge. Since our car didn't go much over forty miles an hour, we all got up early, ate a cold cereal breakfast, and headed for Madison. From there, about two hours away, we would reach the Dells.

It was a great day as we took the boat ride down the Wisconsin River through the area called the Dells. This was the most amazing thing I had ever seen. In our family, it was unseemly for boys to use the word "beautiful," so I exclaimed time and again that the Wisconsin Dells were "neat."

It was past noon when we completed the trip on the river, and we headed for a restaurant that Dad had picked out for lunch on our way to the boat earlier in the day, before it was opened. When we arrived, I think I can speak for everyone; we were starving. The restaurant was still closed. We kind of took it in stride because there were several restaurants in the area. We just went to another one, but it was also closed. We tried a third, then a fourth. All the restaurants were closed.

Out of frustration, Dad drove to the police station and inquired as to why all the restaurants were closed. It was then that we learned that the war was over and everyone was celebrating. *All* local businesses were closed. It was close to dark when we finally learned that there were no food establishments open.

With four hungry kids, the three youngest, including me, were wailing to beat the band. Dad told us that we would surely find a restaurant open in Madison, if not before. Poor Mom and Dad were beside themselves. Since we had not had anything to eat since we left Cambridge early that morning, they were as hungry as we were, but there was nothing to do except to keep driving.

We arrived in Madison and found the same situation that existed at the Dells. He didn't leave the route we were on, just noted to us that nothing was open. With only twenty-two miles to go to the cottage, Dad drove on. That last part of the trip seemed to take forever.

Finally, well after ten o'clock that night, we arrived back where we started. As soon as we got in the door, Mom started cooking eggs. It wasn't long before we were able to eat and get to bed.

We three youngest had quit crying before we got home and after getting our stomachs full, I made a comment about this being a birthday I would never forget. Dad took me aside and said that my birthday party had been planned for the restaurant we had first gone to for lunch, and he was sorry that in the search for food, they had just forgot. That, I understood.

When we arrived back home, school was ready to start. I was entering third grade and in the first week of school, our teacher, Mrs. Halois, had us draw a picture of something we had seen or done over the summer. It was an easy choice for me. I drew a picture from memory of the Wisconsin Dells. That picture hung on my wall at home until after Beth and I got married. Not because it was all that good; it was hung to cover up a hole in the wall made when my brother Bob threw a knife at me, and I ducked.

By the way, that picture placed second in a district-wide art contest. It hangs in my office to this day. The picture was one of two that Mom and Dad had kept all these years. The second was a sketch of the Museum of Science and Industry on the south side of Chicago.

In the spring of 2012, I took a drawing class at PORA (Property Owners and Residence Association) and our teacher asked us to pretend we were about seven or eight years old and for us to draw a picture as freely as we would have then. I did a real lousy job of remembering that picture that I see every day.

It really became kind of funny the way Bob was always throwing things at me. He would try to catch me not looking at him or not paying attention, and then strike. I believe that he intentionally tipped me off, because every time he threw something at me, I always reacted quickly enough that I never got hit, but holes in the wall and broken windows resulted.

I always seemed to be the cause of problems by not doing what I should be doing, or by doing things that I should not be doing. Nothing I ever did was good enough. My picture that I had drawn and colored, which won a second place red ribbon in a district art contest wasn't any good, nor was the picture I drew of the Museum of Science and

Industry, or the essay that won a district-wide contest. If they weren't any good, why did they keep them all these years?

At about this time, I asked Mom and Dad if I could take tap dancing lessons.

You would have thought that I had just asked for permission to kill someone.

"No son of mine is going to be a dancer—that's for Q—-."

I asked, "What's that?" I never got an answer.

Later Mom got me aside and asked me quietly, "Why do you want to take tap dancing lessons?"

I explained to her that I was going to be a first baseman and a first baseman needs to have good footwork around the base. I had read that Hank Greenberg, the first baseman for the Detroit Tigers, was clumsy and his Dad let him take tap dancing to improve his footwork. That's what I wanted to do.

I don't know if she ever talked to Dad or not, but I didn't take tap dancing, but with a lot of work I developed into a first baseman with a good feel for the bag and could effectively cover the bag with left and right stretching techniques.

By the time I reached fourth grade, in my parents' eyes, I was not very bright. It was about this time that I found a book in our living room that I began to read. I don't know why, but I read it through and decided that I wanted to be like the subject of that book. Not necessarily accomplish what he accomplished, but be like him. Honest, truthful, courteous, and humble. This was the first book that I had ever read cover to cover. Before I graduated from high school, I am sure that I had read it, cover to cover, at least ten times.

The book, "Pride of the Yankees," by Paul Gallico, published in 1942, was the biography of Lou Gehrirg, New York Yankees first baseman from 1923 to 1939.

I struggled through each year until the beginning of eighth grade, continuing to be the class cut-up, not doing homework, and without any sense of anything except being a kid. In eighth grade I encountered a new teacher that seemed not to have an idea of who I was. I had always started a school year with a warning from the teacher that this would be the year that I would straighten out and fly right. I always considered that a challenge.

Now in eighth grade, I felt that I could be me and try to do well. It worked. Mr. Eugene Spizzirri treated me like everyone else, and I found a comfort level, finding for the first time that I was being complimented for my work. I later learned that he had turned down the opportunity to go over the records of the students and be briefed on who he should be concerned about. He told the principal that he wanted to start out with a clean slate with each and every student. This was the first man that ever earned my respect.

Well into the school year, I was confronted in the classroom, when Mr. Spizzirri had to leave the room, by one of my tormentors. Without knowing it, I had developed enough confidence in myself to push back when he pushed me. I pushed harder than he did and with a surprised look on his face, he fell backward onto a desktop. I was scared to death (I had never done anything like this before), but I jumped on the desk and straddled him, holding him down. I put my hand on his chin and forced his head backward over the edge of the desk.

With an amazingly calm voice that everyone in the class heard, I said, "This is the last time, or I will break your neck right now. What will it be?"

I could feel his chin pressing against the palm of my hand as he tried to nod yes.

I eased off the pressure as I said, "I didn't hear you." I hadn't noticed that he was as white as a sheet as he responded in a loud voice, "Yes."

By the time Mr. Spizzirri returned, we were all in our seats working on the assignment. After school, when I was expecting a real confrontation, Jim Krause came up to me, smiled, and said, "Friends?"

I gave a positive response, and that ended years of harassment by various classmates.

I walked home with a lighter step and it felt so good that I vowed I would never back down from a bully again, and I wouldn't walk away from a fight.

A ROUGH RIDE

My "rough ride" had more hills and valleys, bumps and bruises than I could have imagined. In 1948 I was eleven years old when Bill came home from school with the news that he had won an essay contest. I just shrugged and didn't think too much about it until he said that he was going to Washington DC for the inauguration of the new president of the United States.

Now, we all gathered to hear about this amazing trip he was going to take. He was one of six high school students in Chicago who had won the trip. Two of the six were from Gage Park. Quite an honor for the school.

The next day it became official, and Bill, along with the other five winners, had their picture on the front page of the paper. Now we were all pretty excited for Bill.

The Chicago Sun-Times came into being in February of 1948 and this contest was a part of the paper seeking an identity. We didn't care why; we were just excited as all get out. No one in the family had ever accomplished anything like this, but *my* brother did. Pride in Bill was at its peak.

Activity picked up and as it seemed that Washington was going to be extremely cold during the inauguration, Mom's brother Bob provided Bill with his military pea coat. I have no idea what pea coat means, but it is definitely not the most handsome coat in the world.

During this time Bob and I would rush to the store as soon as we got home from school to get the Sun-Times with Bill's picture on the front page. He was there to see President Harry S. Truman sworn in as president of the United States of America.

We were one proud family.

Less than eight years later, on November 17, 1956, I married former President Truman's cousin, Beth High, now Rasmussen.

After Bill graduated from college, he spent most of the rest of his life out East and we didn't see much of him. Many years later I was out in Connecticut and his wife, Mickey, asked me to have lunch with her. I was pleased to do so. Unfortunately, I got an earful about Bill's deprived childhood. It particularly caught my attention when she mentioned how embarrassed he was when he went to the presidential inauguration and didn't have a suit to wear to take her to dances when they were in college.

To add insult to injury, he had to promise Dad that he would help pay for Bob's college education. Until Bob graduated this was a great burden for Bill and his wife.

She told me that he promised himself that he would never be humiliated again as he was growing up.

That really struck a chord with me. I didn't say anything in response; I just listened.

Bill was always the most intelligent of us boys, and we were very proud of him and always taught to look up to him and attempt to emulate him. Bob always tried hard, I didn't. Neither Bob nor I could measure up to Bill in Dad's eyes, but I was shocked to hear how miserable and deprived Bill was growing up.

For Bob and I, things got a little bit tougher as Bill stood taller than ever.

Don eight years old

Chapter 3

COPING WITH IRRATIONAL BEHAVIOR

The euphoria of the presidential inauguration behind us in the summer, Bob and I were in our regular routine of playing catch and him pitching tennis balls to me. The new attraction in our lives seemed to be an awareness of girls. Now we were always aware of girls. Mary Burke was a girl. Before now we just didn't pay any attention to that fact. She had always been a part of our group and was just one of the "guys."

We started playing "canasta" in the shade tree in our front yard. Since we had the biggest front yard in the triangle, it was always the magnet for kids activity. In the summer evenings there was always "hide and seek," chasing fireflies, plus just hanging around and talking. There seemed to be more of that this year.

Now, when it came to girls, we were not completely ignorant. Mostly, but not completely. We knew that they were different, you could tell by looking. They all had long hair, dressed differently, and giggled a lot. You see, we weren't completely ignorant. With the exception of Mary, the other girls all seemed to travel in packs. I must admit that Mary had changed since last summer. We generally didn't see much of Mary during the school year since she went to St. Gerald's Catholic School and we went to a regular public school. We didn't know much about religion either.

Mary was always taller than we were, but this year she had small bumps where there hadn't been any before. I wondered what was going on, but I kept it to myself. Then one day while Mary was sitting in on our canasta game, she began to sneeze. Well, she reached into her blouse and pulled out a Kleenex, then another, and another, until she got her sneezing under control.

I guess Mary was just too busy playing with the guys to be bothered carrying a purse or a hand bag, as I heard other girls describe the funny little contraptions they always seemed to have. Yep, Mary was sure different. That's why we all liked her. It did puzzle me, a little, when Mary finished sneezing, the bumps had disappeared from her chest, and some of the other girls, carrying their purses, still had bumps.

As the summer wore on, we came to know some of the other girls that would gather. They all seemed a little less frightening, probably because of Mary, than they had before. But the more that we visited, the more questions we got from Mom and Dad.

Who were these girls?

What were their names?

What were we doing when we would leave the yard with one of them?

All these questions, I didn't understand. The girls were almost just like real people, so, why the fuss?

I had begun to get more and more comfortable with them and one day, Maureen, who lived on the far south end of the triangle, about a block and a half from our house, and I decided to take a bicycle ride. For the occasion I combed my hair. We spent the late afternoon and early evening riding, along with some talking. I wasn't at all sure what girls were all about, but I was getting more and more curious.

It was almost dark when I got home, and I could tell that Dad was in a bad mood. He curtly asked me where I had been. I told him that I had been riding my bike. With that he barked at me, "Don't lie to me; you were with a girl!" As I started to tell him, that I wasn't lying, he took one step toward me and caught me with a right fist to my left jaw. I was stunned that he would do that, and I certainly didn't understand what was going on. I was immediately sent to bed without any supper. That I was used to, so it didn't bother me.

I never told anyone about it. However, I promised myself that he would never catch me like that again. Apparently, he realized that he had overreacted. For the rest of his life, he never raised his hand against me.

Early that summer Bob and I prepared Dad's garden for planting. It was our job to turn over the dirt, pull out the grass, break up all the lumps, and then rake the area smooth. The garden would be approximately twelve feet by thirty feet. This was a pretty big job for eleven and twelve year old boys. We worked after school about three hours a day and all day Saturday and Sunday. We were able to complete the job before the next weekend.

After we finished we could again begin riding our bikes and playing baseball. We probably spent more time riding our bikes than anything else every summer. This year we added some quiet games instead of being on the go all the time. The quiet time was probably the result of Mom's concern about polio.

One day after extensive riding, we were headed home and riding down Melvina, the street in front of our house, when a large Doberman pincher came speeding toward us out of a neighbor's driveway. I was between the dog and Bob. I yelled at Bob to speed up as I did the same. We were not faster than the dog and when he leaped, I got as low as I could and kept pumping those pedals. The dog flew over me and hit Bob. I kept moving and as I hit the yard, I yelled for Dad to come quick—and bring the rake. Dad didn't hesitate, and I turned and headed back to Bob and the dog. Mr. Mariotti was there with his hands prying the dog's mouth off Bob's arm. Bob sat up shaking and sobbing when we arrived. There was some bleeding, but not a lot. Mr. Mariotti told Dad that he was taking the dog in for rabies testing and apologized to Dad and Bob for the incident. Dad asked me how this happened, and although I was shaking pretty badly, I told him what had happened. He was listening intently until I came to the part when I ducked. He looked at me with a puzzled look and asked, "Why did you duck?"

Then he turned his attention to Bob again. I didn't know what to say, so I didn't say anything. Apparently, I had learned when to keep my mouth shut. Dad helped Bob up, and I picked up Bob's bike. We all walked home in silence. I still had that feeling that I didn't belong—and I didn't know why. It would be decades before I got my answer.

We were still mowing Mrs. Mueller's lawn every week during the season as well as occasionally picking up other mowing jobs. One thing that never changed was that we continued to pay Dad rent on the lawn mowers, and he kept the blades sharpened for us. He was teaching us that when you worked for yourself, there were costs for operating. It was a good plan, and we did learn.

As we approached the end of summer, Mom made her annual school clothing purchase. From as far back as I could remember, the process was the same. When the order came in, there were specific items for Bill and Sis (Vivien) and two of everything for Bob and I. This made perfect sense as Bill and Sis were different sexes and Bob and I always wore close to the same size. Mom didn't want us looking like twins so shirts, pants, etc. were purchased in different styles. It rankled me that Bob always got first pick and some years I wore clothes that were too big for me because Bob and I weren't always the same size, year after year. It was a small thing, but with everything else that I was experiencing, it was just another pea under the mattress.

It is important to note that I would do anything to be acceptable to Mom and Dad and on the flip side, I tended to have a short memory when it came to the negative things that happened. I was very inconsistent in my behavior, and I am sure that my parents had as difficult a time figuring me out as I had figuring them out. I was not a violent nature, but when stretched to the limit, I guess I could be. Dad had always taught us to walk away from a fight. Never fight unless there is no option. If you have to, run away and never, never start a fight. Now that can be confusing, and it was to me. As an example, a friend of Bill's by the name of Jerry Stanton would spend a lot of time in our yard. When Bill wasn't around, he thought it was all right for him to boss Bob and me. It was easier to go along with him than create an incident. On top of that he was rather likeable, a pudgy little elf that had simply grown a little too tall to maintain his pedigree. Well, one day I was trying to learn how to whittle. I had some wood and a knife and was working away when Jerry came by. He started in on me and I told him that I was busy and didn't want to be bothered. He continued pestering me and picking up my wood when I sat it down. Finally I had had enough and told him to go home.

Jerry didn't take kindly to my directing him out. He slammed his open hand on the small barrel that I was using for a workbench and began to really let me have it verbally. I took my knife and stuck it in his hand that was right in front of me. To my surprise, he didn't move, or scream or anything—he just stood there looking at his hand. I told him again to go home. He said, "I can't, my hand is pinned to the barrel." I had been looking at him, not the knife or the barrel, so I didn't realize that I had gone all the way through his hand. I don't know what I said, but I did pull the knife out of his hand. There simply wasn't much blood. He turned and walked away. It seemed a long time before I heard him scream, and then he really bellowed. I was amazingly calm about the whole episode, which in itself puzzled me.

When Dad got home that evening, I told him what happened. He took it very calmly and said that I might have been justified. I don't think that he particularly liked Jerry anyway. He talked with Jerry's dad and they agreed that Jerry probably deserved it. That was it!

The following summer Jerry proudly showed me both of his scars, on the back of his hand and the palm. There were no hard feelings. Fortunately, when I struck his hand, the blade went exactly between two bones and hit only soft tissue. That certainly wasn't my plan, I didn't have a plan; I just reacted to what amounted to torment.

My main interest every summer was baseball. That was the one constant in my life that didn't seem to bring any criticism. I had never played on a team, just softball at school. They didn't allow real baseballs at school because they were too dangerous. I guess they could be, because one spring Bill came home with a huge lip and swollen side of his face. He told us that he was hit in the face with a baseball. It happened when he was standing next to the batting cage and the batter swung and the ball hit Bill.

I thought that if you had your eye on the ball, that kind of thing wouldn't happen, and I promised myself that when I get on a real baseball field, I would never allow myself not to know where the ball was at all times.

I knew little of Bill's exploits in high school other than he was an outstanding baseball player. Our source for this was the stories that he related to Dad in our presence.

One series of stories that Bill brought home and shared with Dad was his part-time career as a roller derby star. During that year there was apparently a roller derby star in Chicago by the name of "Wild Bill" Rasmussen and Bill had convinced a segment of his senior class that he *was* "Wild Bill" Rasmussen. When he told Dad the story and the reaction of the other kids in his class, they would both laugh.

I laughed at the time of the telling, but later thought that this was lying on a grand scale. There was obviously something wrong with my perspective of this event. The ruse went on for a couple of weeks in the spring of that year. I never learned if his classmates figured him out, or if he just slid away as the baseball season was starting. Reports from Bill to the family were another star-studded year of baseball. None of us ever saw him play as all games were directly after school, Bob and I were getting out of school about the time Bill's games started, and Dad wouldn't be off work until shortly before the games concluded.

That summer of 1950, Bill played on an American Legion baseball team and had an outstanding season. Unfortunately, we only got to see one game that was held at Hines Veterans Hospital at a time that Dad could take us. It was highlighted by the team having their pitcher give up a couple of runs on well-hit balls off of his slow curve. After the game Bill was furious at the pitcher, George Barvinchek.

That is all that we saw in 1950. Incidentally, George went on to play minor league baseball in the Philadelphia Phillies organization for three years beginning in 1954, the year before I was offered a contract by the same organization.

One day Bill announced to Dad that the Detroit Tigers had offered him a minor league contract. Dad was excited, but Bill told him that he had turned them down because he could get a draft deferment by going to college.

My big mouth and I got into trouble again when I asked, "Why would the Tigers offer a contract to an infielder that can't hit a lick?"

I got a harsh lecture that the Tigers' scout told him that they could teach him how to hit and I needed to learn more about baseball before I asked those kind of stupid questions. I was smart enough at this point to keep my mouth shut and accept his explanation.

I thought to myself about the instructions given to baseball scouts around the country, "Look for fast kids with a good glove and strong arms. Don't worry about their hitting, we can teach them that."

With Bill off to college, Bob starting high school, and me going into my last year of grade school, life at home seemed to be very routine and quiet.

The following summer we began going to Bill's practices, which were for players eighteen years old and up, and I was fixated on the possibility of getting hit with a baseball while standing by the batting cage.

I was thinking in terms of self-preservation. The vision of Bill's swollen face was not something that I wanted to experience, so I was quite attentive in my observations. I decided that if you stayed behind the pipe running vertically on either side of home plate and connected with a horizontal pipe overhead that served as an anchor for the chain-link fencing surrounding the batter to make a cage with a chain-link roof and the only opening facing the pitcher, you could not get hit by a batted ball.

Your exposure to getting hit while in the batter's box was an entirely different matter. With Bob pitching tennis balls to me, I never gave any attention to the possibility of being hit by a thrown baseball. The first time I stepped up to the plate and saw a larger, harder ball speeding toward the plate, I suddenly knew fear and realized that I was afraid of the ball. Thinking of Bill's face caused me to think that maybe baseball wasn't really for me. It was an irrational thought process that I was indulging in.

This wasn't the first time I learned something from Bill being in agony. A few years earlier Bill was having problems with his big toe. It was hurting and it got to a point that he had to tell Dad about it. Unlike my getting my fingers slashed by Bob, Dad immediately took Bill to see Dr. Schusler. Doctors were much more casual in those days, and I was allowed in the room while he examined Bill's big toe. I was fascinated. The toe was huge from swelling. The doctor made his diagnosis. Bill had an ingrown toenail, and it would have to be cut out. I was told to leave the room until after the operation was completed.

When they finished I was allowed back in. Bill had this gigantic bandage around his toe, and he was very quiet as the doctor explained to him what had happened to cause the ingrown toenail. I listened intently, as the doctor explained how ingrown toenails develop and how to avoid it from happening. The "how to" part of the discussion was the most interesting part of the time we were in his office. The big toe is generally the one that pays the price for not cutting the toe "straight across." Then he showed us some pictures. I made a mental note and couldn't wait for the next time I had to cut my toenails. I would cut them straight across and never have that problem. That has really worked out for me to this day.

In college, many years later, a class that was required for physical education majors dealt with non-sport-related physical incidents that are easily preventable. Our athletic trainer discussed this very problem. I was one of the few students that understood the seriousness of an ingrown toenail. Doc Fontenot asked each of us how we happened to know of this problem. All of the other guys had taken a first aid course that taught the same thing. I related to the class the lesson I learned in Dr. Schusler's office.

I was sure Bob had gotten me over the fear of being hit by the pitcher, and the guys on Bill's team knew that I was only twelve years old, and I think they kind of appreciated Bob and I shagging fly balls. Bob and I were able to have some batting practice as the team practice ended. The pitchers eased off the speed of pitches to us at the beginning of the summer. As the summer progressed, the speed of the pitching to me increased, and I thought that was a good thing. I was learning, and Bill was the reason.

As we watched his games, I came to realize that Bill was an outstanding third baseman with a strong arm. He also showed great speed on the bases, when he got on. This was a great summer as the entire family went, every Sunday, to Bill's games. Bob and I watched and learned. The big thing I learned that summer was that I had to become a better hitter than Bill, or I would never make it in baseball.

Unknown to anyone in my family, my mind never shut down; I was always thinking and often analyzing my surroundings and developing conclusions. Sometimes I didn't even know I was doing it, and I am equally sure that I was wrong in a lot of my assumptions.

At the conclusion of each school year, just before graduation, the eighth grade class would take a field trip to Riverview, the large amusement park in Chicago. Every student in every class looked forward to this day. Sure enough, the day arrived when permission slips were passed out. We were instructed to get them signed by our parents and return them the next day.

I don't know if they had the tradition when Bill graduated, but I do know Bob went the previous year. The things he told me about made it sound like that was the greatest day of his life.

Well, I took the permission slip home to be signed and after dinner when Mom and Dad were both there, I handed Dad the slip and asked him to sign it so I could go to Riverview with my class. He looked at and said, "You can't go. The school has arrangements for those of you that haven't earned the right to go."

I asked him, "What do I have to do to get to go?" I was more than a little angry and close to tears.

"Nothing, you're not going."

The next day when Mr. Spizzirri asked for the forms, I turned in a blank piece of paper with my name on it so that the teacher would know that I didn't have any signature. I knew that he would talk with me privately about it rather than make an issue in front of the class. I was right; he waited until the end of class for the day and quietly asked me to stay after class for a minute. Then he inquired as to why I wasn't going, and I told him that I didn't know.

"When I asked Dad to sign it, he just said 'no.'" No discussion allowed.

I had long ago learned to accept my position in the family that allowed Bob to do something and a year later, it was out of bounds for me. All of my efforts to become an accepted member of the family had gone for naught, but having no other choice, I was determined to become an acknowledged member of this family in more than just words.

When the day of the big trip arrived, I decided that I wasn't going to school and just sit around being in everyone's way and broadcasting to the entire school that I couldn't go on the eighth grade field trip.

I went outside and was toying with a baseball when Mom came out and said that Dad had changed his mind, and I could go on the trip. I would have to hurry to get to school in time to catch the bus. I suppose I should have been ecstatic to go since I had been looking forward to this trip for a long time, but I wasn't. All I could think about was how stupid I would look to my class if I showed up at the last minute. I told Mom that I wasn't going on the trip, and I wasn't going to school.

She told me that she wasn't going to have me hanging around there all day, so I got on my bike and left. I spent most of the morning riding my bike up and down the streets within the triangle. Somewhere around noon I went home and made myself a sandwich and then left again. I didn't return home until I met Bob at the bus stop, and I walked my bike home as we talked. Bob was as clueless as I was about my not being allowed on the trip. He had left for school before I got the word at the last minute that I could go. When he heard that, his reaction was, "You didn't go, did you?"

"I told him in a rather incredulous voice, "No."

He said, "Good for you, I didn't think you would."

That was the end of it, and all I could think of now was the end of the school year.

Graduation, summer, and then high school—I could hardly wait.

What I didn't realize was that the biggest irrational thinking that was so far beyond my wildest imagination was about to hit me between the eyes. I had earned mostly Bs and Cs with a smattering of As in eighth grade, which was overall a notch better than Bob had done on his eighth grade report card. I had gone through the entire year without a behavior problem as I had in previous years, so I was struck numb when I heard Mom and Dad talking about finding a vocational school that they could send Don to.

I felt like a black cloud was hanging over my head. I was shaken and near tears when I thought of the Johnny Ray song, and I just had to turn that black cloud into "The Little White Cloud that Cried."

That thought fortified me for the upcoming confrontation.

I knew that they would bring it up to me before long and try to ease me into it. Nothing occurred until after graduation. The next day Mom told me that she and Dad wanted to talk with me. They started out in a relaxed conversation generally about school and wanting to put me in a school where I could succeed. I couldn't wait for what I knew was coming, so I blurted, "I am not going to vocational school!"

That broke up the "ease into it" approach. Dad barked, "Oh, yes you are!" Things deteriorated from there until Dad said, "You have to understand—you are not smart enough to go to a regular high school." I sat in stunned silence and said nothing. He then said in a quiet voice, "We'll talk more about this tomorrow."

I made it a point to talk with Mom before Dad got around to talking to me and worked on convincing her that I could do high school work if everyone else in my class is going to go to high school. A check with the school provided the answer that everyone who graduated was eligible to attend high school. By all measurements that I knew of, which wasn't much more than talking to kids in the neighborhood who were in high school about how tough it was, I was convinced that I could do high school work. Dad wasn't having any of my conclusions after I did all that I could do to convince him that I was smart enough to go to a regular high school.

He had convinced himself that I needed a trade that I could do physically to support myself. After a couple of weeks of standoff with me threatening to quit school the day I turned sixteen unless I could try high school, he told me that if I did that, I would no longer have a place to live.

After a final clash, I made an offer that I thought was reasonable. I suggested that I try high school and if I couldn't pass the first semester, I would go to vocational school. He rejected that immediately.

I was pretty well defeated when he came back and asked if I was open to a compromise that worked for him. I said I would "if I didn't need to kill anyone." I don't know why I said it, but it seemed that this whole mess could use a little humor. With a straight face, Dad responded, "You won't need to do that."

"You can start at Gage Park High School and anytime you fail a semester, I can direct you to go to vocational school and you will do it without question."

"All I asked when this started was a chance. I'll take it." We had a done deal.

Although I knew that we had agreed that I could begin high school at Gage Park, due to other things that occurred throughout my life, I knew that I would have to walk on eggshells all summer, because if I did anything that Dad perceived to be worthy of severe punishment, going to high school instead of vocational school would be reversed. With the exception of going to Bill's baseball games and practices, I made myself as scarce as possible all summer.

When Dad would say was time to mow the lawn, I would jump to it. When the pump in the well malfunctioned, I would grab a shovel and start digging.

By the time school started in the fall, I was eager to get going.

Mr. Eugene Spizzirri
Eighth Grade Teacher
Edited my Master's Thesis

Chapter 4

THE ANATOMY OF A DYSFUNCTIONAL FAMILY

The summer brought not only baseball but the old life in the family kicked up a notch with Bill home from his first year in college. Dad wasn't on my case as much, and everyone seemed happier. Our two dramatic confrontations seemed to slip into the background. Now it was time for baseball. I lived for those baseball practices. And we went to the movies every Saturday night, which had been part of the weekly routine when all four kids were home.

In fall it became Bob and me going off to high school, Bill back to college, and Sis still in grade school. It seemed we were like two different families between the upbeat activity of the summer months and almost like the dark ages when Bill left for DePauw. A few trips to Greencastle, Indiana each year became family highlights. I would usually say something or do something on these trips that would get myself into trouble. One time I made the ill-advised comment about watching Bill play baseball, another time it was a snicker that I didn't think anyone noticed about the painted yellow pants that Bill was wearing. It was some kind of fraternity thing that I didn't understand but still got chewed out about. Then there was the ill-advised excited comment I made about eating really good meals in Greencastle, the only time we get to eat in a restaurant. If only I could keep my thoughts to myself.Back home it was always back to the humorless, dull routine.

After Bill's second year in college, the summer brought my first game activity when one of the players had to leave early. Coach Hunt asked Bob to go out and play right field. Bob declined and said, "I'm sure Don would like to," as he threw me his glove.

Every batter on the other team was trying to hit to right field. It made for a couple of short innings until one batter was successful. A right-handed hitter hit a long slicing fly, and as I took off after it, the ball kept slicing away from me. I ran for what seemed like forever and as I got close to the foul line, I reached out and, miraculously, the ball settled into the pocket of my glove. I don't think I was the only one surprised. As I ran in at the end of the inning, a few of the older guys commented, "Nice catch." That was enough for me to be hooked for life. Bob quietly told me, with a big smile on his face, "Great catch." No one else in the family ever mentioned it, which I felt was kind of weird.

The summer ended, and we were back to the same old grind of work and school. The summer after my sophomore year in high school, I became a member of the Normal Laundry team and learned that if I was going to play baseball, I had to plan for time taking buses to and from the ballparks in Chicago. Bill was going to spend the summer after his junior year in college out in New Jersey, so there would be no family trips to baseball games.

After he came home and before he left for the East, Coach asked me if Bill would play a game with us the coming weekend. I said that I would see if he wanted to and let him know. He said that we would only need to find a shortstop and we could avoid a forfeit. I suggested that I knew a good shortstop that I might be able to get. He asked, "Who?"

"My cousin Harry."

"Can you check tonight and call me?"

When I got home I, asked Bill and he seemed eager, which had me walking on cloud nine. I told him that we still needed a shortstop, and he thought Harry might do it.

"Great idea; let's ask him."

Harry was called, and we had an infield for the upcoming game. I called Coach Hunt, and he was relieved.

I'm a complete blank about the game except that I can still see Bill at third base, Harry at shortstop from my vantage point at first base. We all three played the game without an error, and both Bill and Harry made some good plays and all throws were so accurate that I could have handled them sitting in an easy chair. It was the only time Bill, Harry, and I ever played in a baseball game together. I will never forget it.

This was the summer that I had appendicitis and iced my side every night to make it through the summer.

As a fifteen-year-old tenth man on an adult baseball team, I played a part of complete games more and more as the season rolled on. In an early game, before I began moving up the lineup, as the ninth place hitter, I broke up a no hitter with two outs in the third inning. The poor pitcher was so furious after I stole second base on him that he lost it and gave up another hit, and I scored our first run of the day. We went on to win easily.

Throughout the summer I was going to the doctor regularly for blood tests to make sure the icing was working. When the season was over, I was ready to get it over with and suggested to Dad that it was time. His response was unexpected. "You have waited this long, keep icing until Christmas so you don't miss any school."

I knew it was getting worse and I was willing to chance it for baseball, but not for school. I argued to no avail. We went together to see the doctor, and he told Dad that it was getting worse.

Dad asked him, "Can it wait until December and Christmas break?"

"Possibly, but I want to see him no longer than once every two weeks."

"Okay, we'll see you in two weeks."

I really got to the point where I was sneaking an extra icing session during the day because I knew Dad wasn't going to be deterred.

Finally, the week before Christmas, the doctor told Dad, "You can't push it any further, take him to the hospital tomorrow."

Dad said, "Surely he can make it one more week."

"No he can't—tomorrow, or you may have a dead son on your hands."

Dad agreed to take me in the following morning, very early. I was checked in and taken directly to surgery. I was given a shot on the way and that was the last thing I remember until I woke up in a room.

The following summer was all about baseball. I had made a determination early on that baseball and girls didn't mix, so I didn't date during the summer months. Since most of the guys my age were balancing baseball with dating, I balanced baseball with working and mowing the lawn, which became my sole responsibility since Bob was working full time to earn money for college.

Bob had been inactive physically through high school. Unfortunately, Bob had gone out for football in his freshman year of high school and had to get a physical exam and the doctor found that he had a heart murmur. He told Bob that it was nothing serious, but if he played sports, he would likely have a shorter life span. Instead of dying at age eighty-five—he might die at eighty.

Bob gave it some thought and decided that he would quit sports. That was it. He was done.

I ran into the same thing the following year and made the opposite choice. I told Dad that if I died playing baseball, have them scatter my ashes in Comiskey Park.

In his first year at DePauw, Bob rode a bike on the fraternity annual "Little 500 Bicycle Race" and his team won the race. Many years later I would learn that he rode on the winning team all four years. After he was killed in a plane crash at twenty-four years of age, the university created the "Robert E. Rasmussen Memorial Trophy," which was awarded each year to the outstanding rider in the race.

Back in the summer of 1955 while he was working at the stockyards, I marveled at his acceptance of the stink he picked up every day. Mr. Neat adjusted to his circumstance of smelling really bad when he got home from work. The first thing he did when he got home was to take a bath. He worked a five-day week and was courting Marlene on the weekends.

For the first time in our lives since we got our first baseball gloves, we didn't have time to play catch. I worked every Saturday that we didn't have a game and we had a game every Sunday. I would generally leave for a park somewhere on the south side of Chicago between ten o'clock and eleven, depending at which park I would be playing.

A typical commute to a game would include starting out on a suburban bus and two to three Chicago transit buses or streetcars. Generally a game of baseball would take three to three and a half hours and then two to three hours back home. My average game day would be seven to eight hours. An extra-inning game could extend my game another hour or two.

When baseball was a family outing in earlier years, you could cut two hours off the time and a lot of hassle from not riding public transit.

Chapter 5

BETH

Beth High was eighteen years old and a sophomore in college when I met her in October of 1956. She was a shy young lady with an easy smile and when I got to know her, she became more relaxed and easy to talk with. I sensed that she was as naïve or unworldly as I was. It didn't take long to realize that her circumstances were very similar to mine.

When Beth chose to leave Danville for Eastern Illinois University after one year of junior college, her parents told her that she would be on her own. Her mom, in particular, saw no reason for her not to continue her education at the junior college that they would pay for. Beth's sister, Irene Morgan, volunteered to pay Beth's tuition for the first quarter and Beth would have to work and save money to continue after that.

It became obvious to me that we had a lot in common, as I had been on my own for over a year. I had been working a couple of jobs to support my education, as well as the car I bought the previous summer.

She really impressed me with the quiet manner that she dealt with my parents during homecoming at the school. I had quit dating a bevy of girls and was spending all my time with Beth when in the second week of November, I asked her, "What are you doing this weekend?"

"Nothing special, why?"

"Do you want to get married?"

"Sure—why not."

I had talked with a friend who was planning to elope and learned that Mississippi did not require a waiting period or blood test, so we set the wheels in motion and by Friday, I had wedding rings and Beth had made arrangements for Irene to go with us. Beth took my car and drove to Danville to pick up her sister when she finished working on Friday, November 16th, and they returned to Charleston to join me when I finished working at the service station.

We drove all night and arrived early in Corinth and had to wait for the courthouse to open. Since we had to wait, we decided to have a good breakfast. Somewhere between Charleston and Corinth, we left the Midwest and arrived in the South. Our waitress had the softest Southern accent and was such a pleasant personality that just being served by her was a treat. I told Beth that the South sounds more genteel than Illinois. After a great breakfast, we were all geared up to get things going and the courthouse was open so we headed in and got our marriage license

Irene insisted that we be married in a church and not the courthouse, so we hit the town looking for a Methodist minister. Our search was successful in a short time and we had arrangements to meet the minister at his church.

We had a preliminary meeting to make sure that we really wanted to do this. He suggested that he call Beth's mom because she appeared a little young to be getting married. Irene jumped in and verified that Beth was eighteen years old. The minister, Reverend J.T. Humphries, then turned to me. I thought the jig was up if he were to ask for my age, but fortunately he simply said, "Do you have the rings?"

The ceremony began and all went smoothly until we got to the point of me putting the ring on Beth's finger. He stopped and asked, "Are you a baseball player? You have a baseball player's hands."

A casual conversation continued for about five minutes about baseball before he decided to get back to the wedding.

As the ceremony concluded, we made an offering to the church and he wished us luck and admonished me to keep playing baseball.

In between November 17, 1956 and the same date in 2012, we have had a lot of adventures, highs and lows, and have never stopped loving one another. Periodically in the day to day process of building a life together, there were times that we each forgot or suppressed that fact, but each time we came to our senses before any long-term damage was done to our relationship.

Before we married, Beth had told me that she would probably not be able to have any children. She wanted me to know, just in case that was important to me and I might not want to marry her. I assured her that I loved her for her, not for any children that we might or might not have.

We left Corinth immediately after the wedding and headed back to Charleston and the only hotel in town. I drove most of the way until the sun went down when Irene insisted that she drive the rest of the way and directed Beth and I to the backseat, letting us know that I shouldn't be driving so late on my wedding day.

The one thing we did before heading north was to buy two postcards to send a message to our parents and let them know that we were married. Based on this fact, it is easy to understand how mature we were. On Sunday we drove Irene to Danville and even though we knew that Beth's Mom and Dad hadn't yet received their postcard, we decided it would be well for us to break the news to them. Being really large cowards, we went over to Beth's brother Melvin's house and asked he and his wife to accompany us. They thought it would be interesting, so off we went. As soon as the four of us walked in, Beth's parents knew something was up.

When I broke the news, there was some crying and questioning and I definitely was not the most popular guy in the room. After a short time, things calmed down and I made a promise that I would see to it that Beth would graduate from college. Just that statement seemed to carry a lot of weight and before we left, I felt that our relationship would go forward from there in a positive way.

Since we had school the next day, it was back to Charleston and the grind of working and going to school looking forward to Thanksgiving, November 22 (also Beth's birthday that fell on Thanksgiving that year).

We didn't have to wait long before we got a call from Dad. He demanded our presence at his house "now!" I informed him that we had classes and work obligations through Wednesday, but we could come on Thursday or Friday.

A great deal of one-way bellowing went on, with me threatening to hang up before he cooled off and could talk rationally. We finally agreed that Beth and I would arrive sometime in the morning on Thursday. I didn't ask for an invitation to Thanksgiving dinner, nor did we receive one.

We drove to Kankakee on Wednesday evening and after a leisurely breakfast the next morning, we headed for Oak Lawn and the confrontation. As soon as we arrived, Dad barked at me, ignoring Beth, "How far along is she?"

Beth answered, "I'm not pregnant!"

I jumped in and said, "We want to spend the rest of our lives together."

From there the conversation degenerated to threats of cutting me off financially, to which I pointed out that I had received no financial support since August of 1955.

That brought another barrage of anger and the excuse that it was hard enough for he and Bill to pay for Bob's college. I pointed out that this was not about Bob. That brought an increase in volume and more vitriol.

At one point he blurted, "I will pay for you to get an annulment."

I cut it off at that point and suggested that Beth and I would take a ride to let things cool off.

He said, "Okay, but don't go see Aunt Jeff."

I didn't say anything as Beth and I got in the car and headed to Aunt Jeff's home.

Dad had apparently talked to her and had not gotten the support from her that he expected. She was expecting us and greeted us by giving Beth a big hug and welcomed her to the family.

She had the coffee ready and asked us to join her for some Danish that she always seemed to have on hand. We had a friendly conversation in which she observed that I had made a good choice.

After about twenty minutes, she hit me with the statement that "the family wasn't exactly pleased with your father's choice when he got married, but it was his choice and we accepted that fact. In your case,

BETH

I don't think anyone in the family would not immediately fall in love with Beth as I have."

She congratulated us again as we left to go back to Dad's house and say our good-byes before heading back to Charleston.

When we got on the road, we were both very quiet until the silence was getting to me, so I said, "I think that went quite well, don't you?"

We both laughed and she snuggled up next to me for the remainder of the trip.

It wasn't long before we completed the fall quarter with both of us doing well in our course work. We signed up for the winter quarter and continued our work routine. After Christmas we decided that we needed some money in the bank and the car was beginning to have mechanical problems so we solved two problems with one move. We sold the car, opened a savings account at the bank, and vowed to put money in the bank every payday. This worked out pretty well for a couple of weeks, and then winter hit with a vengeance.

The long walks to and from school as well as being on our feet while at the restaurant began to take a toll on my knee that I had injured the previous football season. After some discussion we decided to go visit an aunt of Beth's that lived in Homestead, Florida, as we figured our next move. This turned out to be one of those amazing decisions that ultimately led to us (me) joining the Air Force for four years and completing our degrees at the same time.

After we left the Air Force with our degrees in hand, we discussed the possibility of adopting. But we didn't have too. During the work on my master's degree and her teaching third grade, we learned that we would be having a baby in October of 1962. We were thrilled, and on October 14, our beautiful daughter Donna Alene was born. To me she had the glow of an angel. As I would sit in my chair grading papers, Alene would lay quietly in my lap looking at me. She was easily the joy of my heart.

As Alene grew, she became an avid reader and was a very quiet child much as her mother had been, yet she had developed a tenacity that was a very positive goal oriented trait. She probably was more like her father in this regard. I remember that she had decided to put on her own shoes. She would have a fit if Beth or I tried to help her. When we were getting ready to go anywhere Beth would get her dressed and give her the shoes a half an hour before time to leave and she would labor at putting them on until she conquered the task. Once she had it down, she would move on to another challenge, and if she didn't get her shoes on that was okay, Mom or Dad would do it for her, but she knew that she could do it if she wanted to.

As she grew she would handle everything that interested her in the same way. In school I recall her getting interested in astronomy. She pursued that interest for months, and the following Christmas all she wanted was a telescope. She was and is an amazing person.

Edie came along next and was a totally different personality. She was a girlie girl from the day she was born and definitely not an introvert. Athletic by nature, most of the time growing up she would prefer not to perspire and thus avoided exhausting physical activity unless she was mysteriously inclined to do so. While in a physical education class in high school one day, the teacher wanted to see how fast Edie could run so she matched her up against a record-holding girl who happened to be in the same class. With no training at all, the two girls took off running and Edie, who didn't particularly care for this young lady, beat her in a mile race.

The teacher asked Edie to come out for the track team. She declined because she didn't like to sweat. Edie explained that she had to do the run she had just completed because it was a part of her class. Track wasn't.

Edie grasped knowledge with ease and when interested would pursue her curiosity until she had an answer that she could act on. As a sophomore she decided to investigate becoming a lawyer, so without our knowledge, she began going to different attorney's offices and asking them questions. In the spring of that year, she inquired of us about the possibility of going to a Baylor University debate program during the summer. It was during this time that we learned of her interest in becoming a lawyer. I asked her if her school had a debate team. She advised that they did not, but she would get one started. With my background I was able to point out to her that any high school club would need to have a sponsor.

Without hesitation she informed me that she knew that and she had a faculty member that would sponsor a debate team if she had enough interest to go to a debate program over the summer, and he recommended Baylor in Waco, Texas. We made the arrangements, and she participated in debate her last two years of high school. The long and short of it is that she graduated from the University of Chicago Law School and became a lawyer.

I guess Beth and I had gotten the routine down pretty well. Edie was born fourteen months after Alene and Dara fifteen months after Edie. I thought Edie was completely different from Alene; well, Dara was and is more different than the other two. She was dark skinned like her dad with coal-black hair and one foot visibly smaller than the other when she was born. The doctor assured us that in time the smaller foot would catch up to the other one. He was wrong—big time. When Dara began to walk, she would fall down a lot.

At a very early age, she developed an indomitable spirit and when she began to talk, she developed a very unique way of using the English language. Her most enduring phrase was, "I decided my mind." We still use it today when the occasion arises—always with a smile. Dara grew to be the biggest of the three girls and in high school became Edie's protector one time when a bully threatened Edie.

Dara became the most physical of the three girls, as well as being a good student, musician, and athlete.

Beth worked very hard at getting the girls working on their individual strengths and pointing out that they were each unique. The idea was to build pride in themselves and not be competitive with each other. It didn't work very well, and it seemed it was always two girls teaming up against one. I guess it was fortunate that they rotated so that the team of two was ever changing.

With me working ten to twelve, sometimes fourteen-hour days, Beth carried the burden of raising the girls with me stepping in only when discipline was required.

She managed all this activity and raising the girls as I worked and did a lot of traveling. Beth had grown from the shy girl I married into a good mother involved in all the girls' activities.

Don Jr. was born eight years after Dara, and the girls had a hard time reconciling having a little brother. Alene was outwardly indifferent yet spent the most time getting acquainted with the little fellow. Over time she developed into Don Jr.'s confidant and trusted big sister.

Edie developed a solid relationship over a lot of years and is a good adviser for him when he has difficult times. Dara was just plain jealous of him.

Don Jr. didn't have the benefit of close siblings and most of his young life was almost an only child. He got it into his head that he could not compete with his sisters and didn't do as well as he was capable of doing in school. After a much-delayed start, he realized that he had the ability to be a student. He graduated from the University of Washington and became a special assistant to Congressman Ron Paul during the 2008 presidential campaign and is now a political consultant in Texas.

Beth and I have developed a unique closeness with Don after years of struggling by all three of us to overcome Don's unwarranted lack of belief in himself. Today he is a confident man about to complete his master's degree from George Washington University.

Beth has developed an outgoing, confident personality that daily amazes me and no, she no longer just goes along with my whims. After fifty-six years of marriage, we have truly become more than just compatible, we are best friends deeply in love with each other. Our four offspring have given us more in learning experiences than we were ever able to give them. Each and every one is a rare and treasured gift as they continue to grow and lead their own productive lives. We are also proud of each and every one of our ten grandsons.

Beth is a reader and has always made sure there were plenty of books around for the kids to read throughout their formative years. As I look back on our time together, I am so thankful for the six years of marriage we had to get closer before we had children. That time laid the foundation for our development as a family.

Chapter 6

MY GROWING FAMILY

During my last quarter in graduate school as we awaited the birth of our first child, I spent the early part of the summer playing baseball in Mattoon, sixteen miles west of Charleston and the town in which Beth taught third grade.

While playing the game always made me feel that there was a constant in my life, during a particular practice, I had hit a couple of knuckle balls off our coach. Apparently, that event got some travel time and caused me to get an interview for a teaching-coaching job in a town northeast of Campaign.

When I walked into the superintendent's office, he got up from his desk and asked if I had seen the baseball field; I told him that I had not.

He said, "Let me show it to you," and we left the school before I had seen anything other than his office, which was strewn with baseball memorabilia. We drove to the park as he asked me if I really did line two knucklers over the coach's shoulders.

I told him that it was just pure dumb luck. He didn't think so.

I was amazed at the structure and condition of the field, particularly in such a small town.

On the basis of a freak incident in a ballpark in Mattoon, I was offered a contract with the understanding that I would play for the town team in the spring while I was coaching the high school team. To a ballplayer, it sounded like a dream job, so without checking out the school, the schedule, or any policies, I signed on the dotted line.

After I was under contract, the first thing the superintendent told me was that I had to get a bus driver's license to be able to drive kids home after baseball practice. Then came the news that I would be teaching five different classes each day, and would be required to submit daily lesson plans to the office for each class.

I made it a point to talk to a veteran teacher, and she tried to counsel me about how the school really ran. "Ferrying boys home is a necessary responsibility because we are a farming community, but forget the lesson plans. He tries to do that with every new teacher, but we make sure it doesn't work, only because it doesn't work," she told me. I followed her directions, and sure enough, he never mentioned it to me again.

Sadly, he was a pretty inept administrator.

In the meantime, Beth was getting closer to her due date. We had rented a house in town and with my birthday coming about a month and a half before the new addition to our family, Beth decided to bake me a birthday cake. We found that the oven didn't work. I called the landlord, and he basically said, "Tough. You want a newer stove, go buy one."

Having just moved and not receiving a paycheck yet, I bought a used one, that not only didn't work, but when I lit the oven, it blew up in my face. It burned the skin slightly and singed my eyebrows, but no permanent damage.

Beth was so upset that I worked with the original oven and got it to heat unevenly. A cake was half-baked. The raw parts I cut away, and we had a mound of cake that Beth frosted. We had my birthday and a good laugh.

On the twelfth of October, Beth was having severe labor pains, so it was time to go to the hospital ten miles south of town.

We packed everything and headed out. Halfway there the car died and refused to go any further, so I began hitching a ride. This was not a heavily traveled road, but within fifteen minutes an eighteen-wheeler came to a grinding halt, and leaving Beth in the car, I talked to the driver. He was a pretty neat guy; he ran with me to our car and insisted on helping Beth to the cab, and we both helped her get inside.

He knew the area pretty well and drove us to the hospital. The attendants were startled to see this huge tractor-trailer pull as close to the emergency room entrance as he could get. Two attendants came and assisted Beth.

I waited with her all night as she began a thirty-eight-hour ordeal of continual labor pains. The doctor would check periodically throughout the night, but by early morning gave instructions to the nurse to call him if the baby began to come. Nothing happened. He came in the next day and checked on Beth before leaving to attend a University of Illinois football game. He came again after a couple of hours and the situation hadn't changed. The nurses were told to call him if she made any progress over night.

With no communication from the hospital, he came in the next morning after over thirty-seven hours of labor pains and decided to break Beth's water. Within minutes Donna Alene Rasmussen was born October 14th. She was a beautiful baby when I first saw her, and I was thrilled to carry her out of that hospital.

The doctor and I had words about him waiting so long. Beth was totally exhausted. Alene's (we chose to call her by her middle name) left leg would go into convulsion during the first few of weeks after we came home. When I called the doctor, he simply said that the nerves were not fully developed and that it would clear up in time. I let him know that I thought it was because he waited too long to take action.

This was first and only time in my life that I did not pay what should have been an ordinary and proper bill. I sent the unpaid bill to him along with a statement of my opinion. He, as of today, has not responded. Maybe tomorrow?

It didn't take Beth long to become her old self again, except that she had a glow that I was unaware of until a couple of days after Alene was born.

To all the family naysayers, we were proud to let them know that after a six-year pregnancy, our first daughter was born.

Due to the fact that it did take us over five years of living together before our first child was born, we determined to have a second child in the not-too-distant future.

The goings on at school had me convinced that this was not a good situation for us. As soon as Alene was born, we called Mom and Dad, who had moved to Utah, to tell them that we had a brand new baby girl. Mom had taken a job at the Intermountain Indian School, in the personnel office, and upon hearing that she had a granddaughter, she checked on the possibility of teaching jobs for Beth and myself.

Now, we didn't know that this was going on until we received a call from Dad to talk to me about the possibility of moving to Brigham City and teaching at the Indian School that had openings for classroom teachers. They had no idea of the depth of my dislike for the attitudes I found in this little central Illinois school and I didn't let on, but I told them we would think about his thoughts.

The idea that I had a place to go made me look at our little school more realistically. In my judgment, I was out of my element and considered myself to be performing as a mediocre teacher in a situation that I had no control over. It was very frustrating.

Beth and I talked it over and decided to take the jobs in Utah, even if it meant breaking my contract. It was something that I really didn't want to do, but I felt that it would be in the school's best interest, as well as mine. I had become adamantly opposed to the lack of interest in what was best for the students and the indifference of the superintendent toward his teachers.

The superintendent had gotten to the point where he simply ignored me and I returned the courtesy. I knew that something had to give before very long. Beth and I had been preparing ourselves to have sufficient funds to get us through the upcoming summer months, so we were also prepared to tear the sheet between the school district and ourselves, if necessary. I had signed a contract with the district for $5,250. Two hundred and fifty of that was for having a master's degree and two hundred and fifty was for coaching baseball in the fall and spring. So my base pay was $4,750.

As the Christmas break arrived, we decided to keep all our essentials and take everything else to Beth's parents' home for storage. We had purchased a small secretary desk in a small chest when we bought our house trailer back in 1958, just before I left for Greenland. That was an essential. Everything else was packed into boxes and left open in case we needed anything.

Being of sound mind and body, we left for a trip to Louisiana to see our friends, Lou and R.J., hoping things would quiet down over the holidays. We knew that they would want to see Alene as soon as possible, so it worked out. We arrived a couple of days before Christmas and were all settled in when we put their kids and Alene to bed on Christmas Eve.

We found that every time we visited the Lagneaux, it was a cause for celebration. On this occasion, R.J. had decided that we needed to share some wine. Although Beth and I didn't drink alcohol and Lou and R.J. drank very little, this would be a long night.

After an hour or so of sipping wine, R.J. asked if I would help him assemble the girls' "kitchen." I readily agreed and as Beth and Lou looked on, we engineers of the absurd dove into spreadsheets of diagrams measuring about four feet by four feet that were numbered and alphabetized in some logical form that we never did figure out. The first direction directed us to "1a/b2—interfaced with 1b/c7."

We decided to ignore the directions and fly on our own. By three o'clock, with Beth and Lou cackling and hee-hawing at us, we realized that we were not going to get the pieces together before the girls woke up in the morning, but we labored on and soon were laughing at ourselves as much as our wives were.

Finally, after we became aware of the sun rising and throwing a different kind of light on our endeavors, R.J. suggested that we capitulate to the facts, and he wrote the girls a letter of apology from Santa for running late and not getting the kitchen finished, but their dad would finish the job for him.

With that, Beth and Lou began making breakfast for us since the wine wearing off was really making R.J. and I hungry.

The rest of Christmas was joyous for everyone, especially the kids. Alene just mostly slept when she wasn't taking everything in.

Our trip to Louisiana was therapeutic as far as my overall outlook toward the future. I had no idea what was going on in the school district.

My hope was that some cooling down was taking place. After discussing it briefly as we left for our trip back to Illinois, we decided not to talk about it again until we actually returned. We had a delightful drive, and Alene proved to be a good traveler. We were becoming different people without knowing it. That little girl made our whole life brighter.

We returned just before New Year's Day to learn that no cooling down occurred and some kind of meeting was being scheduled to resolve several school district problems. No one who came to speak with me had any connection with the school, but had concerns about the impact on the students. I would assure them that they were my only concern, and they seemed to know that.

In early January of 1963, after the New Year arrived, I received a phone call from a school board member wanting to come over and see me right away, as he put it. I agreed and two board members showed up. I would not have been surprised if they were sent on a mission to inform me that I was being dismissed, but I faced an entirely different scenario when they arrived.

When I opened the door and invited them in, I marveled that both were smiling and very much at ease. They informed me that there was an emergency meeting of the school board at seven thirty that evening and they wanted me to attend.

"We have kept the meeting's purpose as quiet we could within the state meeting laws, but we are going to dismiss the superintendent, and it is the unanimous feeling of the board that you should accept the position," they said.

My reaction was immediate and specific, with no room for judgment. "I'm a first-year teacher; I am *not* qualified, or certified, to be a superintendent, and you would be jumping from the frying pan into the fire if you even considered it. My answer is *no!*"

I then asked them to carry a message to the board: "In the best interest of the school, it is my judgment that the school would benefit from both the superintendent and I leaving, as I was a catalyst that brought this bad situation to light. To make it easier for you, I resign my job effective immediately."

When they left, Beth and I gathered our belongings and loaded the car. I called Dad and told him that we were on our way to Utah. Before the meeting was concluded, we were headed west. Although I didn't like the timing or the way we left my first teaching job, I believe that to this day, I did the school and community a service and provided myself with an opportunity to start anew.

Beth and I agreed that since I couldn't step up and do the school district justice, the coward's way out was the best way.

Our trip to Utah had its ups and downs, particularly when we hit the Rockies in the middle of a snowstorm. Driving down Route 40 west of Denver, we came upon "Big Rabbit Ears," a long winding descent from a climb up a mountain we had made. It was a challenge that I hadn't prepared for. Having never driven in mountains, I wouldn't recommend this experience to anyone. The highway was visible when we started down, and I was feeling my way by the time we reached the bottom. We stopped at the first motel we came to and I was still pretty shaken.

The owner of the motel asked where we came from and when I told him, from the east, to which he commented, "Only a fool would try driving down Big Rabbit Ears canyon in a snowstorm like this." I agreed.

After spending a night hoping that the storm would let up, we headed toward Kremmling, Colorado, where we hoped to find Alan and Connie Free, who had lived in the same trailer park we did after I came back from Greenland. They were young and foolish, kind of like us, so we got along very well. It was surprisingly easy to find them, and we spent a couple of delightful hours before heading directly toward Brigham City, where my parents lived.

With the heavy snow, we didn't drive much over three hundred miles that day and were getting weary. Beth was fantastic caring for Alene as I negotiated the two-lane highway. Much of the day, I was driving thirty to forty miles an hour. We stopped early, as I was exhausted. The next and last day on the road seemed to go much better. We arrived at Ogden Canyon as it was getting dark and the snow really began to come down again, this time with huge, wet flakes.

I figured that we could get through the canyon before the accumulation became a problem. As we entered the canyon, there wasn't a car in sight, and I soon learned, no turn offs. I had no idea how long the canyon was, but it took us well over an hour and a half to get through it. The first thing I saw when we got to the end was a state police car that was stopping eastbound traffic, not that there was any. As we approached, he flagged me over. I didn't want to roll down the window because of the cold and the location of Alene's bassinet, so I opened the car door and stepped out to talk with the trooper.

He said that he was surprised to see us, because the canyon road was closed down two hours ago. I think he exaggerated; we couldn't have been in there that long. He was concerned that we were okay and told me that we must have been the last car to enter the canyon, and we were fortunate to get out. The last few miles had been a real sticky wicket.

The roads in Ogden had been plowed and were a lot easier to drive on than Route 40 had been, and the highway to Brigham City was four lanes all the way, so, finally, we caught a break. We arrived at about nine o'clock in the evening.

We introduced Alene to her grandparents and got a good night's sleep. The next morning I went out to the Indian School with transcripts in hand, was interviewed, hired, and assigned an apartment for us to live in. That was easy.

That evening we moved in with furniture from Mom and Dad and their next-door neighbors, Dean and Shirley Hanners. It was unbelievable how quickly we adapted.

Getting indoctrinated to the lifestyle of the Navajo Nation, meeting the kids, and determining the educational level was an interesting and vital part of my training. By the middle of February, I was working with student groups planning dances and other activities. At one point in my evolution to working with the Navajo, I was asked by our principal to address an assembly of all the high school students. The awesome feeling of walking out on the stage and looking at the assembly of two thousand students with ruddy complexion and black hair is difficult to describe. Looking out on a sea of black hair absolutely enchanted me. It is these many years later still very exciting.

Our life was now a happy one, as I found the Indians delightful and talented, each in his or her own way. The pure, simple artistic talent was so unique and fantastic. In an English class I was teaching, I noticed a young man sitting in the back of the room, not paying attention, so after setting an assignment for the class, I walked back to have a private, quiet discussion with the young man. He smiled and said, "I…like…you…so…I…made…this…for…you."

It was a small two inch by two and a half inch piece of paper with an etching he had made on it of a horse in perfect proportion. It was a striking work of art. I asked him how he could make something this small and perfect.

He said, "I…use…a…hair." I must have had a puzzled look on my face as he followed up with, "I…pull…hair…from…head…and…draw."

I carried that beautifully drawn horse in my billfold for over ten years until it finally disintegrated. I don't think any "white-eye" that I showed it to ever believed the story. He was an amazing artist.

Although everything between Beth and I seemed to be going well, there were signs that problems existed that I was totally clueless about.

In order to get a handle on our developing family problems, you have to go back to our childhoods. We were both raised with different, yet meaningful emotional handicaps. The home I was raised in was basically a loveless home where Dad ruled the roost. Bill was born less than a year and a half after the birth and death of our parents' first child. The traditions of the day caused Mom and Dad to marry, then there was the falsification of their marriage date. With all of this baggage weighing them down, Bill was the savior of their marriage, and probably sanity. He became the anointed one. The perfect child.

Bob, Vivien, and I were literally excess baggage. Ours was a loveless existence.

Beth's mother died in childbirth. She was raised by her mother's sister and her husband. When she was nine, her father, whom Beth thought was her uncle, died. Thelma and Bill, the oldest siblings, gave permission for Beth's real aunt and uncle to adopt her. Beth didn't learn that her cousins were really her brothers and sisters, or that her brothers and sister were really her cousins until she was nine years old.

At nine, she appeared before a judge who asked her where she wanted to live. She naturally wanted to stay with the only parents that she had ever known and who had raised her from childhood. The adoption was approved and her life went on, but she was one confused little girl for several years.

Unlike my situation where I figured out at too young an age that I didn't belong, Beth knew that she was loved; it just wasn't expressed. Beth was a shy, quiet, obedient child and a young lady that lost herself in books.

Her mother, Grace High, was the dominant parent in the home, and she and Beth's dad made it clear to Beth that she would have to work and care for them when they got old. This would be a heavy burden for any child to carry.

With these backgrounds, it was easy for me to assume Dad's role in my family, and for Beth to remain silent and obedient in the role of my wife. Neither of us were equipped to being parents.

The sad truth of the matter was that we didn't know that we had shortcomings; if we had, we would have done something about it. We loved our children and provided for them more than adequately, but we sure could have used help in the emotional and understanding aspects of raising children.

We were like children ourselves, carrying baggage that we had to dispose of, but instead of disposing of that baggage, we tended to hide it or in some other way not expose our children to it.

Work at the Indian School seemed to be some glue that kept us going. In March Beth became pregnant for the second time. This ushered in a time of joy and additional stress. At the same time, I was compelled to begin working on my doctorate in education. Beth was totally supportive.

In the spring of the year, Beth read in the newspaper that the next day would be the final day of tryouts for the Brigham City Peaches town baseball team. She read it to me and said, It is a shame that you are down with the flu." I was running a temperature of 105 degrees. The thought of getting out of bed was not an exciting one, but I asked her to give me the time of the tryout. It was to be held at six o'clock in the evening. As I went to sleep that night, I was thinking of feeling well enough to make that tryout.

After a good night's sleep, I woke up the next morning with a temperature of 107. I told Beth that I was surprised because I felt so much better.

She said, "You're going to the tryout, aren't you?"

"Yes."

That was it. We took my temperature just before I left, and it was holding steady at 107 degrees.

I got to the park just fifteen minutes before the tryout and played a little catch. I learned that the team was pretty much set, but as the only new face, they wanted to see what I could do. First, I went through infield practice with no problems, and then batting practice from both sides of the plate, then some simulated base running. The coach created this exercise just for me. I was to show them that I could steal second base.

He just had a first baseman holding me on, shortstop to cover second, a pitcher, and catcher. After two steals that weren't even close, he called me in and said, "I've got a uniform in the car for you."

That was it. I went back home and went to bed. That night my fever broke and though I felt weak; I knew that I was going to be okay.

I certainly would not recommend that anyone do what I did, but I had to make the team.

Later that spring, I went up to Utah State and started the process to get approved to begin working on my doctorate in school administration. When approved I signed up for one class in the summer term, just to get the feel for that level of study.

For me it felt like old times in the Air Force. Working, playing baseball, and going to school. It was different for Beth. She had a daughter to raise and was pregnant with another child.

Even though we had been married for over six years, we were both too immature to be having two children. I think that living among the Mormons had an effect on me and my outlook that put Beth as the parent raising the girls. In the groups that I associated with, the men did man's work and the wife provided a clean house, meals, and raised the kids. I fell into this as the norm, although it was not the norm that Beth expected.

I was totally ignorant to the pain she was going through, being in a new place with a baby to take care of and not knowing any ladies her age that she could relate with. She never complained to me and was as happy as I was when we learned that we were going to have another baby. Edith Ann was born on December 27th, 1963.

It was great having two daughters, but it just got tougher for Beth as I had been transferred to physical education and was coaching the JV basketball team. I had less time at home than I did when I was playing baseball. And yes, I was still driving to Logan for classes.

Dad had commented to me that he wished that he could go to college. I suggested to him that he could, but he rebuffed that possibility, because he had never completed high school. I pointed out to him that he could take a test and be admitted. I told him that all he had to do was tell me when he wanted to start and I would make the arrangements for him. He didn't believe that could happen for him.

I believe that he was a little bit afraid. I just made myself available and waited for him to make up his mind. It was over a year later when he asked me to arrange for him to take the test.

The next time I went to Logan, I set up a time and date for a private testing. The department head understood the circumstances of his age and lack of being in a school setting for many years, and assured me that Dad would be treated with respect.

At the appointed time, I drove him up to the school. He was as nervous as any first-year freshman would be. He took the test and when he finished, he told me that he had just wasted his time; he would not pass. I was surprised at his negative attitude, but I insisted that he return next week; I would drive him up to Logan again to get the results.

I had to tell him that I had put my credibility on the line to set up his test and he would have the results presented to him.

Just as I suspected, he passed. He asked me to explain to him what "ninety-nine percentile" meant. After I explained how it worked, he said that the testing supervisor told him the same thing.

He started college and when away from home, he was happier than I can ever remember. At home it was a different story; Mom did not like being left alone at night while he was going to school.

On March 29th, 1965, our third daughter was born. We named her Dara Jean. She was beautiful and although we didn't need another child so soon after the first two, as soon as we saw her, we fell in love with her and she became the third joy in our lives.

We continued with life as usual with me playing baseball, working, and going to school. Beth taught school until March when Dara was born.

A real problem was developing that would force me to take a stand. Every day during the week, Mom would come over to our home just as we were getting in from picking the girls up from the babysitters and occupy Alene while Beth and I took care of the other two girls. When I had the two younger girls all settled in, Beth would fix dinner. We were so naive. Mom and Dad were treating Alene just like they treated Bill as a child. Alene was everything, and the other children were just excess baggage.

I had a talk with Dad about the problem, and he tried to salve my feelings by paying some attention to Edie, but neither of them could deal with more than one child at a time, and Dad soon just quit coming over and we slid back into the old routine. I finally had to forbid my mother from coming over to the house, unless invited.

Dad was real unhappy over this development and let me know on several occasions that Mom gave birth to me and I had to respect her.

I explained that it was not a matter of disrespect, but necessity for Beth to be Alene's mother as well as Edie and Dara's mother.

Over the years nothing ever really changed in their minds and I had to be constantly on guard, with Beth reminding me when I would have my head in the clouds over something, and I would have to step in.

As Dad was moving forward on his program, he began bringing up negative comments about me being just a teacher, as if being a teacher was not like having a real job. Eventually he introduced me to a fellow he worked with by the name of Chase Nielsen, who worked part time selling mutual funds.

As Chase and I became friends and he helped me study for my securities license, I learned that he was a navigator on a B25 Mitchell medium bomber that flew off the deck of the Hornet in April 1942 as a part of the Doolittle Raid on Japan. He was aboard a plane that crash-landed in China, and he was captured by the Japanese. He was held until the conclusion of WWII and was one of only four raiders that came home. Chase was a very intelligent and interesting gentleman.

Whenever Dad got me alone, I would get the treatment about being just a teacher for the rest of my life. I never made a connection to previous suggestions or recommendations or demands that I seemed to finally accept, such as no baseball, go to New Jersey, and the day I started college, "Oh yeah, I can't help you; you have to pay your own way."

I got to a point where I didn't want to teach and had to try something else. Not long after I began selling life insurance and mutual funds, Dad came to me and said, "Bill thinks you should get into radio. With FM coming along, radio is going to explode."

So I was off to radio school. I was so naïve and pliable due to this crazy notion of needing to belong as a part of the family.

The market place in Utah wasn't ripe for a twenty-nine-year-old Easterner, so we packed up and headed back to Illinois, where I soon found a job as a disc jockey/news director, working for a hundred dollars a week. And that was a seven-day week. Without the hassling of Dad, after four months without a day off, I left the radio business and took a job for one year as a junior high school teacher. School had become a "safe haven" for me to re-gather my being, and then start out in a new direction.

The truth of the matter was that I never got over not playing professional baseball.

Beth was a real trooper and worked to help me find my way. No job, no profession could drive that passion for baseball from my heart or replace it. After a year of teaching and working for an unqualified principal who saw me, a qualified and certified principal, as a threat, he suggested that I find a job elsewhere. I did.

I went back in radio as a salesman and play-by-play announcer in Moberly, Missouri, at KWIX/KRES radio stations.

When I arrived to begin work, I learned of an ironclad rule they had, which was that no member of the staff could socialize with his co-workers outside of the station.

Once again Beth was hamstrung in making friends beyond our neighbors. It was 1968, and that fall my Aunt Florence's husband died of a heart attack on a street in downtown Chicago. She called and asked me to come up to the funeral. Because Alene was in first grade, Beth had to stay in Moberly while I drove to Deerfield, Illinois. Aunt Florence's two sons were, of course, devastated and being pretty well ignored by all the adults, so I made it a point to spend most of my time with them. They were really good kids that seemed lost and scared. When we got through the funeral and said our good-byes, I headed back to Missouri and encountered more hippies and demonstrators on the west side of Chicago than I ever thought I would see. This was in the midst of the Democratic National Convention. I didn't want to think about what was going on closer to the convention site. I kept my doors locked and kept the car moving until I was well out of the Chicago area.

I was pleased with my progress at the station and enjoyed my time doing play-by-play. During the summer months, in between my duties at the station, my immediate supervisor received permission for me to assist him in coaching a ladies softball team. It was a good distraction and helped fill some time with activity. We had a good time and in the fall, I had weekly assignments doing football games and then followed that winter with at least two and sometimes three basketball games a week.

As I was losing myself in continuous activities, Beth was raising our three girls practically as a single mother. When I got my check, I took out what I needed to cover gas and spending money for the time between checks and gave her the rest. She paid the bills and did the shopping. We were in effect leading two separate lives, and I was getting frustrated, as I am sure Beth was also. Neither of us were happy living like we were, nor did we know how to change the dynamic.

Into this environment came a comment that I made to one of our softball players after she got a hit and drove in a run that broke a tie in a competitive game. As Debbie came back to the bag after rounding the base, I casually commented, "I could kiss you for that hit."

There was no intent and she answered, "Okay." The game ended and we continued through the remainder of the season without any word said. I had forgotten about it.

After the season concluded, we had an awards banquet that was to be followed by our first evening workout of the off-season.

As the dinner was concluded, Debbie came over to my table and asked if I could give her a ride to the gym, and would I take her home afterward. She told me that her dad didn't want to come back to town when they got home. I agreed.

After we got in the car, Debbie said, "You owe me a kiss."

"I do?"

"Remember that game when I got to first base? You said you could kiss me and I said okay. Well, I want to collect."

I leaned over and gave her a light peck, she went ballistic and asked, "Do you call that a kiss?"

She really laid one on me, and it felt pretty good. I thought that was the end of it, no big deal.

I learned that her younger sister died and she felt really restricted and hovered over, and that her parents liked and respected me. I spent a few days trying to put all this together in my mind. In the meantime, Beth and I were having one of our "why can't we save any money" periods. I was working so much that I would turn the money over to Beth and she paid the bills and basically ran the home.

During this period, I began living a double life. One relating to when I was totally taken by Judy when I was 17, and the other was my real life as a husband and father. They became confused and separate. With Debbie, I acted out my senior year in high school and yearned to bring that time back again. I maintained my basic and firm moral character with Debbie, although it wasn't easy. At the same time, Beth and I developed a stronger physical bond.

I had to disengage, and the only way I could do that was to take a job outside of Missouri. I contacted Eastern Illinois University and was provided a list of schools in Illinois that had openings in administration for the coming school year.

I selected one and applied for the job of superintendent of schools at a town in west central Illinois that was in pretty bad shape. After the first interview, I was hired.

Beth took a job teaching in Missouri, as I needed time and space to get my act together. In February of the following year, we were divorced. I had a clean slate to work with.

A month after the divorce, I wanted to see my girls, so I went to Missouri for a weekend. I was somewhat surprised to learn that Beth was dealing with teaching, raising the girls, and managing the family finances fairly well. I was paying child support, and with that and seeing both ends of acquiring as well as spending money, Beth had grown interesting and expanded her real world acumen in an amazingly short period of time. That we were able to discuss our situation as equals rather than me dominating the conversation was a new and exciting experience for me. I would like to say that we immediately got our act together, but we had too much to work through before we could reach that point.

Through the remainder of the school year, every weekend, I either went to Missouri or Beth came to Illinois with the girls. Over time I realized that I not only wanted my family back, but I missed them during the week when we were apart.

When June came around, I left the district in Illinois and secured a position in a larger town as a junior-senior high school principal and I wanted Beth and the kids to come with me. We started talking about getting married again.

In July of 1971, we tied the knot for the second and last time. I knew Beth had grown up a lot in the five months that we were divorced, but what I didn't realize was that I grew up a lot more than she did.

Being relatively close to Eastern Illinois University, I got reacquainted with Dr. Bob Carey and also began playing handball again. Being thirty-four years old and relatively inactive, I wasn't in tip-top shape like I was in the Air Force, but I was still able to dominate the college players and the younger instructors. I really got a kick out of that.

We rented a nice, large farmhouse about four miles north of town and had a really good year. The school board that welcomed me was in disarray, with younger members and the older, more settled members in serious conflict over the function of the board. In my years in educational administration, I learned that the inner workings of boards of education in non-urban areas generally do not have an understanding as to their function. As a whole the individuals that occupy these kinds of positions, at some level, think it is their job to run the school.

In fact it is the function of boards of education to establish the policies, in accordance with state law, and to hire professional educators to carry out the policies. A rather simple structure.

At one school I had refused to prevent a high school senior boy from graduating because he broke up with the school board president's daughter. Since the boy graduated, as he was qualified to do, I was told by a prominent citizen of the community that the board president would get me if he ever saw me on the highway that ran by the little community. I thought, "How petty," and dismissed him from my mind. I had a board member seek my dismissal because her brother had led the charge to fire a very competent superintendent in a neighboring town, and she didn't want him to get ahead of her.

I had saved this school district from financial collapse and put them on sound a financial basis. Within three years they were back on the precipice again, having squandered their position.

After Beth and I had reunited in marriage, I was better able to recognize that their inadequacy was not mine and I had gotten to a point where I could separate business life from personal life.

During the midst of this transition, we were blessed with the birth of our son. This event, on January 13th, 1973, completed our family. Beth and I had never been closer than this period when Don was born. I was on the first year of a three-year contract and the future looked good as we approached the end of the school year.

A month before the end of the school year, I received word that my counterpart in the neighboring town had been fired. Knowing about local politics gave me pause for thought, but I had two years remaining on my contract so I had little to be concerned about, I thought. I was unaware of the fact that a senior boy had broken up with his girlfriend. Local politics entered the picture and I ended up taking a buyout of my contract. So at the end of the school year, the family left on a trip to Connecticut to visit with Bill and his family.

We bought a home in central Illinois when we came back and Beth took a teaching job. My health had been deteriorating my last year at the school and I was having serious problems.

The girls were in fourth, fifth, and sixth grade. Beth had Dara in her fourth grade class as a student. Dara didn't like this situation, not even a little bit. Although Dara was a good student, the other students always thought she got special favors from her mother, so Beth had to demand more from Dara than the other kids.

I struggled with my health as I also attempted to find ways to help around the house to make things easier for Beth. I started a business, but it didn't go well. Then I met Herb Price.

Herb and his wife Edith were master coordinators with Shaklee Corporation and introduced me to nutrition and the benefits of eating healthy and taking food supplements.

I began my involvement with Shaklee by taking the products in the middle of February of 1975 with the understanding that if I didn't feel better in some way within thirty days of dedicated daily ingestion of the product, I would get back all of my money by giving him the unused product.

Herb never got any of his product back, and after less than two months, I was feeling well enough to begin looking for an administration job. I applied to a school district just outside of Peoria, Illinois, and was almost immediately contacted for an interview.

After the job was secured, I arranged to rent out our home beginning in the coming summer and squared things away for our move to the Peoria area. I was so pleased that this school board, from the very beginning of our relationship, understood the duties of the board and the function of the junior high school principal. Every trip that I made looking for a livable house to get us started in the area, I met with a couple of school board members.

That summer Beth and I had more fun together than we had in years. The school wouldn't be taking up all my time and we would have more family time than our girls had ever experienced. The big drawback for them was that they would all be in their dad's school for their junior high years.

The girls didn't mind school; it was just the principal of the thing they didn't like. The line became a family joke.

The most pleasant and productive four years of my career were to commence in September of 1975. Beth and I would make it a point to have dates at least once a month and since our girls were getting older, we set up dates with their father so that they could learn how a gentleman should treat them. Each date was a real highlight for me.

All three girls became involved with softball, and all three had unique talent in a given area of the sport. Alene had the perfect left-handed swing. Edie became a good outfielder and hitter, and Dara played longer than both her sisters, showing a real knack for the game, leading her team in junior high and high school. This was a great family time for us all and every family needs as much of that as they can get. Don was still a couple of years away from getting interested in baseball.

I told Beth that if he got interested, it would be up to him. I knew that if I got him started, I would be too demanding, so when the time came, I just stood back and allowed Beth to take the lead.

On September 14 of 1978, Dad called and told me that Bill was in town and wanted to come down and see me. We agreed that he could come down the next day in the afternoon. Ironically, September 15 would have been my brother Bob's forty-second birthday. It would also be the first time since Beth and I were married in 1956 that Bill had ever been to our home.

When I hung up, Beth said, "He wants money."

The arrival of Dad, Mom, and Bill was a little earlier than the appointed time, but I adjusted my responsibility arrangements I had made with another principal so that I could leave for our meeting. I was curious to learn why this visit was taking place.

Bill, who was accompanied by his son, Scott, took charge immediately upon my arrival. He went into great depth about Dad's long-held desire to have a family business with he and his kids. Bill and Dad, along with Sis (Vivien), had spent the last couple of days discussing Bill's idea and plans. Dad was clearly excited about the prospect of the family all going into business together. Sis had given Bill a check for fifteen thousand dollars and Dad gave him one for ten thousand. I had more questions before I would even consider getting another ten thousand for him.

I pointed out that it would take a lot more than thirty-five thousand dollars to build a network. And he very patiently explained to me that they were talking with some major corporations that were finalizing their commitments to ESP TV, and what they were looking for from us were two things: the family involvement and bridge money to carry them through until the large corporate money began to come in.

I finally agreed to see if I could get ten grand over the weekend.

The last thing Bill said to me as he was leaving was, "If you can't get the money to us by noon Monday, forget it."

During the period that we were talking, I said, "If I participate, it would be all the way; I would go to work for the company when my contract was up at the end of May next year."

With Dad sitting there, and Bill committing this whole meeting to developing a family business, he agreed. Because of Beth and me going out east in 1961 and 1974 and me working my backside off doing work for him during the time we were there, he knew that he was getting one heck of a worker.

I called a friend of mine and laid out the program, and he agreed to give me the money. He would have a check for me Sunday evening so that I could get the money to Bill by way of a wire transfer before the appointed time.

I was more excited that I wasn't going to let Dad and Bill down than I was about the prospects of ESP TV at that point. I didn't realize it, but that indoctrination that I received growing up still had a firm grip on me.

When I called Bill to get wiring instructions on Monday, September 18, 1978, I heard whopping and hollering and a lot of commotion going on in the background. Bill quieted them down so he could get the information to me.

I knew from the background noise that this was more than bridge money that Bill was talking about, but I didn't know what or why.

Beth had been correct all along: Bill was after money, and he got what he wanted.

We spent a lot of time that fall and winter talking about the upcoming change that ESP TV would have on our lives. We were excited about it as I received a copy of *Broadcast Yearbook* from Bill that had a section in the back which included vital statistics on every cable television system in the country. This book would become my bible for the next couple of years. I began studying it and learned more about the variations in size and structure of cable systems and the entire industry from reading *Cablevision Magazine.*

I had really enjoyed my time as a junior high school principal and the friends that I made in my years there. With my health getting better and better with each passing year, Beth and I found ourselves giving talks on regaining health and taking charge of your life. The changes in people's lives with just basic knowledge of nutrition and supplementation was amazing.

Our girls continued to grow and develop their own unique skills and personalities.

Having the girls as students in a school that I was the administrator of was harder on them than it was on me. I expected the same of them that I expected of every student.

Unfortunately, other adults sometimes felt differently. The most challenging situation was when the two youngest were in seventh and eighth grade. They, as virtually every girl in school, wanted to become cheerleaders.

I saw this one coming, so working with the sponsor of the cheerleaders, we arranged a completely anonymous judging method. It comprised of two unique factors. First, no students would be known to the judges, and each would be assigned a unique number. Secondly, all judges would be from the high school.

Both girls made the team, and several parents of girls that did not make the team called me to complain about the unfairness of both of my daughters being selected. After a short discussion, most parents were satisfied that the process was fair to all the girls.

There are always the few that want to go as far as they can to reverse the decision of the judges, so it came before the board of education.

The board handled the meeting with parents so adroitly that one set of parents apologized for questioning my integrity and commented that I couldn't have conducted the tryouts any better.

Since the tryouts were held in October, I had converted a small group of annual malcontents into strong supporters of the principal. It made for the best year as an administrator that I ever had.

The key member of the board of education and his wife began to make it a point to invite Beth and me for dinner a couple of times a month. He really worked on me to stay in education. After graduation ceremonies were completed, one of my favorite parents really read me the riot act, because I was leaving the school district.

It was a nice way to leave.

As I was moving on to what was now ESPN, owned mostly by Getty Oil Company, I was required to take a trip to Connecticut to sign papers and get an orientation.

With my career in education over, Beth, our two youngest children, Dara and Don Jr., and I headed for Plainville, Connecticut, where ESPN was functioning administratively in temporary space provided by the Plainville Cable System.

All went well on that front; however, while playing a round of golf with Bill, I got an ear full of problems he was having with Stu Evey.

As we headed back to Peoria to begin building the affiliate base of the network, I couldn't help but think that things were not going well for the "Family Business" that we bought into.

As a whole, the trip out and back were fun and pleasant. The motor home always seemed to make a trip of any extended distance far more relaxing and enjoyable. I'm not sure whether Beth would agree with me when it comes to mealtime. For her, preparing meals instead of eating in restaurants I am sure was kind of like being home. I intentionally avoided discussion of the fun of traveling immediately before or after meals.

If ever there was a trooper when it came to traveling great distances in the motor home and keeping everything together, it was Beth. The kids really loved traveling this way.

By the end of my first year with ESPN, the first of our kids was leaving home for college. It sure was different with Alene not in the home. One by one the kids would be leaving to stretch their wings and fly. As always, there were a few crashes along the way, but they all made it in the world in their own way.

It seemed like, in the bat of an eye, all the girls were gone and we were a small family with just Don Jr., Beth, and I. We eventually gave up on the cold, northern winters and headed for Texas.

Don Jr. was in the sixth grade when we arrived, and he found that a box of tennis balls had been left in the house we rented. He took them out into the backyard and began hitting them with his bat. It wasn't long before he began swinging left-handed. He was doing this by the hour, day after day, as he was having difficulty picking up the new language he called "Texan." Once comfortable with the language, he started making friends, always allowing time for his hitting.

Beth and I were relishing the cool winter weather. Living on the edge of town, we took long walks in the country and discussed what we were going to do with the rest of our lives.

I had been working sixteen hours a day to get ESPN established in the market place and then, with Group W, to find a place in that same market place for TNN (The Nashville Network), SNC (Satellite News Channel), and the Disney Channel. I think Group W, not knowing the exploding world of cable television, tried to do too much out of the chute and confused the industry with some of its innovative approaches.

I was mentally and physically worn out. I decided that I would take a couple of months off and regroup. While Don Jr. was in school, Beth and I explored our new surroundings. On the weekends we would take Don Jr. around to some of those discoveries that we made and he came to love Texas. By the time he was ready for high school, he knew more about Texas geography and history than most of his classmates.

When school was out for the summer, we took a trip to San Antonio and mentioned to Don that we were going to take him to see the Alamo. His response was, "Are we going to Goliad?"

I had no clue as to what Goliad was, so I received a history lesson on the relief column that was to beef up the forces at the Alamo from Goliad, that were over run and destroyed by Santa Anna's troops. Sound information comes from strange places.

We also took a trip to Mexico, crossing the border at Lorado. It's amazing how tourist traps are so international. I had never given any thought to that particular situation. Live and learn.

Beth and I continued to expand our interests in and around central Texas. Day trips and longer trips during the summer when Don Jr. was in baseball camp up in Chandler, Oklahoma. We would pick out a direction and begin exploring, often finding sights that we never imagined we would ever get to see, like the pink sand dunes in southern Utah, Canyon de Chelly on the Navajo Reservation in northeastern Arizona, the seal cave on the coast of California, crossing the Great Divide in Colorado, and enjoying summer snow.

The last of the offspring flew the coup when Don Jr. went to Seattle in the spring of 1992. Choosing to work rather than continue his education, it took several years for Don to realize the importance of a college degree, and sixteen years after moving to Seattle, he graduated from the University of Washington.

Beth and I had been working together in Texas and continued to do that, but we took time off regularly to go to San Antonio, the Gulf Coast, and to Lafayette, Louisiana, to visit with Lou and R.J. and their family.

On one such occasion, sixteen-year-old Larry asked me if I would take a ride with him, because there was something that he wanted to talk with me about. I was more than happy to accompany him, thinking that probably wanting to talk with me was a lure to show off his driving skills. However, I was to learn that he was really troubled about something that he didn't think he should ask his parents about. It had been troubling him for some time.

We drove quite a while, and Larry said, "I don't know how to start."

"Just say it, and we can go from there."

"Your my Uncle Don, but you're not a coon-ass. How can you be my uncle?"

I explained how as children, his sisters and brother couldn't pronounce our last name and our girls couldn't pronounce his last name, so to show respect, his mom and dad and Beth and I decided it would be best if our girls called his parents Aunt Lou and Uncle R.J. and he and his siblings would call us Aunt Beth and Uncle Don.

There was a long silence, and then Larry said, "You may not be a coon-ass, but you are still my uncle." I do believe that is the nicest thing anyone ever said to me.

Long before Don Jr. left home, Beth and I had been remodeling homes and renting them out. In some cases, we would resell them when the people wanted to buy the house they were living in. We saw a need and worked to fill it. I had worked all my life and now it was time to work to help others. I couldn't imagine life with nothing to do.

So, with the girls gone, we busied ourselves and then it seemed like overnight we were having grandsons. We started slow in 1986 when Garrett was born and then they seemed to come by ones and twos. Then one morning we woke up and found ourselves the grandparents of ten boys, including two sets of twins. Now they are growing up and have spread all over the country from Hawaii to New Hampshire and from Texas to Chicago. Where those that are still home with their parents will end up is anyone's guess. I am not the least bit prejudiced when I say, "They are all great kids."

SCHOOLING

Chapter 7

EARLY STRIDES IN EDUCATION

Schooling has been a lifelong odyssey which began at age four and continues today. As I look at the most dominant and enduring aspect of my life, I have touched a lot of bases, beginning in Mrs. Mariotti's kindergarten class in the basement of her home just up the street from where we lived. That was the closest I ever lived to school during my total educational journey.

As a quick preview of my journey, the list of educational institutions whose inspirational doors I opened or were opened for me are as follows:

Mrs. Mariotti's kindergarten
Simmons Elementary School
Harnew Elementary School
Gage Park High School
Northern Illinois University
Eastern Illinois University
McNeese State College
University of Maryland (extension)
Eastern Illinois University
Utah State University
Jack Allen Long Radio Broadcast
PORA Life Adult Learning

Mrs. Mariotti held a half-day kindergarten for neighbor kids that would be starting public school the next year. Since Bob would be going to first grade in 1942, Mom entered him in the school. Rather than wait a year for me to go up on my own, she asked Mrs. Mariotti if I could attend with Bob so Bob could keep an eye on me. It was agreed, and so began a lifetime journey that isn't over yet.

That year we learned our letters, made a clay impression of our hand, and learned how to make candles for Christmas. Those were the highlights. We did have one little problem that was adroitly handled by the teacher. When we started the imprint, she had said that we should place our hand over the oval base that we made. Most of the students put their right hand in the clay, including Bob, who had seen the other students use their right hand, and although Bob was left-handed, he did what everyone else did.

I used my left hand, just because I am left-handed and didn't think about what everyone else was doing. Without saying anything to or about Bob using his right hand, Mrs. Mariotti told me that it was okay that I did it left-handed because "you march to a different drummer." Whatever that meant.

We each had a different size chair and desk, so some of us didn't exactly fit the chair and desk we sat in. My chair was way too low for my desk, and the desk was flat. I had quite a time coloring or working with my numbers.

To make it easier, without thinking, I would half-sit and half-stand while doing deskwork. The result of this awkward position was that I tilted my paper to the left. Left-handed people generally have better handwriting skills if they turn their paper to the right. In the ensuing years, a few teachers tried to correct my paper being turned to the left, but none of them succeeded and to this day, I tilt my paper to the left and twist my wrist above the line I am writing on.

Since this was an informal kindergarten, when it got warm in the spring, school was over in late April.

I was feeling real good about being a big boy and going to school, even though I was only there because of Bob.

Shortly after the end of kindergarten, I had a little money. I don't know where I got it, but I wanted to get Mom something for Mother's

Day. I asked Bob to go to the store on the other side of the southwest highway. That was out of bounds, but I had to get there to buy Mom what I wanted to get her for Mother's Day.

He agreed and when we got in the store, it didn't take long before I saw what I wanted. I had just enough money to buy a little Dutch boy and a little Dutch girl, each holding flowers. When I gave them to Mom, she thanked me and gave me a hug. For me that was real special. Mom displayed those very inexpensive figurines in the living room of our small home.

As the years passed and Mom and Dad eventually moved into larger and more up-to-date homes, the little Dutch figurines always found a featured place. In 1992, when Mom passed away after a long illness, she had put it in her will that I was to have the little Dutch boy and little Dutch girl. Today they stand proudly on display in my living room. They were the only gift from any of her kids that she kept all her life. After she was gone, she allowed herself to let me know "that she loved me."

I had to wait a year to start first grade after Bob started that fall since I couldn't start in public school until I was six.

Getting started in first grade was pretty neat. I had really good-looking teacher by the name of Miss Cain, not the knockout beauty of my Aunt Florence, but close. We had a lot of kids in the class. I must have led the class in missed days, but apparently I made myself known by not knowing what was going on most of the time. For years I heard tales of how every time the teacher walked down the aisle, I would grab the bow on the back of her dress and give it a yank. When I was in school, this happened with regularity.

I guess it really did happen as I heard in the family stories, because when I started substitute teaching in 1961, I was introduced to my first grade teacher at Harnew Elementary School and one of the very first things Miss Cain brought up in our conversation was how a certain little boy always undid the bow on her dress. We had a good laugh over it.

I completed first grade with a surprising result of having been passed to the second grade in what I later learned had to have been a "social" promotion. Having missed most of first grade, I was way behind and I knew I wasn't going to do well in second grade. I was right; a combination of illness and inattention because I didn't know what was going on most of the time left me with the same result. This time I knew I flunked second grade. I should have, but good old "social promotion" moved me forward. I guess that they just didn't want me to turn sixteen in the fourth grade, so I was going to be "socially promoted" right through school.

When Dad died two weeks before his ninety-fifth birthday, he left a box of things that he and Mom had kept over the years for each of the three surviving children. In my box were my grade school report cards. Rather than show that I had missed about a year out of my first two grades, I was more than a little surprised when I saw the actual grade school cards.

In the first grade, I had missed thirty days with illness. The second grade was much improved with only twelve days missed. This was not very good, but not as bad as I was led to believe. The most surprising revelation to me was that after second grade, I missed just four and a half days in third grade, and from fourth grade through eighth grade, I did not miss a single day of school. The reason connected to my lack of intelligence was always tied to the losing of so many school days in first and second grades. If that was the reason I was not very bright, that reason had just bit the dust. So there had to be another reason why I was not the brightest star in the sky.

Dad, as school board president, had been working to get a new school built in District 122 since the early 1940s. Our mom's cousin, Edward Kelly, an Illinois representative in the US House of Representatives, arranged government funding to build Harnew Elementary School which opened its doors for the 1945–46 school year. Since all students in the district had previously attended Simmons School, the district would now have to establish boundary lines to equitably determine who would attend each school. Of course, everyone wanted to stay at the original school due to its fine reputation and very popular principal.

After analyzing the demographics of the district, it was determined by the board that in the triangle, Moody Avenue would be the dividing line. Everyone east of Moody would go to the new Harnew School and those west of Moody (including Moody itself) would go to Simmons.

At the board meeting to formalize the boundary, there was a great deal of criticism because the "Rasmussen" kids would be allowed to continue going to Simmons which was only four blocks from their house, rather than them having to walk a mile to Harnew. Although Dad never permitted any favorite treatment for any of us in school, he chose to rewrite the boundary so that only the "Rasmussen" kids would be affected. The amended boundary came down the alley, around our house, back up the alley, and reconnected with Moody.

That seemed to satisfy most of the people at the meeting except those that were there simply to get the line moved farther east so as not to be included in the Harnew side of the line.

So Vivien (kindergarten), Bob (fourth grade), Bill (eighth grade), and myself (third grade) were now assigned to the new Harnew School.

At Harnew Elementary School, there was a new third grade teacher. That was not an unusual happening; there were new teachers somewhere in the system every year. This one was a bit unusual because the school board's president's wife had baby adfsat the new teacher when she was young.

To those not at the board meeting, and those who didn't get their kids back into Simmons School, the rumor became that the president of the school board had rearranged the school boundary lines so that his wife's friend could have one of the Rasmussen kids in her class.

Sometimes, no matter what you do, you can't win.

I began to outgrow the almost constant yo-yo of being well and being sick. I missed less than five days of school and began to develop a belief in myself that I didn't always have to be wrong, except when it came to math. I really couldn't see the need to memorize the "times tables."

Somehow I made it through third grade where we were introduced to multiplication. I just looked at the word and decided that it must be some kind of disease that I haven't had yet.

In fourth grade I ran right into multiplication like it was a brick wall that I certainly couldn't budge. Before we got to Thanksgiving, Mrs. McDade had called my parents and told them that I didn't know my multiplication tables. Although they didn't think I was very smart, Dad sat me down at the kitchen table and told me that any dummy could memorize and I had better get started because every day I was not in school, I would be memorizing the multiplication tables every waking minute of the day. I knew that he meant it.

I started in. I remember it well to this day. That first Saturday was long, laborious, boring, and virtually nonproductive. By the second day, I figured out that trying to memorize the whole thing just wasn't going to work.

I started with 1 x 2 = 2 and repeated it numerous times, then added the next one, and on and on.

By the time I got to Sunday evening, I was worn out, but I crossed the half-way point. After repeating 5 x 9 = 45 several times, I could go back to 1 x 2 = 2 and go straight through without making a mistake. The next weekend was sixes through nines. Another weekend saw hour after hour of random selection of cards that I made.

I thought after I conquered the math dilemma I had to have gotten Mom and Dad to a point where they could think that, maybe, I wasn't as dumb as they thought.

Although I had gone through more agony than I care to remember in the fourth grade, I knew that I would be passed on to the fifth grade. I had learned more in the fourth grade than in the first three grades combined.

Probably because I was having some success, I wasn't nearly the cut-up I had been in previous years.

Fifth grade was going to be a great year. My teacher was an old hand and very encouraging. Mrs. Lefoldt had experience, and it showed. She also had what I call presence.

The first part of the year, I was feeling pretty good about myself and all was going well, and then a big adjustment was made. We had between forty-eight and fifty kids in the fifth grade and the crowded room soon became too much. A second teacher was hired. The class had to be split in two, but there were no classrooms available, so half the class had to be put on the stage in the all-purpose room.

With no one wanting to go with the new teacher, the administration had to make the decisions as to who would be going to the stage. We didn't know what was happening when we went to school on a Monday morning and were called out by name and directed to go to the stage.

Once there we saw a teacher's desk and student's desk set up as in a classroom. A somewhat round man with a balding head told us to take a seat. He introduced himself and made the announcement that he was our new teacher. Although there was about half of our class on that stage, we really filled it up. I didn't know what to think. I had never seen a man teacher.

The way he conducted himself from the very beginning didn't quite set right. When we got to recess, we went outside and gathered to talk. No exercise on this day, we were trying to figure what was going on. After a confusing start, things settled in somewhat. I believe most of us didn't like the situation. I responded by going back to a non-behaving smart mouth and comedian. From the very beginning, I considered Mr. Johnston a non-teacher. I readily admit, and have from the first day that I met him, that I didn't like him.

Yet these many years later, every time I write a check, I think of Mr. Johnston. As I thought of the relationship between education and earning capability, I would think of Mr. Johnston. When I have traveled through our country to far-flung states, I think of the pictures Mr. Johnston showed us.

I made a terribly poor judgment of this man and by the time I realized it, he was gone and I never saw him again. Even in that act of poor judgment, Mr. Johnston taught me to be slow to judge and quick to praise.

After the year split between Mrs. Lefoldt and Mr. Johnston, Bob really got me excited about sixth grade. He had Miss Schatzman, who was a first-year teacher, and he simply raved about her.

I arrived for sixth grade with great expectations for myself. The first day of school, Miss Schatzman had a talk with me. She knew I was a slough-off and enjoyed creating havoc in the class. She would have none of that and would be watching me like a hawk. That year went to hell in a hand basket with only nine months of school remaining. I had been beaten down enough and just quit for the year before it started. I had my fun during recess and the lunch hour. I did just enough work to pass and was glad to see the year end.

If she were rookie of the year when she taught Bob, the next year she sure suffered a "sophomore slump" when I was in her class. Unfortunately, I wasn't the only one in the class that felt that way. From talking with the guys in our group, she should not be allowed near a classroom.

At Harnew School seventh grade was always considered tough but good. Mrs. Botta was not liked by students, but she was respected. We paid attention as the year started and then ran into a series of substitute teachers who were just filling in. We heard all kinds of rumors regarding difficulties she was having. Mostly the rumors concerned her health, both physical and mental. I know I had been accused of driving teachers crazy over the years, but I plead not guilty on this one—she wasn't around long enough for me to infect her.

Having made it through seventh grade, I was simply going to eighth grade to finish up elementary school. I had no hopes and no expectations; I was just going to be there.

Was I ever blown away. We were having another first-year teacher. This one had character and was a bit bullheaded. He took us all as we were and we were going to move forward from there. I never behaved so well, or worked so hard in my life. I liked it. I was getting good grades and feeling good about myself.

The guys all knew he was effeminate, but it didn't matter, he was a straight shooter.

Every Friday was boy-girl relationship time. Sometimes we met as a class and sometimes he met with just the girls and at other times it was just the guys. He frankly talked about grooming, manners, treating a girl the way you would want your sister to be treated, talking with girls, not about girls. We had a nine-month, one-hour-a-week class on how we were going to change as we got older.

The information we received taught me more about being a gentleman, and it made me less intimidated about getting into serious discussions with the opposite sex.

That year I grew confident and looked forward to going to school. What a great sendoff year before starting high school.

"A little white cloud that cried" had to be lurking somewhere overhead.

Chapter 8

HIGH SCHOOL AND A TASTE OF NORMALCY

Traveling from home to high school was the beginning of a new adventure. Bob and I caught the suburban bus on Ninety-Fifth and Melvina Avenue and rode it to Western Avenue, where we transferred to a Chicago Transit Authority (CTA) bus that carried us to the turn-around on Seventy-Ninth Street and then boarded the CTA street car to Fifty-Sixth Street From there it was a two-block walk to Gage Park High School.

On the first day there, I was directed to the school auditorium after Bob told me when and where to meet him. In the auditorium we received a pep talk and orientation. After the orientation those that did not have a class schedule were directed to a table to receive our class schedules. When I finally worked my way to the front of the line, I was told that my name was not on the list, and since they were so busy that day, I should go home and come back tomorrow and see Miss Roche and she would work up a schedule for me.

I had been at the school for about an hour and really didn't know how to get home. There wasn't anything to do except wait around until three thirty to meet up with Bob.

I found another lost soul that was sent home and he wasn't anxious to leave so we hung out for a while. He was a little slow on the uptake and I figured that he could use a friend, so I promised myself when we got back the next day, I would look out for him. His name was

Bruce Flowers and we became locker partners when we returned. After a short time, he decided that he had better get going, which left me with better than three hours to wait for my brother.

In a strange and new world, I was fascinated. It didn't take long for my head to start working in the wrong direction. What if Dad is playing a cruel joke on me and when I get home, I will learn that I am going to be going to a vocational school?

What if Bob forgets me?

The nervousness and anxiety that I had felt earlier in the morning was returning.

I was really letting my head get ahead of reality, so I made myself stay calm with a "wait and see" attitude.

It worked out well the next day. I now knew how to get to and from school. I went directly to Miss Roche's office, and she asked me why I wasn't there the day before. I laid out for her my activities and to my surprise, she apologized. She had my schedule in her desk, and I was supposed to have been directed to her office by the lady that told me to go home. She took out my schedule and went over it with me, even including how to get from class to class. She was a very nice lady to help me the way she did.

I started out each day with ROTC at nine o'clock and finished with English at one fifteen. I decided right then and there that I liked this high school thing.

I had the same schedule every day. Even though I had no study halls scheduled, I soon got in the habit of finding a quiet place to study and complete my school homework before I headed home. It didn't take long for me to decide, with encouragement from Bob, to get involved with extracurricular activities. The first one was the science club, which introduced me to a lot of new ideas and opened my mind to the fact that school can be more than just classes. My homeroom classmates elected me as their representative on the student council. I was amazed, since when I first walked into the homeroom concept less than two weeks earlier, I didn't know a sole besides Bruce.

I spent extra time in the ROTC room some days looking for something to do. Before long, Sargent Roland asked me to be the office clerk.

I had no idea what the office clerk did, but I was willing to do it. I really didn't know what the service club was, but by becoming the office clerk, I automatically was part of that club. I was further surprised near the end of the first semester when I was awarded the *Chicago Tribune* silver medal, which was a big deal as only a limited number of medals were awarded each semester. Ironically, both Bill and Bob had been awarded the same medal that is only awarded to one freshman each semester.

In this first semester of high school, I had made a lot of friends and probably, without thinking as to why or how come, I had developed a great excitement and enthusiasm that was far greater than I ever could of imagined. The semester was topped off by my making the honor roll. Without any planning or thought for that matter, I was emotionally and psychologically finding acceptance that I had never before known. It was invigorating.

The biggest negative was my algebra class. My teacher was pretty much retired on the job from teaching and I learned zilch, even though I earned an "S," which in Gage Park talk was an "A." Since it was a required class, I knew that I would be in deep trouble in the second semester.

Before I got into the second semester, I had to get a parent's signature on my report book. I proudly took it home and handed it to Dad. He looked at it, signed it, turned away, and left me standing there without saying a word. I was dumbfounded. Oh well! What did I expect anyway?

My second semester started out with a bang. The aforementioned algebra class was to be my first target. I had planned to talk with Mr. Yasnoff, my second semester algebra teacher, about the fact that I didn't learn much in algebra in the first semester and ask for help in catching up. I didn't have to bother, as the first thing he did when the class started was to ask each student who his or her teacher was in the first semester of algebra.

In his introduction to algebra, he then advised the class that "some of you are going to have to work harder to get caught up, because you will not pass this class without being prepared for geometry."

Although I had heard horror stories about him, I found Mr. Yasnoff to be one of the toughest, meanest, and best teachers I ever had. He poured on the work, and I worked harder in his class than I ever had to date. At the end of the second semester of the year, I understood algebra well enough to look forward to my sophomore year of geometry. All my other classes went well and I continued my activities that I had begun in the first semester and added drum and bugle corps.

When spring came around, I went out for the baseball team. I thought I stood a pretty good chance of making the team, as we had about thirty-five guys going out for the team. After the second day, having fielded one ground ball and getting a couple of swings off a batting practice pitcher, I was cut. I couldn't believe it. I had no choice but to accept Coach Stanger's decision.

The team ended up with one freshman on the team and a couple of sophomores and the rest were upperclassmen. I certainly respect the fact that upperclassmen dominated, but the lack of opportunity was appalling to me. Having been cut from the baseball team was the greatest disappointment.

With the spring "federal inspection" coming up for the ROTC, I had plenty of work to keep me busy until the end of the year. The federal inspection was practically a full day of individual, squad, platoon, and battalion scrutiny from regular Army inspectors. Being in the drum and bugle corps provided extra attention. It was not unusual for a half a dozen or more cadets to pass out during this grind. When we finished there was a general feeling of accomplishment. In the office, which was also inspected, we received a superior rating that made Sargeant Roland beam. Although I had been working to get everything in order, I hadn't realized that what I was doing was a part of the inspection.

Once again I made the honor roll. I felt certain that Dad would lift the threat of vocational school from my shoulders. I was wrong as I got the same reaction from him as I had before when I got those grades. He looked, signed, and walked away. Not a word. This was peculiar.

After a fruitful summer where I learned a lot about baseball watching Bill's games and occasionally going and practicing, along with

Bob, by shagging fly balls during batting practice. I returned for my sophomore year with one big concern, and that was that I didn't get Miss Scannell for geometry. I was relieved when I got my schedule and learned that I once again had Mr. Yasnoff. Most of the guys that I ran around with thought I was nuts. I didn't argue with them.

I spent a lot of time studying and memorizing theorems, but learn I did. I was ready to tackle the second semester of geometry.

The rest of the first semester went very well and I really kind of thought that maybe I wasn't as dumb as my parents had so often reminded me.

I was still working as a clerk in the ROTC office, now with sergeant stripes on my sleeve and a terrific coworker and good friend Janet. I joined the ushers club so that I could be at all the Friday night dances that came up periodically. Janet was a senior, so my parents would never let me date her, especially since I was only fifteen. But we had a great time when I was off duty at those dances.

Toward the end of the first semester, I received the DAR medal. A lot of the guys razzed me about the award since my initials are D.A.R., with the *A* standing for Allan.

The end of the semester brought another honor roll report to be signed by my dad. This time I wasn't going to be disappointed. I handed him the report book with a very serious look on my face and no comment. He took the book, smiled slightly, and when he looked at the book, the smile went away and he signed the book and handed it back. Not a word was exchanged between us.

I was really apprehensive about the scheduling for my second semester. My hope was for Mr. Yasnoff and my fear was for Miss Scannell. I liked Miss Scannell and she liked me, and especially all of the activities I was in. I never understood all of her reasoning, but she told me one time that I added to the "spirit" of the school.

On the last day of the semester, we received our second semester schedule in home room. The schedule hit me like a ton of bricks. I had Miss Scannell for the second time. I knew immediately two things. First, I would get another "S" and secondly, I would waste my time and learn nothing. Having planned to move on to calculus in my junior year and continue toward a goal of studying architecture or engineering in college, I would end my study of the only really challenging academic discipline I felt that I could conquer.

I started out the second half of my second year in high school knowing I would not have a feel-good semester. I had to kick myself in the rear, knock myself in the head, and get over it. It took about a week, and then I was ready to go. I never told anyone of my disappointment and buckled down to do the best I could, even in geometry. Sadly, I was not equipped to teach myself from the textbook and so I resolved that at the end of this semester, I would not sign up for another math class. My various activities continued unabated, and I had a lot of fun. With an hour and a half bus and streetcar ride each way and a Starlight Drive-in Theater opening about a half a mile from our house in the early spring, I knew that I would be applying for my first job as school wound down, and that further motivated me.

Once again I went out for the baseball team, and once again I was cut in just a few days. This was really frustrating since we had already begun play in the eighteen and over twilight league, and I was playing well.

When the final day came, I once again made the honor roll. Except for the fact that honor roll now meant to me that I would not be threatened with being sent to vocational school, so it didn't mean much. I knew Dad's approval would not be forthcoming. And so it was, I silently handed the book to him. He took the book, signed it, and said, "Bill didn't do that!" Then he handed the book back to me. I didn't know whether to laugh, cry, or what. "BILL DIDN'T DO THAT!" I repeated the words over and over in my head, "BILL DIDN'T DO THAT!"

That phrase just kept reverberating through my head. I really couldn't get a handle on it, but I was sure of one thing, since I did something that Bill didn't do, that was good, and it meant that after two years I didn't have to concern myself about going to vocational school anymore. Just the elimination of that from my mind made me think of all the fun I was going to have in my last two years of high school.

I added band and orchestra to my schedule, which was a fun thing and really made me humble. I had been a fair trumpet player in grade school, but the high school musical organizations were loaded with trumpet players so Mr. Loman made me a french horn player. To maintain a reasonable level of civility, I will simply say that after the first day on the horn, I really found music to be a most unlikable activity. Fortunately, I was still playing the bugle in the drum and bugle corps, which allowed me to maintain some level of musical sanity.

The only positive contribution I made to the band and orchestra was to mention to Mr. Loman that my brother used to play the trombone. Bob was not pleased with me, but he did agree to play after school for Mr. Loman. I waited outside the music room for him to finish. When he came out after his audition, he looked at me, and I swear that it looked like his grin was touching both of his ear lobes. He had not played the trombone since eighth grade and he walked into the music room and in less than ten minutes, he was in the band. It was awesome to see.

I was carrying the largest class load that I had ever had. We had ten class blocks in the schedule, and I filled them all up. I had two ROTC classes with the picked platoon extending from an hour before school into first period ROTC, then I had four periods of academic classes, another ROTC class division/lunch, Engager (school paper), band, and orchestra.

After my sophomore year, I said I was going to have fun. This class schedule shows that philosophy. The Engager first period after lunch was a loosely organized group of students interested in journalism, and me. I was investigating journalism and practicing tomfoolery. That period was just so much fun with the greatest kids and too much time on our hands.

With no challenging classes, I concentrated on a subject that I really hadn't paid much attention to: trying to figure out what the opposite sex was all about. It shouldn't take more than one semester. Now in my mid-seventies this is a long, long semester.

When I left the hospital after my appendix surgery, I had specific instruction to wear wool trousers until the incision was completely healed. I knew I had a few days before school recessed for the Christmas holidays, and I really wanted to go back to school for those days. When I got home from the hospital, I was worn out and I knew that there was just no way. I was down most of the rest of the holiday season and just before school was about to start, I was back in the doctor's office and was told that I needed another week.

Several days after school started up again, I went to school wearing my ROTC uniform trousers. The first thing I did was go down to the ROTC and talk with Sargent Roland. I explained that until I healed better or the weather warmed, the doctor insisted that I wear wool trousers, and the uniform trousers were the only pair I had.

I had seen Sargent Roland smile on several occasions, but never had I seen him bust out laughing as he did in response to my explanation. He asked if I had spoken to anyone else about this. I said, "No, I came in the door and right down here." He then told me to use my own judgment as to when I could return to normal use of my Army-issued trousers. Boy, was I relieved.

The ROTC was called upon to form an honor guard to assist the veteran organizations with the conduct of funerals. With the Korean War in full swing, the American Legion and the Veterans of Foreign Wars simply didn't have enough men to do the job. Bob and I volunteered. Since he was a drummer and I was a bugler, we were in the first group. Since we could both handle a rifle, we could be used in any of three positions in the conduct of funerals.

At the end of the first semester, I missed the honor roll for the first time since I started high school. When I took my report book home for Dad to sign, I figured that I would get a different response than I had been getting. I was right. I gave Dad the book; he looked at it and hit the ceiling. I was now a lazy, good-for-nothing, plus a few other words that I don't allow into my vocabulary. For the first time, after two years of total frustration of not knowing what to expect, Dad reacted the way I thought he would. It was so much easier for him to tear down than it was to build up.

The spring semester brought a sense of accomplishment in that I didn't even think of going to vocational school. I may not be the brightest star in the sky, but I sure liked where I was and I thoroughly enjoyed being who I was. I had all kinds of plans when the winter would turn into spring.

I ended up wearing the wool uniform trousers for less than a week. When I returned to the doctor for a checkup, he was pleased that I had healed so well. He told me that I shouldn't have any problems, except for a curveball, and trying to do too much too soon. So, take it slow, he told me.

Every time we had a funeral to do, I became a little less of a kid. These guys weren't that much older than I was, and they had gone to some place I had only read about and been killed in a "police action." Bob was a senior and one funeral we did was for the brother of one of his classmates.

It was a Greek family, very emotional, not only at the graveside ceremony, but for weeks afterward. I couldn't get the sight of the solder's mother grieving as she hugged the casket out of my mind.

For this service I was the echo for taps. That put me some distance from the gravesite, but I had a clear view of the proceedings after I finished taps. I know how deeply it affected me. I can't even imagine the agony of those senior cadets, whose classmate's brother was about to be laid to rest. Although Bob and I often discussed honor guard performances after a funeral, on the way home, this time we didn't, and we never did discuss that one. I feel that it must have been even harder for him than it was for me.

I didn't realize it, but the camaraderie between Bob and I was beginning to wind down. After graduation he would be taking a full-time job at the Chicago stock yards to save money for college.

We still had spring activities ahead, and I was bound and determined I would enjoy the rest of the school year. My classes by now had become primarily the anchor that kept me tied to the school. I did enough studying to make sure that I would pass every class. I was still on a college-prep schedule, but in spite of the fact that I wasn't playing even though I was on the high school baseball team, I knew that baseball was in my future.

When the call for ballplayers went out, I was there and ready to play. I got little more attention than I had the first two years, but this year I wasn't cut. I don't know what the difference was, but I was on the team.

One day after school, Bob and I were walking down the hall, headed toward the Kedzie bus route. He said to me, "It's that time of year, when boys start thinking about what girls have been thinking about all winter." I was a bit surprised and asked, "I didn't know girls thought about baseball all winter?"

Bob looked at me with this weird, pained look on his face. I don't recall that we ever discussed girls and baseball together again, although I did create quite a stir from Marlene (Bob's girlfriend) on the way home from school one day. I told my girlfriend Betty that I was going to be playing baseball all summer and that I would not see her until the fall. Of course, Marlene was the first to hear of my thoughtlessness, and according to her, I had dumped Betty. She unloaded on me all the way from Seventy-Ninth Street to Ninety-Fifth, and she wasn't finished when we got off the bus.

Betty had accompanied me to our junior prom, me in a tuxedo and her in a beautiful evening gown. The highlight of the night was going to a concert by Nat "King" Cole. Our table was right up front and we had a fantastic view of this great singer. We were at the first show of the night and showed so much appreciation of his talent that he decided to extend the show. When he finished to a raucous ovation, we left the Palmer House and I couldn't believe my eyes. I looked to my left and saw hundreds of teen gentlemen and their ladies lined up eight to ten people wide and down the street and around the corner as far as the eye could see.

It was all in all a great night that I knew I would never forget.

As spring was just beginning, each club sponsor submitted a list of qualified candidates for specific offices in the club. I hadn't been paying much attention to the goings on and didn't know the procedure until a fellow student brought me a ballot with the list of offices and a number of candidates for each. I was listed as a candidate for treasurer of the service club along with guidelines for campaigning. It was all kind of weird. It became weirder when Marlene, who was a senior, announced that she and her sister, who was a freshman, would be my campaign managers.

After I had agreed, they invited me to their home for a strategy session. I arrived and the strategy had been determined and we started working on posters to be placed around the school. Marlene's idea was to have more posters than anyone else. Other than that night, I didn't have anything to do with my campaign. I really didn't think I had much of a chance of winning so I didn't talk to anyone about it.

You can imagine my surprise when I won. As a senior I would be the treasurer of the service club. I kept the notification ballot with my name circled that I received and took it home to show dad. Since I wasn't really involved except for one night, I didn't think it was a big deal, but apparently Dad did. When I showed him the ballot, he somberly responded, "Bill didn't do that!"

There it was again—"BILL DIDN'T DO THAT!" As if I shouldn't have done something positive that Bill didn't do. I was bewildered and couldn't understand, but now having better understanding of my role in the family, I just accepted the comment silently without berating myself.

I was so used to hearing that type of comment, that I didn't give it another thought, but I apparently logged it in my memory bank.

In the last week of school, a tradition was for the graduating senior ROTC cadet officers to pass off their officers hats to a recently promoted junior cadet officer. Bob was passing his hat to me. I suggested that he leave it home and just move it to my closet. He said we would do it at school so everyone would know that I had become an officer. Since this was not a uniform day, I had to carry the hat back home. Now, here comes a great benefit to doing things Bob's way.

As I was walking toward Kedzie, this very, I emphasize, *very* attractive blond girl walked up behind me and said, "You're Don Rasmussen, aren't you?"

I said something like, "Yes," as I looked her over.

Now, you have to understand teenagers of the mid-fifties to put what happened next into proper context. She said something like this, noticing that I am carrying a cadet officer's hat, "You're going to be one of our class leaders next fall. I'm so excited to meet you!"

I was pleased, not only because she was a walking, talking doll, but no one had ever said that they were happy to meet me. It was really kind of cool; I hoped she didn't notice that I was embarrassed. Her name was Pat Shea, and she was in the service club.

After taking my report card home and receiving a somewhat toned-down series of disappointed comments from Dad, I was ready for the summer. I did notice I preferred the negative comments about lack of academic performance more than I did the total silence of my academic achievements. There has to be an answer to some of this continued attitude that I was feeling. The answer would come to me years later.

Bill, Vivien, Bob, and Don

The picture above is one of a very few photos of all four siblings together. Bill had just graduated from DePauw University in Greencastle,

Indiana, and Vivien (Sis) would be graduating from eighth grade just a few hours after this photo was snapped. Bob would be graduating from Gage Park High School later in June, and me, I would be completing my junior year at Gage Park.

Bob and I had been working whenever time allowed and saved to buy suits to wear for special occasions. We definitely added class to the photo.

After an interesting summer of baseball, I was eager to get back to school. It was a strange beginning, because many of my good friends were gone. I hadn't realized how much I had interrelated with members of Bob's class. It seemed like my circle of friends had just become a half-circle.

Although I didn't allow it to affect me, I just figured I would spend more time with my half-circle and look for the opportunity to make new friends, either in my class or classes below ours. I had no idea how things can change so quickly.

I had seen some kids kicking and throwing a football during lunch; I knew a couple of them, so I went over and joined in. Before long I was kicking and they were retrieving. A crowd of kids started gathering as the bell rang. Thank goodness. I was not trying to draw attention to myself; I just saw a chance to join in.

Since the seventh or eighth grade, kicking a football was something I did in our front yard. We had two trees that made rather narrow goal posts and when I had reason to feel good or was frustrated, I would dropkick the football. Some days I might kick a hundred and then not kick a ball again for a week. Sometimes I might kick ten. It was merely a random thing that I did, that I enjoyed. I had never thought, planned, or schemed to do anything with it. It was just fun for five or six years.

After a day or two, word had gotten to our football coach, and he sent word for me to go and see him. I did, and when I left his office, I was on the football team.

I knew my first practice would be an initiation or a physical test, I just didn't know what. It came on the first snap from scrimmage on an extra point attempt. We lined up in a short punt formation. The ball was snapped, and as I caught the ball and started to kick, I caught eleven defensive linemen and backs. It seemed that my blockers wanted to see if I could survive the onslaught. Well, if you have ever seen an eclipse turn day into night, that's what I saw.

As they peeled off me, the defensive players moved to the goal line, the offensive players formed back in the huddle. They were all apparently waiting to see if I was alive. When the last player got off me, I got up and headed for the huddle without saying a word. The first words I heard came from Al Fonseca. As I was getting to my feet gingerly (if I do say so myself), Al pronounced that I was okay. We lined up again a couple of times, and I kicked a couple of practice points.

Without intending to, I expanded my half-circle of friends' potential.

With the class schedule I had, the last thing I needed was a study hall. I had not taken any difficult classes as a senior. In the fall I took "careers," which looked at various careers that we might consider. We also had to write an autobiography. In the autobiography I stated that I was going to be a professional baseball player. I had never thought I would be anything else. All my other classes were just as much of a strain on my brain as that one. That study hall was the first and only study hall I had in four years of high school. It was in that study hall that I met Judy.

I was able to use various reasons to get excused from classes during my senior year. There was always important work that needed to be down in the ROTC room. Another good one was that I needed to see the coach. Miss Scannell, the scourge of serious math students, was in charge of college planning. I had more questions about college than you could shake a stick at, and Miss Scannell was always glad to see me. Sometimes we would talk for an hour or more. She really was a nice lady. Then there was service club business. This was good toward the end of each semester as we were planning the service club breakfast that the officers always planned for all members to honor the graduating seniors.

Of course there was picked platoon in the fall and federal inspection in the spring, which always had problems that required attention.

The fertile mind of a senior could miss a lot of school and still receive passing grades, which I did.

With the conclusion of the first semester, I received all passing grades and went through the routine with Dad that I think he was beginning to tire of—I knew I was. None of it had any meaning now, if it ever did.

The previous spring I had received a baseball letter and had not appeared in a game. That fall, having appeared in a couple of football games, I did not get a letter because I was not on the team at the beginning of the season. It all seemed to be a choreographed dance to satisfy some goal that was never understood nor ever shared with the students under any circumstance.

In the second semester, I needed a different direction and something to do. I began working with the committee planning the Valentine's dance. I met some people that I had gone to school with for four years and never noticed. I am quite sure most of them had never noticed me either. One girl in particular caught my eye. Her name was Lori Ledeika, and I believe she was the chairman of the group. She was smart as a whip, directed, and determined that we were going to have the best Valentine's dance ever.

We met at her home for planning and creating, and we did a lot of the latter. I was assigned to design and develop a slogan sign for over the doorway into the gym. Now, that was going to be fun. As others at the meeting began various art projects and theme development, I designed the entrance. All I needed was the measurements that I would get on Monday and I could have it in place by the time we left school on the day of the dance.

I showed the drawings to Lori, and we kept them under wraps until it was time to put the them up. I surely believe we set the standard for originality and appropriateness for an entry to the dance. I completed the top of the display, and a picture for the yearbook was taken as we finished the entryway.

My main interest in the spring was our sales club. This club should be listed as a club to maximize time away from school under the guise of getting advertising for the yearbook. A primary ingredient to make this a successful adventure on a weekly basis was to have a member of the club have a car at his or her disposal.

Frank Karnoscek fulfilled that requirement and as the only two male members of the club, we had to take long and distant drives to get our advertising assignments completed. Even though the same businesses advertised in the yearbook every year, they had to be sold anew by each graduating class. This took a great deal of time and persuasion. All of this attention to duty basically provided Frank and I with a four-day school week throughout the spring.

I did save time for baseball, even though I had eliminated the school team from any of my plans of being discovered to play professional baseball. I was not disappointed. I was upgraded to keeping the scorebook. I was able to get more time in the batter's box as well as fielding time, but we had a big homerun threat that couldn't move enough to play anywhere except first base. So I was able to keep score and continue to play my third season in the Chicago Public Parks eighteen and over twilight league. I would probably still be the youngest player in the league.

Graduation finally came on June 21, 1955.

Chapter 9

HIGH SCHOOL: EDUCATION BEYOND THE CLASSROOM and FRIENDS

From the day I entered high school, I had this feeling that "*this* is where I am supposed to be." I was determined that it would be so. I soon found friends and a precious few people who had significant influence on me.

Through my class in science, I had thrust upon me a realization that I needed glasses. Very early in the year, Miss Jordan told me to stay after class. I didn't know that I had done anything wrong, but I was nervous about what might be happening. She advised me that she thought I needed glasses, badly. I was instructed to speak to my parents about it immediately and report back the next day their plan to get me glasses.

I wasn't eager to do this, but I had no choice. I knew by implication that if I didn't talk with them, Miss Jordan would be calling them about her concerns. When Dad got home from work, I told Mom and him that Miss Jordan said I needed glasses. Dad's immediate response was, "We can't afford to be buying glasses." I knew better than to object.

The next day Miss Jordan asked me privately, "When will you be getting an eye examination?"

I just told her what Dad had said. I had no idea of the firestorm that I created by being honest. After all, after a serious period of time when I told a lot of lies, Dad had taught me to always tell the truth, no matter what. I did

Miss Jordan had someone in the office call Mom to offer services that the school had to cover the expense of my glasses. I don't know how Mom responded.

When I got home, I was chewed up one side and down the other for discussing family business with a teacher. I tried to explain, "She asked a question, and I answered it honestly."

That just didn't seem to make any sense to them. Boy, talk about being confused.

Dad said, "What's done is done. Saturday morning I am taking you to an eye doctor. We'll see how bad your eyes are."

The next Saturday, sure enough, I went to see an eye doctor and within a week, I was wearing glasses. What a different world I was now seeing. For the first time since I could remember, the world wasn't blurry.

Having come to Gage Park without knowing anyone and being apprehensive about how I would fit in, it was probably natural that the first member of our class that I met would be Bruce Flowers on my first abbreviated day. Just by coincidence we ended up in the same division (homeroom). Locker assignments were made initially by kids just partnering up. After that was completed, the division teacher, Mrs. Dennison in our case, would match the remaining students. No one knew me, so I wasn't bothered by the process, but Bruce had been passed over. Seeing that, I instinctively raised my hand and asked to be partnered with Bruce. His face lit up like a Christmas tree.

When we received our locker, we had to put a padlock on it. I had known this from Bob, and so I had one at the ready. We were dismissed to go put the lock on our assigned locker. We opened the locker and divided it up and then locked the locker. Bruce had a little difficulty learning the combination, but he did conquer it.

I made sure Bruce was included in different things that I was doing since, although he came from a "feeder" elementary school, he didn't appear to have any friends. He remained in school for all four years and graduated. During that entire time, I got to know him and his strength and weaknesses. I was always his friend and he mine.

After high school we went our separate ways and I never gave much thought to Bruce until I became a school administrator. When I began working with special education supervisors, I realized that if Bruce had

HIGH SCHOOL: EDUCATION BEYOND THE CLASSROOM AND FRIENDS

come along fifteen or twenty years later, his experience would have been a disaster.

Special education protects students that it determines have mental limitations or are educability handicapped. I must also say that in the typical "expand your domain" philosophy of modern educational concepts, no discipline has been so outrageous in its analysis than the hierarchy of special education.

In 1976 I met with a new special education supervisor who had been assigned to our school district. During our conversation, she was explaining the new knowledge developed for placement of students in special education. She interrupted herself to express her sympathy to me for having grown up in an unenlightened time.

She stated, point blank, "Mr. Rasmussen, you should have been placed in special education. You are 'educationally handicapped,' you are left-handed." I maintained my composure as I informed her that: number one, I had to approve her for this position in our school, and number two, "You're nuts!" and number three, "You will not be approved, so I suggest you leave this building immediately." She was insulted. Unbelievable.

When she left, I thought of Bruce and what he accomplished. He was not protected, he was challenged, and he flourished. The student needs to become the center of development possibilities again, not a number to expand educational empires. I'm proud to have known Bruce, and I believe I helped him reach his success in school.

Although he has passed on, in my heart he is still my friend.

With no natural clique to belong to since I didn't come from a "feeder" school, I instinctively moved rather easily from one group to another and generally found acceptance and inclusion. This, more than anything else, allowed me to overcome doubts that had been instilled in me at home.

Bob had really emphasized to me that I become involved in school activities. The first activity I joined was the science club, whose president was Barbara Kluth.

For some reason, she took a liking to me, a reasonable, quiet, and insecure kid with less than a month of high school experience. She was a very pretty girl, a bit stocky with a personality that could shake the world.

Over the next several months, a close bond developed, and Barb helped me become more self-assured. Bob and I were invited to a Christmas party that Barb was also at. The group was mostly sophomores and I may have been the only freshman in the group. That party was a catalyst that over the next three years helped me develop a number of friendships with Bob's classmates. I didn't realize how many friends until his class graduated.

Barb was the first young lady that I had a date with. I took her to a movie at the Colony Theater on Fifty-Ninth Street just west of Kedzie, a theater that was once owned by my Uncle Ed Qualkenbush, my Aunt Jeff's husband. Sometime during or after the movie, Barb became the first girl I ever kissed.

I learned a very important lesson one spring Monday afternoon when I was walking Barb home from school. She asked me if I had noticed anything different about her.

After contemplating the question, I answered honestly, "No."

That answer really hurt her feelings. After what seemed like an eternity, she informed me that she had gone on a diet the previous Friday. Lesson learned.

Any time a guy is going with a girl regularly, he should notice her hairstyle and color, because when you are asked that kind of a question, there are only two answers: "You changed your hairstyle (color)—and you had better be sure you got it right—or, "You have lost weight and look terrific." And you had better get that one right also. Answer number two is almost always right since girls are always trying to lose weight.

Barb was one terrific person. I hated the idea that I wouldn't see her over the summer, but there was baseball and she had some definite plans. I don't know what she did over the summer, but when she returned for her junior year, she had morphed from a cute, pudgy girl to this beautiful lady with a gorgeous face and a goddess-like figure. When I saw her, I knew immediately that she outclassed me. We just

HIGH SCHOOL: EDUCATION BEYOND THE CLASSROOM AND FRIENDS

never could connect again like we did a year earlier, but I continued to admire her for the next two years, and still do.

Without Barb to pal around with, I dove into other activities, which included ROTC. I was in the picked platoon, drum and bugle corps, and the ushers club. This caused me to spend a lot of time in the ROTC room. Our lead instructor, Sergeant Roland of the US Army, appointed me again to be the company clerk. That meant that I would be spending even more time in the ROTC designated rooms.

I worked with the ROTC secretary, who was a senior. As she organized, I filed and we got to know each other pretty well. After we had been working with each other for just a short period of time, maybe a month or so, she came up behind me while I was posting something on the bulletin board just outside the main drill room. She asked me what I was posting, and as I turned around to tell her, we came face to face, and then lips to lips. I hadn't thought of her as a possible girlfriend, after all, she was an older woman. I hadn't planned to kiss her, and I don't know if she planned to kiss me. It just happened. We both took the incident smoothly, as if it were an everyday happening, and discussed what I was posting on the board. A day or so later, I was working on my filing after school, and she came into the office to pick something up and then came over to where I was working and we kissed again as she said good-bye.

Now, I really didn't know what was really happening, but I liked it, and I really liked Janet Meike. As we got to know each other better and I began to know her as an individual, I learned that she was very intelligent, hardworking, and had a quiet confidence in herself. Since I was not allowed to date as a fifteen-year-old, I volunteered for usher duty at every evening dance, as did Bob. He became my cover with Dad. It was unusual for any cadet to usher at every dance, much less a sophomore. Every one that mattered knew what we were doing, and no one complained or minded that I got every assignment.

Jan lived west of Kedzie Avenue, so I began using the Kedzie southbound bus so that I could walk Jan home after school.

One beautiful spring day, we were walking down the hall toward the back door of the school, when she tugged at my sleeve and stepped into a recessed doorway and kissed, and kissed. This was a big no-no, students kissing inside the school building, but we didn't get caught. As she walked toward Kedzie, I just floated beside her on a cloud. Jan had to think I was the most naive creature she ever met (which I was) or dumber than a brick (which I was). I just knew that I really liked her.

When she graduated, I felt a little empty, as I knew I would never see her again. I haven't seen her since, but every now and again, I think of her and say a little prayer that she is happy.

I dove into my summer activities, which included working, mowing, and baseball. The summer flew by, and it was time for my junior year of high school.

As I entered my third year of high school, my main goal was more social than academic. Having completed two years of high school with the threat of vocational school hanging over my head, I now felt liberated. I concentrated on my extracurricular activities and ROTC.

Early in the year, picked platoon took center stage. Beginning in the middle of September, those of us that were selected to participate, through an elimination process, began working an hour before school. Within a matter of a couple of weeks, we had learned our program and began refining it. Having been in the platoon the previous year, both Bob and I began to feel that we had a special platoon this year. Every member of the platoon had a greater sense of purpose than the previous year. Our biggest competitor was going to be Lindbloom High School, which was the perennial city champion.

As the date of the district competition approached, we were rounding into a cohesive, disciplined unit. We were eager for the big day to arrive. Personally, and Bob agreed with me here, getting up at five o'clock in the morning every day was beginning to wear on us. With my other school activities, I would generally get home between six and seven o'clock in the evening, often as late as nine.

The last two Saturdays before the competition, we reported to the gym at eight and worked until noon. We were ready. On November 7, 1953, we arrived at the armory ready for inspection and then the drill competition. There were seven schools in our district. We came away both disappointed and excited. Morgan Park HS placed first in what was a surprise to us and everyone else. We came in second—but the big news of the day was that we both beat Lindbloom. Several cadets from various schools mingled with us and felt that we had a good chance of winning the city championship, including some cadets from Lindbloom.

The top two teams from each of five districts would compete for the city championship.

We reported for practice the following Monday at seven o'clock a.m. to learn from Sergeant Roland that we were only a few points out of first place. For the next two weeks, it would be practice, practice, and practice nonstop. Six days a week and a volunteer session on the first Sunday. Everyone showed up at every practice, even the volunteer practice. When the evening of the twenty-first arrived, we knew we were ready.

While all of this was going on, I had been seeing this very pretty and intelligent redheaded girl. We had gotten together earlier in the year when a friend of mine pointed her out to me one day in the cafeteria at lunch. She was sitting a few tables away from me and I couldn't get a good look at her, so I went over and introduced myself. By the reactions of her girlfriends when I approached their table, I think they all knew that she wanted to meet me. They were all very quiet when I approached, then they finished their lunch and left the two of us alone. It all worked out very nicely, and we began seeing each other every day.

I wanted to take her to the city championship, but I knew my parents would not agree to me taking her unless Bob also had a date. Bob was real sweet on a girl in his class, but having never had a date, I knew that he wouldn't ask her without some help.

My girlfriend's name was Betty Endlicher, and the girl Bob liked was Marlene Kus. I talked with Betty, Betty talked with Marlene, and then we arranged a meeting with the four of us, and I suggested that Bob and Marlene go to the armory with us. Bob agreed and asked Marlene to accompany him to the city finals. Everything was set except for the problem of getting our parents to agree to pick the girls up and take them with us.

When we were alone later, Bob said, "We have a problem. Mom and Dad would never agree to you having a date, and when you ask them, they are going to say no."

I told him that I had that all worked out. "I won't ask them, you will."

He responded, "You're nuts."

"Just think about it, you've never asked them about going out on a date. They will be so happy that you like a girl, they will say yes."

Although he wasn't very keen on the idea, he couldn't think of a way around it, so that night he got them together and asked. They were very pleased and said yes.

After it was agreed and since Betty didn't live too far out of the way, we would pick her up too. Then Dad asked Bob, "Did Don put you up to asking us?"

Without using the good sense that the good Lord had given him, he answered, "Yes."

When Bob broke the news to me, he said that after he told Dad it was my idea, Dad just smiled.

The big night arrived and the girls were picked up, and we all had pleasant conversation on the way to the armory. When we arrived Bob and I had to split as soon as all were seated. On our way to meet up with the platoon, in his quiet manner, Bob said to me, "I hope they get along."

Out of the ten schools represented in the city finals, the worst spot to be in was number one according to the averages of the finish in all the preceding years. Fortunately, we didn't know that. We drew the first number.

After the opening ceremonies, we took to the floor. Tonight belonged to us. We knew it. We were sharper than we had ever been in practice. We hit every move perfectly. When we left the floor after our performance, we felt terrific. Sergeant Roland did not exude the confidence we did. He instructed us to return to the staging site when the tenth platoon took the floor.

Bob and I went up and joined Mom, Dad, and the girls. We were nervous, yet confident. Time dragged on. We could pick out flaws in

HIGH SCHOOL: EDUCATION BEYOND THE CLASSROOM AND FRIENDS

every platoon. We didn't know it, but every sponsor of every platoon told their crew that all they had to do to win the competition was to be perfect. If we had known that, we wouldn't have been nervous.

After the last platoon completed their routine, they remained on the floor and the other nine marched in in reverse order. We were the last platoon to enter and await the judges' decision. The third place platoon was announced and then the second. At that moment we knew we had won. As the chief announced, "First Place, Gage Park High School," my chest swelled, a huge lump constricted my throat, and I had to fight back the tears.

We had to come to attention and then marched to a predetermined location on the floor. The whole platoon became confused, and we made our first mistake, then recovered and all ended well as we were presented our medals.

Nothing was said that night, but on the first day back at school, we learned something about our performance. At the beginning of the presentation, each platoon had a thousand points. For each group mistake, twenty-five points were deducted (a group mistake is three or more members of the platoon making the mistake), each individual mistake resulted in one point being deducted. The judges checked stride and cadence. Perfection was a thirty-inch stride and a cadence of a hundred and twenty strides per minute. It was required that the judges make this measurement once for each platoon. They checked us three times and came up with the same perfect measurements each time.

By the way, we scored 972 points, a deduction of twenty-eight points—a new city picked platoon record.

When we returned to meet our parents and the girls, the girls congratulated us and Dad suggested that we stop for a piece of pie on the way home. While we were gone, the girls must have wowed our parents because the rest of the entire evening went as smoothly as could be. Back at school Betty told me how nice my parents were. I thanked her.

I continued to see Betty on a regular basis in school and shared time with her at school events. The winter of our junior year was lost due to my hospitalization and recovery from the appendix operation.

I had no concept of how long the recovery would take or if it would have any lasting affect through the spring on baseball. It was of no particular concern, as I was confident that I would snap back.

Betty and I had become more comfortable with each other than I had with the girls I had as best friends in my freshman and sophomore years. We went to dances with my parents' approval. The highlight of our friendship was the junior prom. Betty was a most precious friend, and I am very pleased that we have remained friends through all these years after reconnecting in the early 1980s

In the spring of that year, my brother Bob's best friend decided he wanted to fight me. To this day I have no idea why he felt compelled to do this. When he initiated a challenge, I had two choices. I would have to back down, which I swore to myself I would never do again, or I would have to fight him. As casually as I could, I said, "Okay."

A benefit of belonging to the ROTC was that you could always use the rifle range to settle arguments in private. I suggested that we go there for privacy. He agreed. So, we went downstairs and he waited as I took off my glasses, and then he took a fighting stance and began dancing around as if he were in a boxing ring. I raised my right hand as if in a defensive position and then threw a left that caught him on the right side of his head in the vicinity of the right eye. The area of the eye immediately swelled up. It must have jarred him pretty well, because he said, "That's it, I've had enough."

I was glad to see that response, since I didn't want to fight in the first placc. This was the first fight I had had since eighth grade, and I really didn't want another one.

Bob's graduation was a big deal for me. I was an usher, so I was seating people and directing them to areas where friends were waiting. Just before the commencement was to begin, I went over to the graduates and bid a number of friends good-bye and good luck. When it was over, there were more good-byes and I began to wonder what my senior year was going to be like with so many friends gone.

That was a question that would be answered in time. Now it was time for working and baseball. This was my fourth year of following

HIGH SCHOOL: EDUCATION BEYOND THE CLASSROOM AND FRIENDS

Bill's team and coach Bob Hunt. That year would be without Bill, as he went out to New Jersey to work for the summer.

I was working at a shoe store for my first legal-age job.

The summer went very well as I worked regularly, and my hours were such that there was no conflict with my baseball playing.

I will note that at the conclusion of my junior year of high school, I was halfway to achieving an even split with the honor roll. The first four semesters I was on it, and the last four semesters I wouldn't be.

After the summer was over, it was time for school to begin and another shot at the city championship in the ROTC picked platoon. We started two months in advance of the district event. The feel of the previous year just wasn't there. Taking the bus without Bob and not having him to discuss our development as a team definitely gave me a different perspective. I wasn't the only one that noticed. Sergeant Roland attempted to pump some juice into the group with more constant and sometimes vitriolic rants.

I came up with an idea and met with the Sergeant about it. He thought it might help, so he brought it before the group one morning. He suggested that it would improve our appearance if we all had identical shoes to wear. He explained that I could get a quality shoe that I had shown him, but everyone must agree to buy their own pair. Everyone bought into it, and we set a time for me to measure each cadet's feet for proper fit. That was accomplished and we marched forward.

I was beginning to feel better about our chances as November approached. We were starting to get the team feeling that we had the year before, but we never quite got to the level that we needed to be at and when the district competition was over, we were sent home. We didn't even make it to the city finals.

Our poor showing seemed to set the stage for the entire year in the ROTC. At the beginning of the second semester, I decided that finishing the year as an ROTC was not something I wanted to do. I switched to gym, which really suited my ambitions better.

In the fall semester I worked just hard enough to assure that I would have easily passing grades. It wasn't that I didn't want to make the honor roll, I just preferred Dad chewing me out for not doing better than the total indifference that I drew when I did well.

Our honor guard did occasional funerals, but thankfully not as many as the year before. Although I had quit the ROTC, Sergeant Roland kept me on board with the honor guard and with the federal inspection, he asked me to lead a platoon. It was a nice gesture.

I really enjoyed gym. The physical activity suited me, and I definitely got into it. Since I was going to major in physical education when I got to college, it was appropriate that I have some idea of what it was all about at the high school level.

In the first semester, I met Judy in a study hall. She and a friend sat right behind me and concentrated on driving me up a wall. It's a good thing that I didn't have much to do in the way of studying. Judy decided that I needed a nickname, so after a few study hall sessions and a lot of nonsensical foolish discussions and derisive comments, she decided that my nickname would be "Snake." I'm sure glad that never caught on.

My initial feeling about her was that she was a juvenile flake and her friend was slightly less mature.

As they got past that teenage girl thing and began to get into some serious back and forth, I learned that she was very intelligent, had a great sense of humor and was pretty good looking.

It really didn't take too long to go from antagonizing one another to exchanging class schedules to walking her home from school before I headed out to catch a bus home. I actually ended up dating Judy more than girls the previous three years combined. This was a combination of circumstances that included age and having a driver's license. As with the previous girls I shared infatuation with, I learned from Judy. Her enthusiasm for life and constant sense of humor lifted my spirits beyond anything I could imagine. She got a bang out of my being so naive. She would say something like, "You are so backward that if you decided to take me, you would *epar* me, that's *rape* backward." She would laugh so hard that she never noticed that I had nary a clue as to what she was talking about. I guess I really was backward in a lot of ways.

That year we went to two proms. My senior prom we went with a group of guys and their dates and concluded the night at the Ice Show at the Palmer House Hotel. One of the guys in our party worked at the hotel and had set up reserve seating for us. We had the front row and when the skaters would do a quick stop at the front of the stage, we would get showered with ice chips. It really was pretty neat.

We attended Judy's junior Prom in a lower emphasis due to my financial capacity at the time. A working guy in 1955 could budget handling one prom a year, but two was quite a strain. We nevertheless had a fantastic time and spent the night in another couple's basement, dancing all night. In the morning I went home, changed, and we went to the Indiana Dunes, where we spent the day and early evening and then back to the basement for another night of dancing. Sunday morning I headed home to get ready for a ball game we had scheduled at one o'clock that afternoon.

I hadn't slept since I woke up Friday morning and really needed to get some sleep before leaving for the game. I asked Mom to wake me up about ten o'clock so I could get ready for the game.

Dad stepped into the conversation and directed me to mow the lawn before I took a nap. I suggested that I take a nap, go to the game, and mow the lawn after the game.

"Your job as part of this family is to mow your half of the lawn on Saturday. Since you weren't here to do it, I told Bob to leave his half for you to do today. You have to learn to schedule your fun around your responsibilities," he said. I pointed out that it would take three hours of mowing nonstop to complete the job. His response was, "You had better get going."

What choice did I have? I mowed the yard, grabbed a bowl of cereal, put my uniform on, and headed for the bus stop. I'm surprised I had my shoes and glove with me.

I played the game, had two hits, stole a base, and made no errors. When the game was over, I headed for our bench and looked down as I crossed the foul line. Then, it was over; we won the game, and I collapsed in foul territory.

Coach and a couple of guys on the team moved me to some shade and shortly later Dad showed up to drive me home. Dad apologized to the coach for me sleeping through the game. The guys told me at the next practice that Coach told Dad that I hadn't missed the game and turned and left before he did something he would regret.

My Dad's logic and sense of propriety had something lacking.

I got a good night's sleep that night and went to school as usual. I determined that I wouldn't initiate any conversation with Dad for a while. After a few days, Dad asked me about the game last Sunday. I told him we won. He kept pressing me for more, and I only fed him what he asked for. Finally, he gave up and just shook his head.

The one thing that came out of all of this was that I knew for sure: I was going to be a ballplayer. I didn't know how it was going to come about, but I was going to be a professional baseball player.

Between the junior prom and graduation, I had an occasion to accompany an ROTC friend to lunch one day at a small restaurant just a couple of blocks from the school. His name was Don Hackbar. We were both wearing our ROTC uniforms. As we walked past the alleyway, a student I knew stepped out of the alley and confronted Don with a switchblade knife.

He very quietly, and in a controlled voice, told Don that he was going to cut him. Poor Don turned as white as a sheet. The kid then addressed me, and said, in effect, that his beef was with the other Don and that I had treated him well and he meant no harm to me. I addressed him with a wild, spur of the moment plea. I said something like, "Man, you picked the wrong day to do whatever you plan to do to Don. This is uniform day and he is wearing an Army-owned uniform that is loaned to the ROTC. In just a few days when school is over, they will come to the school and check all the uniforms. When they find one that has been all cut up, you will be in more trouble than you want."

It was wild, it was crazy, and it worked. He looked me right in the eye and said to me, "All my buddies know you have always been straight with them, and so I will catch Don at another time." He put his knife away and left.

It took Don a few minutes to compose himself, and then he told me that he had never heard such a ridiculous story in his life, but he was sure glad that it worked. I told him to remain calm and act as if he knew that everything I said was fact. He agreed and we had lunch and headed back to school.

I never saw Don or his nemesis again.

Graduation was held on June 21, 1955. Judy's sister, Jan, graduated in my class and Judy's mother had arranged to take Jan, Judy, and I to a celebration dinner at the Sabre Room on Ninety-Fifth Street in Hickory Hills. This was one of the Chicago area's top nightclubs and restaurants. We had a wonderful evening.

Chapter 10

TRANSITION: THE HARD, COLD FACTS OF LIFE

The final weeks of school prior to graduation were once again spoiled with an ongoing verbal battle with Dad. Unlike the one shortly after graduating from elementary school that I had to win, this one I wanted to win, but could see the logic in his thinking.

We were a couple of months into the baseball season and were looking pretty strong in our search to make the National Babe Ruth League Tournament being held in Bethlehem, Pennsylvania, in late August. I certainly felt that I was a viable part of the team. I had a couple of places I could stay for a week while the family went to New Jersey for Bill's wedding.

Dad was adamant that I would go and be a part of the wedding. Bob would be the best man and I, an usher. (He would also emphatically assert that when the time came, I would be the best man at Bob's wedding, while Bill would serve as usher and at my wedding, Bill would be the best man, while Bob would be the usher.) Even at the age of seventeen, I knew that he would probably get one out of three in that plan, and that would be the first one. I was fighting tooth and nail to stay and play baseball, because it was important for my team.

Even with the fantasy of his future planning, I could see the logic of his wanting the entire family to go to Bill's wedding.

I lost the battle, and the morning after I graduated from high school, we loaded the car and headed for New Jersey. It would be a two-day trip with an overnight stay at a Howard Johnson Motel. Once we arrived, we were caught up in a whirlwind of activity to get ready for the wedding. Bob and I had to get fitted for our tuxedos, meet our counterparts for the bride, return to the formal wear shop and pick up our monkey suits, and then get back to the home we were being housed in and change into suit and tie for the rehearsal dinner that, because of our late arrival in New Jersey, had been scheduled immediately after the rehearsal.

Bob had alerted me a week or so before the trip that it would be a rush for us to get everything together and get to New Jersey in time for Bill's wedding with my graduation being so close to the wedding. He brought it up because he thought Mom and Dad might ask me to skip the ceremony. Even if I weren't there, I would still be a high school graduate. I told Bob that there was no way I was going to miss my graduation. "Bill went to his graduation, you went to your graduation, and if he thinks there is any chance of carrying out his future plans for our weddings, I will go to my graduation."

I was sure Bob had been encouraged to discuss the possibility with me. My response, if relayed to Mom and Dad, must have made some sense to them, because they didn't ask me to skip my graduation.

The trip out contained a lot of grumbling about being rushed due to circumstances, but nothing specific. I just figured that if they hadn't been grumbling about that, they would be grumbling about something else. It's just the way they were.

Well, everything went off as planned. Bill and Mickey were married and off to their honeymoon as Bob and I and the girls in the wedding party went out and partied. It was this night that I had my first drink. I don't think it was Bob's first. I didn't particularly like the taste, so it took me a long time to get to the second one. Not so with the third. Bob didn't have any problems at all, so I figured that he had learned something in his first year of college. We simply had a blast. My girl gave me her gloves as a remembrance of the evening, and we made plans to get together if my Colts made it all the way to Bethlehem.

By the time we got in early in the morning, our game, back in Chicago, would be played later that day. I was really praying that they would win without me. We needed a strong record going into the first round later in the summer.

We got a late start back to Illinois the next morning because Bob and I were not up at the crack of dawn. I must have had better sense than Bob. He woke up with a headache. I didn't.

The trip home was a repeat of the trip out, except for subject matter and direction. Grumbling was now concentrated on the fact that at the rehearsal dinner, Mrs. McDonnell asked Justin, her husband, which was the flavor of pie that she liked so well.

Mom, Dad, and Sis (Vifafddfvien) went round and round about this for eight hundred miles over two days. Bob and I just sat back and tried to ignore the whole thing.

Back in Oak Lawn, early the next day, I called Coach Lyons to see how our game came out the previous Sunday. We lost. He asked if we were back in town, and when I told him that I was, he asked me to come out early that coming Sunday for some extra batting practice, and concluded, "Don, I'm really glad you're back."

When I arrived earlier than expected, I went to first base and shared infield grounders with a couple of other regular infielders and our utility guy. As more of the players arrived and we began our pregame routine, Coach called me over and introduced me to a priest from St. Rita High School. This gentleman was to be my batting coach for the next twenty minutes or so.

I stepped into the batter's box with my left-handed stance and hit a couple of pitches. I was instructed to move my weight more to my back foot. I did as I was told and immediately felt I was hitting the ball more solidly. After a few good shots up the middle, my new coach said, "More weight on the back foot." Feeling like I was about to fall backward, the next pitch I drove hard toward right field. I had never been a pull hitter, so I felt like the first specific hitting instruction was going quite well.

As soon as I hit the ball, Coach told me to step out of the box. It was time for some talk before I would hit again. This man of the cloth was moving up the steps of a pedestal of respect very rapidly in my mind.

As we sat down away from the field, and he told me that I had a good eye and had developed sound fundamentals except for weight distribution. After about a seven- or eight-minute discussion, he had me get into the box again and hit four or five pitches. I was very pleased with the results. He didn't even know that I was a switch hitter, but I crossed over to the right-handed batter's box and took five or six swings from the right side of the plate. Except for the one I swung at and missed, I did pretty well.

During the game that day, I didn't feel a lot of difference. I had a couple of singles and stole second each time. That set up runs for us, and we won the game. The main thing I noticed was that both my outs for the day came on decently hit fly balls. I had never been much of a fly ball hitter.

The following Sunday was a day I will never forget. For all the wrong reasons. Our pitcher, Ted Kucharski, threw a no-hitter, but we still lost the game because of me. I was not very pleased with myself after this one.

It was a nip-and-tuck game with neither team hitting well. In the later innings, we got a runner on first with two outs as I came to bat against a left-handed pitcher. He got two strikes on me quickly and then threw a fastball on the inside part of the plate that I jumped on and hit a scorcher over the third baseman's head. It was obviously fair the last time I saw it, but it was bending toward the foul line. Sure enough, as I was rounding first, the umpire yelled foul ball. I looked toward left field as the left fielder was chasing the ball into foul territory.

I was back getting my bat when the ball got to the umpire. As I stepped back into the box, the umpire said to me, "Sorry, kid, I missed that one; there's chalk on the ball." The ball I hit would have easily been a home run and scored two runs to put us ahead by a score of 2–0. I stepped out of the box, shook my head, and tried to get my head back in the game. With two strikes on me, I was determined to focus on the ball. I swung and missed for the final out of the inning.

We made it until the ninth inning when our opponent got a runner on first base. He was a speedster, and I was holding him on first. On the first pitch to the next batter, the runner took off for second base. I yelled "going" as I moved from the base farther into fair territory. The batter hit a hard grounder right down the first base line directly toward the bag, where I had been just a second or so ago. I dived back to my left and caught the ball as I was sliding into foul territory. I got up and turned toward a throwing position to throw to second base. The runner didn't slide; he just made the turn and headed for third. I adjusted and threw to third in the ground and past the third baseman. The runner that was on first base scored all the way from first on my error. Ted's no-hitter was intact, but we just lost the game on what turned out to be my only error of the season. I had a hard time getting that game out of my mind.

In the middle of the next week, we had a three-game non-league series with the University of Chicago baseball team. This turned out to be a lot more than I expected when Coach Lyons informed us to make sure everyone would be able to make the games. We had a couple of guys that had work commitments, but they said they would make adjustments so they could play in these games. We would be playing at Stagg Field.

Stagg Field! Just those two words made me excited, just to know that I would be playing on that famous turf from the days when Amos Alonzo Stagg commanded one of the first great college football programs in the country. This was a stadium in which legends and history were made. It was under the stands that the Manhattan Project provided the United States with entry into the nuclear age.

Our team, the JC Colts was made up of high school kids and recently graduated high school players.

We were supposedly over matched. I was leading off, as I did in most of our games that summer, and I started the first game off with a single and a stolen base. I only occupied one other spot in the batting order that entire season, and that was third in the lineup. The whole series just got better after that. In the three games, I had three walks, four singles, and a double in twelve at-bats along with six stolen bases. I played error-less ball at first base, with a .556 batting average for those three games

In my last at-bat of the third game, I pulled a line drive over the first baseman's head and cruised into second with an easy standup double. I later scored the last run of the game.

The University of Chicago had a small, but loyal following of fans that had been obviously supportive of their team throughout the series. After I scored the last run of the third game, as I was heading for our dugout, I heard a fan say, "We've seen a special player during these games." He said it loud enough for me to hear, and I instinctively put my head down and continued to the dugout. I have always had a difficult time accepting praise.

In just a matter of days, I was approached by a scout for the Philadelphia Phillies, who asked me if I would be interested in playing professional baseball. When I said yes, he suggested that we meet somewhere and discuss the possibilities.

"Since you graduated from Gage Park, why don't we meet at the field house after your game today?"

I said, "Okay."

"Will your Dad sign for you"?

"I'm sure he will." With that he gave me his card and told me to call him after I discussed it with Dad.

He said, "By the way, you will be going to Ft. Walton Beach, Florida."

I couldn't wait to get home and talk with Dad. I should have known better. When I told Dad that I had reached my goal and "the Philadelphia Phillies have offered me an opportunity to play professional baseball, but I need you to sign the contract when I get it," he said, "No, all my boys are going to get a college education."

I jumped in and told him that this was my dream. He cut me off and said, "This conversation is over, period."

He refused to talk about baseball the rest of the night.

I called the scout the next day, and he told me that he was sorry to hear that.

Just like that, my dream was over.

I was devastated, but there was nothing I could do about it.

The rest of the season was a blur. I don't remember most of the games the rest of the year. There was a particular play in one game that is really etched in my mind simply because it was so weird.

A right-handed batter swung hard and hit the ball right off the tip of his bat. The ball was spinning dramatically toward the foul line after it hit the ground in foul territory thirty to forty feet from the plate. I started for the ball and then thought that it might make it back to fair territory. I stopped at the bag and waited. The ball kept spinning and turning toward me. I checked the batter. He was standing back from the plate, taking a practice swing, not running to first. I had time. The ball finally rolled fair just as it reached me. The ball had slowly rolled three or four inches fair and touched the home plate side of first base.

I looked up, while standing and making no move toward the ball. The umpire was looking at me and saying nothing.

I yelled, "Mister Umpire." He didn't respond. I tried it again, "Mister Umpire—this is a fair ball!" With that I leaned over, picked up the ball, and made an exaggerated stomp on the base.

The umpire yelled at me, "You're right, the batter is out," as he raised his right arm—with vigor.

After the game the umpire came over and talked with me. He told me that it was the smartest and most patient play he had ever seen by a first baseman.

I was taken out of my doldrums by a game we played in Kenosha, Wisconsin. This was a summer college team sponsored by the Pittsburg Pirates, filled with college juniors and seniors that were pro prospects.

The Kenosha ballpark was well manicured and a joy to play on. I scratched out one hit by slapping a grounder just out of the reach of the third baseman into left field. Since I was batting left-handed, it was a lucky shot. I did steal second, but died there. Our pitchers did an outstanding job, but we lost one to nothing.

After the game we had a nice bus ride back to Sherman Park on Garfield Boulevard. This was the first time I had been through downtown Chicago at night, and I just marveled at the lights. It was really awesome.

We made it through the rest of the season and broke a tie by losing our last game of the year. The game we lost while I was in New Jersey and the game we lost on my error put us out of the tournament.

After the last meeting, Joe Lyons called a meeting at his home and we turned in our uniforms and selected the MVP of the team. Two of us were nominated. I lost by one vote. I felt uneasy voting for myself, so I cast my vote for Charlie Wisniewski, a pitcher/outfielder with a great arm and a solid stick. Charlie voted for himself. I think my negative image of myself cost me. Oh well, Charlie had a real good year and was a great guy.

We had one last event. The JCs was sponsoring a barbeque and swim party for us at the Sherman Park swimming pool. We were all expected to bring dates.

As it turned out, I was the only player that wasn't dating during the summer, so I had to find a date. None of the girls I went to high school with was available, so I ended up bringing a girl from the neighborhood to the event. After that night I never saw any of the players again except Charlie, who I ran into a year later.

I just couldn't get over not being able to play professional baseball and it affected me very negatively as I was preparing to go to college in late August.

JC Colts - 1955

Chapter II

COLLEGE ON MY OWN

As summer was winding down it was time to get ready to go to college. My heart really wasn't in it, but just turning eighteen and knowing each year I would be less and less likely to be able to make it in baseball, I was totally frustrated.

My experience with high school baseball had me pretty well convinced that educational institutions did not produce the kinds of coaches that would provide the stepping-stones necessary to develop professional baseball players. I was naïve with that outlook. The one thing I was sure of was that in the summer of 1955, I had solid coaching and some special coaching from a Catholic priest.

Over the last couple of years of high school, it was made clear to me that I could not think of going to DePauw as Bill had done with the aid of a scholarship and Bob, who was attending without a scholarship. Dad had worked out some kind of deal with Bill to help Bob financially get through his four years.

I had selected Northern Illinois University because it was the closest teachers college to Chicago without being in the city. The sole purpose of my selection was Judy. I thought I might be able to get back often enough to see her.

My scholarship paid tuition and books and I was responsible for the rest. My Grandpa O'Connor had given me two hundred and fifty dollars to help me get started in college. As we drove to Dekalb, Dad let me know that after the money, which he was keeping for my initial room, was gone, I would be on my own. He followed this up with a statement that "you have been good at making money, so keep it up."

I was dumbfounded, frustrated, and frankly, mad as hell. As soon as we got there, he dropped me off with my belongings in front of the administration building and left. Starting out in baseball, I would have been paid more than I had earned in my part-time jobs through high school, and he had refused me that opportunity.

Now to fulfill his ambition to have all of his boys getting a college education, I was to get a job and put myself through school, for which he would take credit after I graduated. I had thought for a long time that I was out of step and had problems to overcome.

As I started college, I was beginning to think that my place in the family was not about me, but something that bothered my dad about me.

He worked to help Bill, he and Bill worked to help Bob, so it was reasonable in his mind that I work to put Don through college. There seemed to be some inequity going on here.

Apparently, in Dad's mind, it made sense somehow.

I could just not get comfortable with being at Northern. I worked in the school cafeteria for both breakfast and lunch. Worked my schedule around those two time periods, worked on making the JV football team, played touch football on the quad after football practice, and still found time to be frustrated about baseball.

There wasn't anything I could do about it, so I started going into downtown DeKalb for coffee at night and engaging in conversation with anyone I could meet up with. It ate up a lot of time and made for some short, deep sleeping when I hit the sack. The only highlight of my time at the school was one weekend that Judy came up. My grades were barely acceptable, but I made it through the first semester.

As soon as I finished my last final exam, I got on a bus and headed home.

Had I had any other place to go, I would have. As soon as I got home, Dad ordered me to go and get a job, "because you are not going to stay here free." The next day I went out and began looking for a full-time job. Taking a bus and walking was not the easiest way to look for a job. The only job I came up with was just not acceptable to me due to a sickening sweet aroma that you couldn't escape from, and it was a dead-end job. With each passing day, I became more and more frustrated.

At one point I told him, "I guess all I'm good at is playing baseball."

He yelled back at me, "Forget baseball, by the time you are old enough to sign your own contract, they won't want you."

He never ceased to amaze me! But why?

I got some part-time jobs to hang on to until I could get out of there. In March I enrolled at Eastern Illinois University using the same scholarship that I had used at Northern and immediately got a job at the A & W Root Beer stand a couple of miles east of the campus. I was making and saving money to buy a car. Going to classes was something I just had to do. I began studying the teachers as well as the classwork and would learn the different concepts and techniques various professors used in their classrooms.

As an example, one history professor I liked had an approach that each student pick a specific event or historical figure and concentrate his or her reading efforts on that event or person. We had an assignment to read five historical books for the quarter. I read one on the life of Teddy Roosevelt and turned in information on his life that was significant with the names of authors from five different books, highlighting a different aspect of his life on each card. Another history professor always called on the people in the middle and back rows to respond during oral finals. Although I always sat in the back row of the room during class, when it came time for the final exam and only grade of the course, I arrived early and sat front and center. As the professor walked back and forth in front of me, so close that I could smell his aftershave (it didn't smell very good) for two hours, he never saw me. His eyes focused on the back rows because he knew that the students in the front row were prepared and he didn't want to waste his time. A friend of mine who thought I was a little "nuts" for abandoning the back row for a seat in the first row was called on five times and had no clue. He failed the class and I, never called on, easily passed. He was the brother of the lady I worked for at the root beer stand.

I lived in basketball coach Bob Carey's house and had a couple of interesting character's that were noteworthy. One was a Korean War veteran attending school on the GI Bill. I don't believe that he was ever sober during the entire quarter. I don't believe that he attended class and by summer session, he was gone from the house. I didn't know why, but I felt sorry for him and couldn't understand what he was doing in college. He was very likable when he wasn't being obnoxious. The other was "Chick" Hearn, my roommate, who was a pitcher on the baseball team that concluded the season with a 1–11 conference record and overall lost twice as many games as they won. I never talked baseball with Chick because I didn't want him to know that I was a ballplayer, especially one that had been offered a pro contract the previous July.

During a game I attended, I noticed that the Eastern Illinois coach was really old. I had been enrolled in three institutions of learning since leaving elementary school. All three, Gage Park, Northern, and Eastern, had old, worn-out coaches.

I went to watch a couple of Eastern's baseball games that spring and ran into an old friend from the previous summer. Charlie was a pitcher and outfielder for the JC Colts and was playing for St. Mary's. As I was standing around before the game, Charlie spotted me and came over to say hi. It was good to see him. He expressed concern that I wasn't playing.

Not wanting him to know that I had to make a living as well as go to school, I relied on the old standby that I had transferred from Northern and was ineligible for a calendar year. He seemed satisfied with my answer.

Because Charlie was playing, I watched the entire game, which ended in a tie. As he was heading for their bus, he yelled to me, "They could sure use you!" I yelled my thanks to him as well as luck for the remainder of his college career.

With the end of the spring quarter, I still needed a summer quarter to complete my first year of college. By now I had fully accepted Dad's admonition that I pay for my college education. If I were to get through this phase of my life, the only thing I could be sure of was that Dad would proudly boast that he had been successful in getting all of his boys through college.

The only cost to me was losing out on my dream and plans of playing professional baseball and the cost of my education.

By carrying a full load in the summer, I not only completed my first year but also had some credit hours as a sophomore. By continuing to take a full load each quarter year round, I could graduate after the summer quarter of 1958 and be able to sign a contract to play professional baseball. The only thing that would still be hanging over my head would be my required military service, which could create a problem, especially since I hadn't been able to play baseball since 1955. Things just didn't look good.

There wasn't anything I could do beyond just keep trucking along. That is what I did. I carried a full load in the fall quarter and upon completion of that, I signed up for a full load in the winter quarter.

By the time we got to January of the winter quarter, the combination of studying, long walks from downtown Charleston to the campus, and working fifty-plus hours a week on top of the burden of not playing baseball got to me

We headed to Florida primarily with the hope that the weather would relieve the pain in my knee. What a brilliant decision that was. Nothing could change our course.

We had a definite destination when we arrived in Florida. Beth had a aunt that lived in Homestead and we were on our way there when we drove through Tampa. Everything was looking good until we reached the southern part of town.

We weren't far from being out of Tampa when a police car pulled up behind me with lights flashing. A knew that I wasn't speeding as I pulled over to the side of the road and came to a stop. I placed my hands on the steering wheel and waited for his arrival. No movement from the officer, instead a I received a barked command, "Exit the vehicle and keep your hands in clear sight."

I knew this wasn't a normal situation so I just followed orders. When I got out of the car, he told me to turn around and face the patrol car, which I did, slowly. That's when I saw it. It was the biggest looking gun barrel I had ever seen and it was pointed directly at me.

The officer asked me several questions that I must have answered to his satisfaction since he lowered his gun. I asked him, "What is this all about?"

He advised me that within the last half an hour there had been a bank robbery and the two men were driving a gray car with the same body style as yours and a temporary license taped in the back window. Since I had bought this car just before leaving on this trip we had a temporary license taped in the back window.

A very relaxed officer now was smiling as he recommended that we find a motel and get off the road as soon as possible or you will be stopped again. We followed his advice. I had handled the crises pretty well I thought, but as I was getting my identification out at the motel I noticed that my hands were shaking.

The following morning after we left Tampa and found a restaurant for breakfast a police car pulled in beside us. I thought, "Here we go again."

Fortunately, the officers that got out of their car were both smiling and just wanted to tell us that the bank robbers were captured last night. They just knew we were the couple that got stopped as possible suspects shortly after the robbery.

For me, as I thought about it, this was a once in a lifetime experience that I would never forget! (In thirty-eight years this robbery scare would become miniscule).

We made it all the way down the coast to Homestead and had a good visit with Beth's cousins and aunt and uncle. One of their daughters had married an airman stationed at Homestead Air Force Base.

I knew that I had a military obligation ahead of me so I asked airman Richard Varney a lot of questions. The long and the short of it was that in a matter of two days Beth and I were headed back to Illinois.

On the way back north we stopped in a beautiful town that we had made note of on our way down to Florida.

Macon, Georgia was an idyllic picturesque city that had really stuck in our mind and we planned to get a room in a tourist home, have a nice dinner and take in a movie as a highlight of our belated honeymoon. All went well until early in the morning after our night on the town.

Neither Beth or I could sleep. I had a strange feeling that we just shouldn't be here. As I was trying to figure things out, Beth felt my shoulder to see if I was sleeping. When I responded, she said that she had a premonition of danger and we needed to leave. That made it two out of two, so we got up, packed our meager belongings and stealthily made our way down the stairs and out the front door. We pushed the car out of the driveway and drove a block away before slamming the doors closed and turning on the lights.

We felt a little foolish as we drove north and listened to the music on our radio to calm, what I now thought were irrational fears.

About a hundred and fifty or so miles out of Macon at six-thirty a news report informed us that a tourist home in Macon had burnt to the ground earlier this morning, two people are missing.

Beth thought we should stop and call the Macon police and let them know we left before the fire. I was just scared enough to say, "No."

We had decided that the Air Force would be good for us. We had no idea how good it would be.

That decision led me to join the United States Air Force, and had me back in college in less than a year in September of 1957. In January of 1958, I became a full-time college student, performing my military duties at night and weekends. I was able to remain a full-time student through that summer before I was shipped to Thule, Greenland, for a year. While in Greenland I attended the University of Maryland extension program and completed some tough courses that required a lot of concentration, meaning that I had the remainder of my classes more adapted to a full course load and full-time military work.

In September of 1959, back at McNeese College, I took twenty credit hours and followed that with twenty-two credits of courses in

January of 1960. By taking nine hours in the summer, I only needed thirteen hours in the fall of 1960 to complete my bachelor's degree.

From the time I first stepped on a college campus in September of 1955 until I completed my bachelor's degree and completed my four-year Air Force tour of duty in January of 1961, I had devoted five years and five months to the effort. That was really a "brilliant decision" we made way back in January of 1957. And as an extra bonus, I even had the opportunity to play a year of baseball.

During the fall of 1960, I received a phone call at the gym from Major Carmichael advising me that I would be required to attend a company assembly, and summer dress uniform was to be worn. He gave me the date and time and reemphasized that attendance was mandatory. Since Captain Miller was in the office, I asked him about the assembly because our company commander had always made a point to assure me that I was excused from such formations. Rene basically advised me that he had no clue, but you had better be there.

When an assembly was held to honor our baseball team at the end of our season, I wasn't even informed. When I arrived for duty that night, Captain Miller presented me with my trophy. He didn't want me to miss any school. He really wanted me to get my degree before I left the Air Force

So, why was this assembly so important?

The entire company was called in so they could witness the presentation of a certificate from the Strategic Air Command headquarters located at Offutt Air Force Base on behalf of General Thomas S. Power, Commander in Chief of SAC, presented by our company commander, Major Carmichael.

He spoke for about fifteen minutes about the uniqueness of this award and how rarely it is presented. It seemed to me that this must have really been something, and whomever he was talking about, he must have been feeling pretty good about then. Then he read the certificate and as soon as he said, "The certificate states, 'Certificate of Distinguished Educational Achievement,'" I thought that it might be for me, yet when he called me to come to the front of the assembly, I was still surprised. I had no idea that such an award even existed.

When I arrived at the front of the group, I saluted the major and he saluted me back as he offered me congratulations.

Major Don Carmichael presenting SAC award to Don

Chapter 12

I DID IT MY WAY
MASTER'S DEGREE DOCTORAL STUDY

I turned down the opportunity to stay in Lake Charles and play baseball for McNeese after receiving my separation from the Air Force. The week that we had completed our requirements for our bachelor's degrees, we talked about the future and life without going to school all the time. I had made all the arrangements for getting our financial ties concluded in Louisiana, and we left with more than sufficient funds for us to be able to take our time getting acclimated to a complete civilian life.

After a final check with the school on the first of February, we went out for breakfast and pointed the car north toward Illinois.

Before we even got close to Illinois, I was having some problems, mentally, about whether or not we had a future together. Ever since I spent a year pretty much isolated from the world, I couldn't get my mind off Judy. The only thing to do was to discuss it with Beth, and trapped in a car for a long road trip might be the best time and way to do it. So we did.

After a while I told her that I just had to go and see her, then I would know. Beth is the greatest, but I hadn't come to that understanding by this time in our lives.

When we reached Illinois, we decided to go to Charleston, where we had met at Eastern Illinois University. As we were walking around, reminiscing, I decided to go over to the gym and see if any of my old professors in physical education were still there. I ran into basketball coach Bob Carey, whose home I had lived in while I was attending Eastern before Beth and I married and left for Florida. Coach Carey asked me what I had been doing the past four years. I told him that I had served four years in the Air Force and finished my bachelor's degree. The look on his face was one of astonishment. He said, "That had to have been a gargantuan job. Fill me in."

After we discussed judo, handball, weight training, baseball, intramural supervision, earning 104 semester hours of credit, the SAC award, baseball, and handball trophies, I also pointed out that Beth had completed her bachelor's degree.

He suggested that if I were at all interested, he thought that what I had accomplished in the last four years would make me an ideal candidate for a graduate assistantship.

"While you are here, let's go talk with Dr. Masley and get the paper work started and if you decide to do it, you'll be all setup."

We met with Dr. Masley, who, as I recall, was always next to impossible to get an appointment with. We had a short conversation, with Dr. Carey doing most of the talking, and I ended up with an application and a set of instructions longer than the application. As of yet, I made no commitments, and neither did Dr. Masley, other than to promise me that I would get due consideration.

As we left, Dr. Carey told me that having discussed many candidates with Dr. Masley, the head of the Department of Physical Education, his use of the words "due consideration" was more than he had ever heard him give.

Then he said, "I think that if you carefully fill out the entire application, you will get your assistantship."

As I left, I assured him that one way or the other, he would be hearing from me.

When I met up with Beth, we discussed the possibility, along with the rest of our discussions over the last couple of days. It seemed like everything was going by so fast and at the same time, in slow motion.

We finally arrived at her parents' home in Danville, where we split up the money I had from selling our trailer home and separation from the Air Force and said our good-byes.

I was such a jerk, but didn't know it.

I drove to Chicago, not knowing whether I would ever see my wife again. Once I arrived, it took Dad less than ten minutes to tell me that he knew a lawyer that would handle a divorce for me. I told him there was no hurry on anything.

I had some things I had to get in motion and they were the first priority. I worked that night to get my material sent off to the State of Illinois Department of Education, called the scout from the Phillies, and began looking over the Eastern Illinois assistantship papers. The situation was better than first appeared. I would basically get my education paid for by working at a specific assignment from the head of the department, plus there would be a monthly stipend.

After I completed that and set some things in motion, I called Bob Hunt and told him I wanted to play some baseball. He immediately invited me to their first practice.

With everything in order, I went to see my friend Roy at the flower shop. He was able to tell me where Judy was. I left the next morning for Macomb, Illinois, and Western Illinois University.

Before sending word to her, I looked up Dan Waskevich, who I knew from high school, as he graduated in my class. After visiting with him and his wife, I called Judy.

She was surprised to hear from me, but we agreed to meet the next day. The day dragged on until the appointed hour finally arrived. I felt like a teenager again as I anticipated our meeting. When we met, it was very disappointing for me. She was very casual in appearance and manner. She asked me very little, but did share with me the fact that her parents had insisted she break up with me because I wasn't Catholic, but she never had a chance to tell me before she had heard I was married. She presented herself to me in a fashion that I knew there was no chance for me in her life. We had spent less than an hour together when I reluctantly left.

There is a special place in my heart for her even today, and I occasionally think of her, and pray that she is having the good life that she deserves.

I left that day and headed back to Chicago and my parents' home. I had nowhere else to go.

After spending the summer in New Jersey, Beth and I headed back to Illinois and Eastern Illinois University.

For the first time since graduating from high school, school was fun again. I had Dr. John Masley as my adviser. It was to him that I had to present my subject for my master's thesis.

There were six graduate assistants in the physical education department. For each and every one of us, the thesis would be the first important decision we would make. I had made up my mind as to what my subject was going to be before I enrolled for the fall quarter.

When I met with my committee, Dr. Masley laid out the importance of my decision and that it should not be taken lightly. When he finished, he asked me, "How much time do you think it will take you to research and determine a subject?"

I told him, "I decided what I wanted to do over a year ago, before I knew I would have an opportunity to work on my master's this soon after completing my bachelor's."

"Well, don't keep us in suspense."

"I want to do an experimental thesis titled 'The Effect of Resistive Exercise on the Velocity of a Thrown Baseball.' I haven't worked out the details yet, but I want to determine if resistive exercise will have an impact on the speed and power of throwing a baseball."

"This department has never sanctioned an experimental research thesis. And, I must admit, I have never seen such determination on a candidate's face, as I just witnessed."

"It's unusual, but not unheard of to approve a project on the first meeting, but, with the approval of my fellow committee members, I move to accept Mr. Rasmussen's subject."

After a unanimous vote, I had my project.

I could only think, "What have I gotten myself into?"

The first thing I did was to go to the library and begin looking up books, reports, articles, and research papers in the broad area of "Weight Training related to Sports." I must admit that I was surprised that there hadn't been much done in this area.

One article really jumped out at me. "Weight Training in Relation to Strength, Speed and Co-ordination" by Masley, John W., Hairabedian, Ara, and Donaldson, Donald N.

I was working on experimental methodology for measurement of strength as a means of establishing pre- and post-experimental activity results. I had the extreme pleasure of working with Dr. P. Scott Smith, professor of physics on development and structure of a measuring device, and later in the process the statistical analysis of the collected data.

The first idea we came up with was constructed, tested, and came down in a flaming crash of disappointment and frustration after a couple of weeks of wasted study and work. Back to the drawing board.

Our second attempt showed a simpler measuring technique, as well as a favorable statistical application for pre- and post-testing. I ran this development past Dr. Masley and he not only approved our plan, but he also volunteered to find a location, and the Department of Physical Education provided all the materials.

As this was moving forward, I was assigned as the assistant coach of the extramural soccer team working under my supervisor, Dr. John Hoddap. This went back to my undergraduate days, when I did extremely well in the course I had taken in soccer.

One of the frustrations of my previous stint at Eastern was concentrated on soccer. During the fall the school's fraternities were recruiting freshmen in a process they called "Rush." I had the two most athletic fraternities trying to recruit me. The one fraternity was up front with me and stated that it wanted me for their soccer team, which was a compliment, and I took it under advisement. The other fraternity was playing defense with me but were honest when its members told me in the interview that they didn't want me playing against them on the soccer field.

No one in the class had ever played soccer, so we were all pretty much even when it came to learning the game. I did have one advantage in that I was a left-footed kicker on the football team in high school and had practiced kicking for four or five years before I joined that team. In our soccer class, I played on the left side of the front line and never scored less than two goals in each class session. The most I ever scored in the forty-minute class was five. I had just accepted the results and hadn't given it much thought until the battle of the fraternities for my services.

In the long run, I determined that I didn't want to be tagged for just that one reason for being "rushed" and turned them both down. So, now as a graduate student, I had my first coaching experience.

As I worked my way through this first quarter of my master's program, I realized that this was the first time since high school that I was enjoying school. I was free from having to work to provide myself with a living; I was free from the frustration of a total lack of support from my parents; and Beth and I were moving forward together in a positive way.

Since this was a calendar year program, I was only permitted to take twelve hours each for each of the four quarters. That meant that I had three classes a day four days a week plus the work I was doing on my thesis. When summer would roll around, I would receive my credits for the thesis upon its completion, so I would only have two classes in the summer. I did take an extra class when the time arrived to have an experience of lower grade curriculum.

Needless to say this year and program were a blast. The slower pace from my twenty and twenty two semester credit terms while playing baseball and doing my military responsibilities made this seem a whole lot less stressful.

From soccer in the fall, I became deeply involved with intramural basketball in the winter. My job was primarily scheduling and supervising the progress of the program.

There was also time to learn a new game in a competitive fashion. Mr. Bob Hussey, an instructor in the department, was an accomplished badminton player and had established a group of faculty members, graduate students, and upper class athletes to play the game. I joined the group and with my aggressive attitude, I worked my butt off until I was winning more often than not. That is not a game for the light-hearted when played competitively.

One day, while trying to curtail that wild "bird," I dove, swung, and made contact, not with the bird, but with the floor, my chin leading the way. For my efforts I was awarded with a gash that bled like a gusher. Bob laughed and said that I would probably be the first person to get a broken jaw playing badminton.

It was a fun experience that lasted until the winter winds ceased and we began to put the spring intramural program together. I was blessed with working with the softball program.

While all this was going on, the work with the "Effect of Resistive Exercises Upon the Velocity of a Thrown Baseball" continued. I was assigned three physical education classes for non-majors. In other words just regular kids that were taking required courses. One class would be assigned as a control, to determine consistency of the methodology. The other two classes would be put on a specific weight-training program of doing the same exercises twice a week for ten weeks. One group would be doing specific arm motions with weights determined to be optimal for each student's strength and flexibility. This would be the isotonic group.

The third group would be the most difficult to observe. This would be the isometric group. They would be applying pressure against an unmovable object from different arm and shoulder positions to force muscle contraction without muscle movement. Each position would be held for six seconds, before moving to the next station. Each station would have multiple sets.

Prior to beginning, each student would throw a baseball at a target with a normal throwing motion as hard as was comfortable for him to do. Using a rebound-measuring formula that sought out an average of a specified number of throws, a standard for each student was established. After ten weeks of class, all students were retested.

A comparison of pre- and post-measurements would determine the results of the experiment.

The third quarter of the school year was dedicated to writing the thesis, after analysis of the data. I completed it early and since Mr. Spizzirri was an English major in college, I called him and asked if he would proofread my thesis and note any changes he would recommend. He was pleased to do that for me. I drove up to Chicago to hand him a copy and asked him to call me when it was ready for me to come back and pick it up. Within a week, he called and I went back for a consultation to pick up the result of his endeavors. I was quite pleasantly surprised that he recommended a few minor changes and those only in the area of proper written language.

Mr. Spizzirri told me that as far as the content was concerned, he didn't have a clue as to what I was talking about. At the same time, he stated that it was well written.

With that assurance, I made final copies and turned in my thesis, which would be studied by the committee and form the basis for my oral final that had to be passed to receive my master's degree.

I was the first of the graduate assistants to present their work to their respective committees. I thought by working hard and completing my work early, I would be able to devote most of my summer to playing baseball on a team in Mattoon.

I didn't realize that one of the procedures used by the committees was to make the graduate student sweat a little, or a lot, depending on various factors. My final work sat on Dr. Masley's desk for over a month. However, I was the first to have my orals, and I got little heat treatment. The oral examination was more of a discussion of my background that led up to the "experiment." Dr. Maynard O'Brien, a professor of physical education, made the offhand comment, "In my recollection, I don't ever recall having a twenty-four-year-old, four-year military veteran qualify for a master's degree at this institution." Dr. William Groves, the third member of my committee, concurred. Dr. Masley wrapped up our meeting with congratulations.

The entire meeting lasted less than a half an hour.

I had five happy compatriots that were waiting for me at our usual coffee spot when I finished. They were ecstatic that I was out in such short order. They just knew if my orals were that short, then theirs probably would be too. Unfortunately, none of them finished in less than two hours, and one went on for more than three hours.

Mine was the first experimental thesis in the history of the physical education department, and wanting a smooth conclusion of that pioneering effort, I think I was let off the hook easy. Nevertheless, I did it *my* way!

In the spring of that year, I was presented membership in Phi Epsilon Kappa, the honorary men's physical education fraternity. After turning down two fraternities as a freshman, I was not even aware that this honorary membership was coming. My friend Bart Zeller was president of the club and signed the certificate. It made me feel more a part of the school.

Graduation was bittersweet. Mom and Dad came down from Chicago for the ceremony and participated in small talk with Beth and me before I received my degree, afterward, they had to get back home, but Dad shook my hand and said, "I'm glad we came down for this."

After all these years of trying to please Dad, it was probably never going to happen. I knew there was something terribly wrong with his thinking and his treatment of me over the years, but I had no clue as to what it could be. One day I would learn, but it was now time to begin my coaching and teaching career.

Little did I know that in less than a year, I would have played on a baseball team that won the state title in Utah, qualified for the annual National Baseball Congress Tournament, and would be back in school as a student.

Driving from Illinois to Utah, I was thinking about the last impression I had of the Buckley-Loda school district and the offer I turned down to take the position as superintendent of schools made to me by two school board members. I was considering going back to school and becoming a certified school administrator. Well, maybe someday. That someday came far sooner than I thought it might.

As a teacher at Intermountain Indian School, life was a little slow for me, so I began working toward my doctorate in educational administration at Utah State University. I was teaching Navajo children at the largest off-reservation school in the country. I was hired as a classroom teacher, but within a year, I became the junior varsity basketball coach.

Working with these young people with very little exposure to the American culture (Bureau of Indian Affairs [BIA words, not mine]). In my view I had not had any exposure to the Navajo culture, which in terms of tenure was more an American culture than ours.

Dad had gone to Utah with Thiokol Chemical Corporation after not finding work in the Chicago area. When he arrived in Brigham City, Utah, he contacted me about the opportunities at the Indian School. Still trying to please him, I packed up Beth and our three-month-old baby girl, Alene, and headed for the great state of Utah.

In the following summer, I was back in school at Utah State University, having been admitted to the doctoral program at that school. That summer I dipped my toes into the advanced program by taking one course in public relations in education. It went well so I continued in the fall with a second class. I was beginning to get a handle on a program that was rather strict in its application, as it needed to be. Any grade less than a "B" put you out of the program, no questions asked and no excuses accepted.

I took the winter semester off to analyze the program and reevaluate my chances of success. That old "you're not any good" syndrome I was indoctrinated with as a child began to creep back into my head. By that summer I had conquered the demons and signed up for six classes, or eighteen semester hours. I passed them all easily with a tremendous amount of support from Beth. I decided to continue.

In the fall I took a single two-hour course, followed with a three-hour course in the winter semester to keep my program on schedule. The summer was another heavy load with seventeen hours. The scary one for me was applied statistics. The class had over fifty students, which indicated to me that there would be no individual help and since the days of Miss Scannell, I had been a disaster when it came to any kind of mathematics. I knew that it would take a gargantuan effort for me to make it through this class. After the first day, I went directly home and advised Beth that I would have to dedicate myself to pass this class. I went to the basement and studied until dinner and after dinner, back to the basement. After the second week, our class was cut by more than half. I obviously had a handle on the subject matter by then, and a young man sitting next to me asked if I would spend some time with him and help him to understand what we were doing. In another week our class was down to fifteen. I continued helping the fellow student as he said that without passing this class, he would have to drop out of his master's program. He worked really hard, and when I would finish with him, I would head home and hit the basement for more studying. Every day, including Saturdays and Sundays, I spent every hour possible in the basement. When the class grades came out, two of us had "As." My student and I made it. Everyone else in the class had either dropped the class or got a "C" or below. I knew then that I had the "stuff" to complete the program.

After that summer, as a part-time student, I had completed seventy-two percent of my program. I was gleefully looking forward toward what would be my final year, and receiving my EdD (Doctorate of Education).

* * * *

Dad decided to go to college and asked me how to go about it, so I led him through the process, set up his test, and drove him up for it. He was as nervous as a March hare. After he finished he was not relieved. He just knew that he probably didn't do well enough to make it into college, but he said, "At least I tried." I told him not to kill his chickens before he had them. "You might be surprised," I said.

Then I asked him, "When do you go back to get your results?"

He gave me the time and date, then I told him I would pick him up and drive him up to Logan.

Well, the day came, and he was no less nervous than the day I drove him up for his test. I waited for him, and it didn't take long. He got into the car and didn't say anything. After we got on the road, I asked him how he did.

He said, "I can study anything I want and all I have to do is decide and then register. I asked him what his test result was. Now it was my turn to be amazed. He scored in the ninety-ninth percentile.

He then expressed his concern that he couldn't figure where he messed up. I explained to him that he did as well as it is possible to do. He replied that if he hadn't messed up, he would have gotten a hundred.

"Dad, it is impossible to get a hundred on this type of test."

He responded,

"No it's not. You can always get a hundred!"

"Dad, I have been dealing with this type of test for the last several years; I know what I'm talking about." Then I changed the subject.

He started school the next term and received his two-year associate's degree. I did not learn that he had achieved that degree until several years later.

* * * *

In the fall of 1965, I took one course, as I had all through the process. During that semester my adviser called me in for a consultation. He kind of hit me between the eyes with the proverbial baseball bat. "Don, you need to plan to be on campus to finish your program. You have three more courses and your dissertation to finish, and you are in great shape, but the university requires that a doctoral candidate spend one school year on campus. All of your work has been as a part-time student and you have completed seventy-seven percent of the program."

He suggested that I work it out for next year. I thought about it for what seemed forever. I had two children at home and a third one on the way. Beth had been teaching so I could pursue this high level of education.

I discussed it with Beth and she was willing to go through another year of teaching for me to finish. With three children under four years of age, I didn't think she needed to do that. She had gone way over and above what I asked her to do to this point. It was time for me to take the certification I had earned and walk away.

With the motive of moving forward, I became disenchanted with teaching at the Indian School and sought other challenges.

I started selling life insurance and before I left the Indian School, I began studying for a security license and joined the NASD (National

Association of Security Dealers). It wasn't long before I was the leading salesman for Utah in our company in life insurance. Unfortunately, I remained in the middle of the pack of the organization in securities.

I was moving along slowly when Dad came to my rescue. He was talking to Bill, who, he said, told him that "if Don is out of education, tell him to get into radio. That industry is going to be making a giant leap forward." This was according to Dad. I never discussed it with Bill. By now I should have known better. When Dad and Bill get together to help me, disaster follows, but I was still hung up on becoming accepted in the family. I moved forward.

I did some reading up on the requirements, and the FCC regulations required that any one in radio that is on the air must have one of a variety of FCC licenses. I picked up a newspaper and on that day, KJAL Radio Broadcasting School was opening up in Salt Lake City, Utah. I hurried down and became their first student. After passing a barrage of tests that, in my mind, turned out to be rather easy. After the testing, I was then examined by a speech pathologist. I was told to return the next day to see if I was qualified to be a student there.

I left the small studio and office thinking that the whole process was pretty painless, and I was confident that I would be attending a school that would give me a new direction.

When I returned the next day, I was stunned to learn that I had been rejected. It seems that I failed the speech test. I advised Jack Alan Long, the owner and director of the school, that I was determined to attend radio broadcasting school and earn my FCC license. I requested a meeting with the young lady who had failed me to learn what I had to do to correct my speech deficiencies I had with my speaking abilities to become qualified. He initially turned me down and said that my problem could not be corrected by anyone my age.

We had quite a discussion before he called the young lady in to explain why I would be wasting my time. She was very kind and considerate when we started, but became condescending and authoritative as she got into the nuts and bolts. I wasn't going to be dissuaded. She finally explained that I had a "lateral s" and that when I spoke, the sound I made over the air would not be pleasant to the listener at all. I asked her, "How do I correct it and overcome my problem?"

She repeated Jack's statement word for word. I rejected the assumption of failure before tackling the problem. After discussing my background that overcoming the assumption that I was not bright enough to go to a regular high school, I was allowed to give it a try and made the honor roll my first four semesters of high school and had earned a master's degree, she relented. She showed me, with the use of a mirror what I was doing when I said the letter "s." When she concluded she stated, "Now you can see why you cannot reverse a lifetime of slurring the letter 's' the way you do and say a proper 's.'"

I told her to make an appointment for me in two weeks to retake the test. "I will conquer the speech impediment by then." She shook her head and said, "Okay, but don't be disappointed when you finish." I told her that I wouldn't be and left.

As I drove home from the studio, I read every billboard on the way, concentrating on the letter "s." In the next two weeks, virtually every waking hour was spent reading aloud and talking with my wife, using every word that I could think of that had an "s" in it.

Beth was quite the trooper during that time, and my daughters thought that their dad had lost his mind. They did chip in by giving me words and laughing a lot. This really became a family that everyone was enjoying in their own way. The girls really liked taking rides into Salt Lake while listening to me read billboards. On these excursions, Beth would drive, so I could concentrate on my task at hand. When I would goof pronouncing my "s," everyone would catch it and let me know.

It was kind of neat. At first no one corrected me, but then slowly they would catch a mistake, and soon they were all catching my mistakes. During the second week, the mistakes became less and less, until the last few days before the retest. There were no more mistakes, and I approached the retest with confidence.

I went to the studio fully expecting that I would have to be over-the-top perfect to make any kind of impression on the speech pathologist. She was blown away. She said, "You, sir, have just done the impossible."

After that test, which, needless to say, I passed with flying colors, I was accepted into the school and the weeks flew by. I mastered the board, wrote commercials and read them on the air, as well as read the news and carried on conversations with the audience. My final was to conduct a half-hour interview on a real radio station on the subject of my choice.

I met with the interviewer, and we worked out an introduction before the start of the program. The subject was education, so the interviewer provided my background of study and work in the field. We started out simply and then let the callers determine the direction of the program. The interviewer soon became a coordinator between myself and the callers.

I was surprised at the number of callers, as that aspect of the show was not emphasized in any of the preliminary discussions. I soon understood why.

Just before the half hour was completed, the manager of the station came in with a note, asking if I would stay an additional thirty minutes. It seemed that they had just had more calls in the first half an hour than they have ever had, so I agreed to stay.

I didn't have any idea that my education philosophy was so readily understood and accepted. Before that half an hour was completed, I was once again asked to extend my stay for the same reason. This time I agreed to extend for an hour. I was having a ball, and we ended up turning a half-hour course assignment into a two-hour call-in talk show, which included several callers suggesting that I run for state superintendent of education. One caller called in from Wyoming asking if I would consider moving to that state for the same purpose.

It turned out to be fun and very flattering. It showed me that I could think, respond, and provide logical answers and comments on the fly.

The next day I had to go back to the studio for a critique of my final examination.

Jack Long provided me with a very good and positive assessment of my appearance on the show.

The general manager of the station had called him before our meeting to tell him that we had broken all records for a two-hour period at the station. I passed.

WORKING

Chapter 13

JOBS

Working is something that adults do to support themselves and their families. When kids work voluntarily, it is usually to buy something that they deem important and their parents cannot afford or do not think their kids desires are worthy of their consideration. When my brother Bob and I began working, it was to buy baseball gloves. Not being old enough to get a job, we went to work for ourselves, mowing lawns. We did pretty well.

That initial experience brought us our goal and a good friend, as well as a way, for a few years, to take care of any needs that we wanted to take care of ourselves. I do believe that the development of confidence became a double-edge sword for me as I grew older. I knew at a young age that I could work successfully, not only for payment, but also for satisfaction of a job well done, when money was not the primary goal.

As far as function goes, what is the difference between mowing lawns for payment and mowing a baseball field to play baseball?

Even mowing lawn for your parents as a chore brings the satisfaction of not having your dad get on your case. So satisfaction can come in many shapes.

After a few years mowing lawns, at age fifteen, I secured my first job for a paycheck. I pushed a refreshment cart up and down the aisles of cars at the Starlight Drive-in Movie Theater on Ridgeland Avenue, just a few blocks from our house. When I began working, the manager of the concession operation for the drive-in asked each new employee if they wanted to work on an hourly wage or commission. I waited until the others hired that first night answered, and only then did I make my decision. The other guys chose the hourly wage, so, out of curiosity, I selected commission. At the end of the first night, five hours without a break, the hourly workers each made two dollars and fifty cents. I made a little over eight dollars and sold more refreshments than all of the other guys.

I never stopped the entire night; I was back for refills more often than the others, and I took less time getting my cart reloaded for my next trip. We were not told how much we earned, but five hours at fifty cents was easy to figure out. The other cart pushers didn't know how much I made, simply because they didn't know how much I sold. I never became a part of the group because I was there for one reason only: to work.

With school starting in the fall, I cut back to just working at the drive-in theater on Friday and Saturday nights until it closed for the winter. Even on the slow nights as the nights grew colder, I seldom left for the night with less than ten dollars.

At the beginning of my junior year of high school, I turned sixteen and Bob introduced me to the manager of the R & S shoe store, where I began a two-year stint as a shoe salesman. Now, this was fun once I became acclimated. Using the same enthusiasm that I had at the drive-in, it wasn't very long before I regularly sold more shoes than anyone else. We rotated turns waiting on customers as they came through the door, and sometimes a salesman felt too tired to take his turn. I was always ready to jump in. It was just natural for me to talk with the customers and learn as much as I could about them as I worked with them.

I recall, quite vividly, an older lady (probably in her thirties) that one of the other guys was working with, and he showed her about everything we had. He was getting frustrated and had spent a lot of time with this lady when he gave up and asked me if I would take over for him. I did, and I immediately struck up a conversation with her and approached her as a brand new customer, even though she had been sitting there for at least half an hour. She loosened up and before long was smiling as I went through our inventory again with her. To make a long story short, she walked out after having bought ten or so pairs of shoes. She became a regular customer and if she came in and I wasn't working, she would check with the manager to find out what time I would be coming to work. I never saw her outside the store, but she always bought a pair of shoes or two.

When the second summer came along, it was a no brainer. I ended up working at the drive-in theater for two years. It was hard work and the second year I was the only refreshment cart pusher that returned. By staying on my routine of hustling from the moment I got there until I left, time flew by. I would hear other workers complain of the hours and the night moving along so slowly, and I made the determination that I would never be a slacker. Where other workers were seeing a long night of work ahead of them, I saw a relatively short time of having fun, meeting people, and earning money while doing it.

When I turned sixteen, I opened a bank account at the Oak Lawn Bank and always made sure that I had some money in the bank. Dad never asked me for any of the money I earned and during the school year, he always paid for our bus tickets and streetcar fair, as well as thirty-five cents a day for the school lunch. Since I always had a couple of dollars in my pocket, Bob and I would stop at the "Cameo" at Fifty-Ninth and Western, which was kind of like a modern convenience store with a coffee shop that was laid-back, on the way to school.

In the spring of that year, I was planning on going to the junior prom. I was discussing it with Mom when she said that it would be kind of expensive and asked if I could afford it. I pointed out to her that Bob did not have to pay for his junior prom, that she and Dad had covered his expenses.

She acknowledged I was correct but said, "Bob has a senior prom this year, and he doesn't make as much money as you do, so you can help out by paying your own way." This was the beginning of my conditioning for college.

She went with me to Sixty-Third and Halsted where I was measured for my tuxedo and ordered flowers for my date. I made arrangements to go to the Nat King Cole show in downtown Chicago with a buddy to drive us. I didn't realize it but by not objecting, I would be buying my dress clothes from that time on. During my senior year, I paid for two proms and another trip with Mom to buy a sports coat and tie for another spring dance.

In that last year of high school, I sold over thirty pairs of shoes to the picked platoon for our annual competition. Working at the shoe store was fun every day I went to work.

During the Christmas vacation of my senior year, I worked at the post office doing a minimum of four routes a day. The regular carriers would post the mail and stay inside where it was warm and there was so much mail coming in that the regular carriers didn't have it easy. I think that slogging through the snow better suited our young legs than it did the older guys. We would arrive at the post office, pick up our first route, and be delivering mail by eight. A couple of hours later, we would get our second route and finish before the noon hour. We would grab a bite to eat on our way back to the post office to pick up our first afternoon route. Generally, Bob and I would meet up again between five thirty and six o'clock.

Although it was hard, fast work, it was invigorating and extremely educational. If we received envelopes from the people on the route, we took them back to the regular mailman on that route. In the two weeks we were running those routes, I had a couple of residents that specifically handed me bonuses with the express statement that it was for me, not their regular postman. In each case, they were people that had given me an envelope for their regular mail carrier in the first week on the job. There are a lot of gracious, good people out there, if we just look for them and acknowledge their kindness.

After the holidays I was back on a regular schedule at the shoe store, which by now was more like visiting old friends and getting paid for it. I continued to maintain a high volume and was so comfortable with the manager and the customers that I was always anxious to get to work when I was scheduled. Things did get a little tougher after Ted Kucharski introduced me to the JC Colts baseball team. With my bench-sitting duties at the high school and practice and games with the Colts, my time at the store was, out of necessity, getting shorter and shorter and would conclude before I had to go off to college.

My next work experience was to come the day I arrived at the campus of Northern Illinois University. It seemed that everything I had been striving for had fallen apart when Dad dropped me off with the news that I was on my own. Seventeen years old, denied my dream, and then told to work my way through college. Was it any wonder that I felt betrayed, abandoned, frustrated, and very much alone?

On the brighter side, I had come a long way from not being smart enough to be able to go to a regular high school rather than vocational school.

I began working in the school cafeteria for breakfast and lunch and set my schedule around that. I made enough to get by, but not much left over. I was looking forward to Christmas break. So I could make enough money not to be strapped when I returned in January.

During my first semester in college, I again worked at the post office and really enjoyed my encore, although I had totally different routes and the snow was not nearly as rough as the year before. In less than a month, I would be back in Chicago, looking for a more permanent job. Those employment opportunities that would have been good for a high school kid on a part-time basis just didn't fit my vision of a full-time, permanent job.

One such job was offered the day I made an application at Nabisco on the southwest side of Chicago. After an oral interview, I was put in this little room to take a written test. I was not told how I did on the test, but I was offered a job as a driver, courier, and general go-fer. The salary was good, $5,000 per year, with the possibility, determined by performance (likeability), to enter the Nabisco administration-training program in a few years.

The aroma of the facility and musty feel of the offices I had been exposed to during the process caused me to think there had to be something better than this. I was really thinking, "I'll be locked into this for a long time with long, defined hours and no chance to play baseball." I just couldn't get my blown chance out of my head.

Within a month I was running out of money, so I pulled out my scholarship and headed to Eastern Illinois University, since it was on a quarter system.

Now, with some limited restaurant experience, before completing my enrollment, I was job hunting. I found several options and decided to go to work at the A & W Root Beer drive-in. I then went back and completed my enrollment, so as not to interfere with my work schedule.

Having worked two meals a day at Northern, I didn't want to get in that cycle again. The root beer stand was only a mile and a half from the campus and as such, it was the shortest walk to and from work. I worked from three to eleven and then an hour for cleanup, so on average I was in bed by one o'clock in the morning.

I would get up, have cold cereal (no milk) for breakfast, a ten-cent can of pork and beans for lunch, and after I got to work, I would have a root beer float and a burger for dinner. I would prepare another burger as I closed down the grill and eat that before heading back to my room. My life consisted of classes, work, and sleeping. I was saving up money to buy a car. A car would provide me with more options.

Working eight hours a day, not counting cleanup, which was not paid time, I was making twenty dollars a week. I figured that in five months, I would have enough money to buy a decent car. That was too long a time for me to make it on the regimen that I had laid out for myself, so in the summer, I left the root beer drive-in for a job as a gas station attendant during the afternoon and early evening and as a pin boy at the local bowling alley at night. I beefed up my eating habits in order to make it through until the close of the bowling alley. I trained myself in the first week to handle three alleys at a time. I would receive seven cents a line.

With an average of four bowlers on each alley, playing three lines each, I was making $2.52 per game. In an average evening, I would do between three and four different groups, earning between $7.56 and $10.08 per working night, sometimes more on Friday and Saturday.

At the gas station, I made fifty cents an hour to be there, extra for doing grease jobs and oil changes, and even more for changing tires.

JOBS

When I sold a set of tires, I earned a commission, separate from everything else. Working three to four days a week, I would average earning ten dollars a day.

I was now earning sixty to seventy-plus per week. Much better than the root beer stand. By the middle of June, I had earned enough money to buy a car. I bought a 1950 Ford two-door coup, with a Pontiac grill. It was pretty cool. Dad put me on his insurance for twenty-six dollars a year.

I now had transportation, and I cut back to just working at the gas station and picked up a job working the grill for a couple of hours a day at Owl Drug Store. That was a fun place to work.

I also attended a couple of classes at the university and completed my first year of college. In the fall I would be a sophomore, back on schedule. Through it all, I really missed not playing baseball. It couldn't be helped; I had to make a living, so college took a back seat. Unfortunately, baseball was now even further behind.

As the fall quarter was getting under way, it became clear that I could not continue at Owl Drug Store. I was taking seven classes and the lunch hour was not available for me to work. A new restaurant was opening on the square called Kurr's, named after the owner, Bill Kurr. I made an appointment and went for an interview. He liked my references and work experience, so I was hired on the spot. We worked out my schedule to allow for my classwork, and it looked like I would be set for the school year.

Kurr's and the gas station were the last places I worked before going into the Air Force. I enlisted in the United States Air Force in January of 1957.

For one year while overseas, I worked as a masseur that was arranged by our base commander, and I bought hair clippers and taught myself the art of barbering to make extra money. I also worked at the base gym at night for extra pay and would do the overnight chow hall subbing for assigned GIs that would pay me just so they could get a good night's sleep. I also received overseas pay. All of this helped keep Beth in school during the year I was gone.

My first job after I was separated from the Air Force was substitute teaching in southwest Chicago suburbs.

I was lined up to work a summer program with the YMCA when Dad intervened with the story that Bill was having difficulty coping with Bob's death and needed family. I was the only one that realistically could go. He had talked with Bill, and Bill had lined up good jobs for Beth and I for the summer. He also had a baseball team that would give me a tryout so I could keep playing baseball.

The latter was the trigger to get me to go (see "New Jersey Fiasco" chapter).

My job as a graduate assistant carried a monthly stipend to help with expenses as I worked on my master's degree.

After graduating I became a teacher-coach at Buckley-Loda school district for four months before leaving to go to Utah where I became an academic teacher of Navajo Indian students and later a physical education teacher and basketball coach.

Next on the ladder of experience was Hamilton Mutual Funds and Life Insurance. After a relatively short period of time, it was easy to determine that this was not my cup of tea and thus, on to becoming a radio announcer.

My first job was as a news director and weekend disc jockey at a radio station in Danville, Illinois, for the sum of one hundred dollars per week, while also being on call twenty-four hours a day. This seemed to be way more work than the pay justified, so at the first opportunity, I again became a schoolteacher. I couldn't believe that I left a job I was good at to teach seventh grade history and science in an industry that was notoriously low paying and I enjoyed a large pay increase.

I did keep my hand in by doing play-by-play announcing for football and basketball games in the evenings.

At the conclusion of that year, I found a small market AM/FM combination in Moberly, Missouri, and was hired as an account executive and play-by-play announcer that was more in tune with paying a living wage. This worked out for a few years when I soon converted to com-

JOBS

mission rather than salary. My income began to move up quite nicely until management decided that a couple of us were out distancing other account execs and shuffled accounts to be more "equitable."

When a few of my bigger transferred accounts began to cut back on their advertising, the station's management pressured the current account exec to get with the program without stating any specific actions. What had been a reasonably good and positive team soon showed deterioration.

I began to emphasize my unique accounts that had potential for large commissions, such as Edina Wild West Days, farming expositions, and rodeos. I also was able to expand my play-by-play assignments to include some baseball and junior college sports.

Time to spread my wings as a school administrator. After all, I didn't get my certification for nothing. I determined to apply for some jobs in Illinois to learn the process. Learning didn't last long as I was offered the first position I applied for and became a superintendent of schools in 1970.

This was a failing school district that had not received state aid for several years. My first task after I developed a pretty pathetic budget was to get the district qualified for state aid. With a month to go before school started, I had everything in place and in October we received out first state aid check. I knew that the school district would not be in operation for very many more years, thus I began looking for greener pastures in the spring.

I have a bad habit of getting the first job I apply for, so I became a junior-senior high school principal in a larger district and thought I had found a home. But alas, the superintendent was fired at the end of the year and put the onus on me, as I was qualified to succeed him. After the fact, however, I was asked to leave also. That was unfortunate because I really liked that town and would have enjoyed staying there.

Finally, I ended up in East Peoria as the junior high principal where I remained for four years after being introduced to Shaklee, where as a part-time thing, Beth and I became senior supervisors sharing my health improvement.

In September of 1978, I became involved with ESPN as one of three outside investors, along with an agreement that at the end of my school contract, I would become an employee. I eventually resigned from ESPN under consistent pressure from my brother. He was no longer with ESPN and had started a new company called Enterprise Radio and was going to hire me, along with a handsome raise. The company went belly-up in a matter of months.

Thanks to Shaklee, I kept my head above water until I received a call from Lloyd Werner at Group W that was going to develop a new cable TV network giant. That went in the tank at a loss of millions of dollars.

I didn't think a return to a school district was in my future, as I had seen too much of the country and different ways of living, so we packed up the family and headed to Texas.

We built three businesses in Texas over a twenty-year period before we decided to sell out and move headlong into retirement in 2005 at the age of sixty-eight.

Chapter 14

THE AIR FORCE YEARS

We went to Danville, Illinois, where Beth's parents lived, and they were happy to have her stay with them while I was in basic training. Then I went down to the recruiting office and started the process that would lead me on a four-year adventure and complete an obligation that every male citizen of our country must sign up for on their eighteenth birthday. That obligation had been in the back of my mind for over a year, and it would be good to get on with it.

After completing the paper work, I was given a bus ticket to Chicago for early the next morning where I would get a physical and something short of a hundred inoculations to protect all those Texans from invasion from the North that we represented. The thing that stuck out in my mind was that I received the first series of tetanus shots that, when concluded, put me into double digits of tetanus shots in just over a year. I felt pretty safe from lockjaw. As a matter of fact, I will probably always have the loosest jaw in the country!

Now, they had to get us to San Antonio to begin basic training. They put us on a train that we were told would get us to Lackland Air Force Base in a little over twenty-four hours. I stretched out in my seat and fell asleep. The events of the previous several days must have caught up with me, because I woke up about an hour before our arrival.

We arrived in the early morning hours and I assure you, the stars were not "big and bright," deep in the heart of Texas! The greeting DI (drill instructor) did have a loud mouth that would probably cause an earthquake if it didn't have our ears to absorb the kinetic energy. After some disparaging, wild, and apparently out of control ranting, we were marched to the chow hall for an early breakfast (three o'clock in the morning) then to the barracks to locate our bunks, then move them to one side of the large room so that we could scrub the floors before putting the room back together again. At five o'clock we were greeted by another DI, who just happened to be bigger and had louder mouth than the first. None of us had been spoken to in a civil manner as a group or individually since we had arrived.

The big DI simmered down a little after he assembled us and asked us a few questions. Have any of you had any college? Have any of you been in ROTC? I was the only one that raised my hand to both questions.

I was now a squad leader of squad number one. Two others raised their hand and were assigned to squads two and three. I hadn't realized that we had thirty men in our group, which made up a platoon.

Our next activity was haircuts, and I do mean haircuts! Down to the scalp. More than a couple of the guys had the popular DA haircut of the urban 1950s cool cat. Some of them were literally in tears as they came out of the barbershop. Having seen the identical results of everyone as they came out, when it was my turn, I sat down and told the barber to "take a little off the sides and lot off the top." He laughed and said no one ever has asked for a lot off the top—and then he did it. It made me feel good that he got to follow my orders.

We were now a platoon of skinheads, and the next stop would be to get our uniforms. The supply people were very good at making sure we got the right size shoes. After this it was their judgment of trousers, shirts, jackets, caps, etc. When we left there, we checked to see if they were somewhat close to getting our sizes right. Surprisingly, when we got back to the barracks, somehow, all my clothes fit, as they did for just about everyone else.

Whoever it was that said you couldn't take complete chaos, throw stuff at it, and bring order to it had never met an Air Force supply sergeant.

The first week was set aside for us to learn close-order drills. With my background in high school with the championship picked platoon in Chicago, I became a third instructor, teaching drill techniques to the members of the platoon that were having difficulties catching on. It really was kind of fun.

Once we got that down, it was classes for "military customs and courtesies," where we learned proper wearing of the uniform and aptitude testing, as well as the typical IQ tests. We were told that after the results were in, we would have individual counseling sessions with the administrative personnel that would determine our placement in a field or a job.

When I met with my administrative adviser, I learned that my verbal skills, administrative skills, and grasp of military customs and courtesies were all high. Math and mechanical were below average. So in putting this all together, he decided that I should volunteer for the Honor Guard in Washington, DC, and play football on the Air Force team. I had a couple of questions to ask before giving a definitive answer. The first question was in regard to the meaning of "volunteer" in this setting. Getting a positive response, my next question was in relation to the quality of the team.

He advised me that they had a very good team; that Ralph Guglielmi was their quarterback, and they had a few other All-Americans on the team as well. I looked him right in the eye and said, very calmly, "Are you nuts? I was a kicker in high school and a second- or third-string halfback at a small college. That level of competition would be so far above my head that standing as tall as I could, I would be looking up to their shoe laces."

Next on his list was joining a physical conditioning team at a Strategic Air Command (SAC) base. I had no clue as to what a physical conditioning team was, but I knew that I would have a better chance of coming out of that with my body in one piece, so I said okay.

He pointed out to me that this one wasn't voluntary; he was making it the assignment. Then he suggested that I ask my DI to arrange for me to take the five level test in my field of expertise, which was physical conditioning specialist. I took the test and passed easily. My specialty number became 74150. My DI told me that not too many airmen left basic with a five level and even though I did so well on the five, I couldn't take the seven until I became a staff sergeant, simply because the Air Force didn't want airmen with a higher rating than their supervisor. I would learn what he meant when I arrived at my first assignment.

Having all this determined, I was then scheduled for the second phase of basic training at Lackland, as my field had no technical school and I would get my training on the job. The second phase of basic was more of the same, except they threw an overnight hike in to spice things up a little. That was the most fun part of those three long months in San Antonio. We had a week of preparation. At the appointed time, we were all set to go, even though it was pouring down rain. We were marched to the assembly area where the staging area was. We were left standing out in the cold rain from six o'clock in the morning until early afternoon.

We were all getting edgy (to be polite), and some of the guys were wilting under the weight of the backpack, which surely doubled in weight as the rain continued to pummel us. I was getting pretty light-headed when the word came down that we were to return to our barracks and get into dry clothes before marching over to the chow hall for a late lunch. Our war had been called off because of rain. We were given the rest of the day off, which after lunch, meant catching up on some sleep. I was looking forward to the rescheduling of our camping out, but apparently it wasn't a high priority in our training.

As the days of basic training dwindled down to a precious few, I learned that I would be assigned to Lake Charles Air Force Base in Lake Charles, Louisiana. With the travel time and authorized leave, I had enough time to go up to Danville and pick up Beth for what appeared to be a long drive to southwestern Louisiana. The trip down was a lot of fun, as we began to get reacquainted. We had been married six months and for just over three months, I was in basic training. We spent two nights in small motels on the way, as we did not hurry. Each motel was two dollars a night for a neat, clean room.

We went into Hammond in eastern Louisiana and bought some fixings for a picnic lunch and began looking for a clearing to have our picnic. I obviously did a poor job of selecting the site, because Beth had no more than put everything together when she was stung by something. We never figured out what it was, but she was very concerned and it hurt. We stopped in the next town and got some ice, but neither of us was sure that we wanted to be in Louisiana!

When we arrived in Lake Charles in the late afternoon, we immediately began searching for an apartment to rent. Price was a primary concern, as I didn't know how much I would be paid when I reported to the base the next day.

We found a little two-room apartment in the back of this house that we rented for a month. The next day I reported to the base, was directed to each and every office that was needed to let folks know that I had arrived, and the last stop was the finance office.

The whole day had been pretty good until the finance people told me that I had been overpaid in basic training and I wouldn't be paid until the next regular payday, which was a little over two weeks away. When I returned home that evening with the news, Beth was a little shook up, but pulled herself back to the facts very quickly and started planning meals using flour, pork and beans, and macaroni and cheese. Pork and beans sold for five cents a can and I believe macaroni and cheese was about the same. We took a long walk then and started building each other up. As long as I was in uniform, I could eat in the chow hall, so I ate my noon meal on base.

I'm not sure how we did it, but we made it through the two weeks-plus without suffering any permanent damage to our bodies. We got our nightly exercise during this rather down period in our lives when we returned from our evening walk. Beth would quietly open the door, and I would then walk to the center of the room. When I was in position, she would flip on the light switch and I would begin stomping tree roaches that infested the little apartment. I would generally get between twenty and twenty-five before the survivors scurried to safety. Fortunately, those two-inch critters stayed on the floor, so we slept well at night.

Our landlady was a nice lady, and we didn't want to hurt her feelings, but those roaches were just a little too much. We gave her two weeks' notice and she understood, with "you being from the North."

We began looking for another place to live and hit the jackpot. We found a two-bedroom house trailer located in the backyard of this really cool Cajun couple, Adam and Dora Sonnier. Their Cajun neighbors, R.J. and Louella Lagneaux, and Beth and I became good friends and remained so the remainder of their lives.

With my full month's salary and Beth's allotment, to which I contributed forty dollars, gave us just under fifty dollars a week to live on. We learned to not only get by on this, but by the end of the summer, we paid for each of us to take two night courses at the local college.

At the air base, my training was enhanced by the Kodokan-trained Judo instructors in our unit. The training was intense, and I was soon teaching hand-to-hand combat to the B 47 crews. Handball became a training activity to enhance our speed and dexterity. With no other assignments, except for auxiliary air policing during base alerts, being in the Air Force was like any other low-paying job while trying to go to school.

Taking classes in the fall allowed us to meet Captain Philip Young and turned the military into a challenge to complete our bachelor's degrees by the time we separated from the Air Force in January of 1961.

In January of 1958, we began going to school full time and for the privilege of going to college during the day, I worked the night shift at the gym. This was a job that everyone assigned to it in the past did everything they could to get reassigned to a day job. I also was required to work half-days on Saturday and Sunday with the dependents recreation program.

The neat thing about this job was that I was judged solely on results, as I was the only airman working in the gym at that time of day. I supervised the activities, resolved disagreements, did my homework, cleaned the facility after an activity was completed for the night, and had the gym ready to open the next morning. I always managed to have some quiet time before locking up, in which I went into the gym and got some exercise running and shooting hoops. I had never played basketball, so this was interesting to me and challenging at the same time.

I was all settled in at the gym, Beth and I had some good friends, and life was good. I finally was in a position where I could look forward to a consistent way of life on a day-to-day basis. Life was good. Then Uncle Sam stepped in.

In July, I was assigned to overseas duty in Thule, Greenland. With lead-time, I was able to complete the summer session at McNeese College and spend some relaxing time with Beth before heading north.

Thule was not a choice garden spot on the planet. Situated in northwestern Greenland approximately nine hundred miles south of the North Pole, that part of the island was desolate with a shoreline of permafrost that extended perhaps three miles inland, where it met the permanent ice cap that covers ninety percent of Greenland.

When landing on the island and stepping off the plane, one's heart sank at the view. When I arrived in September, the days were already growing shorter and in a little over two months, we would be experiencing darkness twenty-four hours a day. Ironically, after a few weeks, we adapted to living and existing in that environment.

My duty assignment was as a weight-training instructor and supervisor of gym activity. I was also expected to participate in activities when a troop wanted to engage in individual activities, such as boxing, wrestling, and handball. I was given instruction by a young man on the technique of amateur wrestling. He was a state high school champion from Iowa.

He had no idea as to my physical conditioning, such as a judo background and status as a handball player, so he approached me as a weak opponent that he could handle easily. To say he was a bit arrogant would be an understatement. He was, in fact, a lot arrogant. After being talked down to during the instruction and demonstration, along with the referee, the match began.

At the young airman's suggestion, I was to escape, so we got into position and at the referee's signal, he pulled my right arm to collapse me, as I pushed with my right leg and arm so that when he collapsed me, I rolled over him for a reverse. Grabbing his right arm, I had him on his back with this right elbow on my left leg and my upper body on his wrist and hand in perfect position to dislocate his elbow. When he tried to roll up on me, I simply put more pressure on his elbow and he would lay back to ease the pressure. In less than fifteen seconds, he submitted. I complimented him on his knowledge, as I was sure that had to be easier than being on top. He didn't know what to think. He looked confused and without any sign of his earlier arrogance, he got down to escape. When he dropped his left shoulder to force me to release him, I let him go and instinctively he raised his right shoulder and the left shoulder went down. I took the movement of the right shoulder and kept it going in the direction it was, bringing him toward me and on his back. Within seconds we were in the same position as the previous round. This time he recognized his plight and immediately submitted.

The young airman became a regular at the gym, working on weights to develop more strength, but he never asked anyone to wrestle with him again. He would talk with me, as well as my partner Al Brekke, about judo, speed, and technique. He never asked for instruction, which we would have been glad to give him, or a match.

I really had no idea how the judo training would work out against a wrestler, so it was an interesting experience.

Boxing was another story. I had never been inside a boxing ring in my life, so we requisitioned one. The only place it would fit was in a corner, just outside the weight room. We were set, and again I went through an instruction period with an airman that was a weight or two higher than I would be, but we were just going to box. I wasn't too concerned about my conditioning; after all, I was playing handball three to four hours a day. I should have been in good condition. By the time we got to the third round, my legs were feeling like jelly. About a third of the way through the third round, I couldn't move away from the side of the ring by the wall. My opponent flicked a jab toward my chin and as I pulled back, the back of my head hit the wall and I was down and looking up at dancing, crooked, little white lights. The next day the boxing ring was dismantled and was not used during the rest of my tour in Greenland.

As we worked with the airmen and officers in the various activities of the gym, we took great pride in the dedication to their objective of becoming stronger and in better physical condition when obvious improvement was made. A 140-pound airman that in six months became a 170-pound airman was not an unusual occurrence. We also had our failures. Some individuals wouldn't follow instructions and concentrated on their strengths to the exclusion of their weak areas. A 125-pound young man refused to work on his legs and in a matter of six months had done a good job of developing his upper body and increased his weight to the range 170 pounds. His skinny legs were having a difficult time carrying that heavy upper body around before he realized that he should listen to the instructors. He then expected to correct the problem within a few weeks. When he was transferred back to the states, he was a very frustrated young man.

Another example was a barrel-chested lieutenant that would only work on bench presses with a wide grip and extremely heavy weights, easily pressing three hundred pounds. We had several long discussions with him to no avail. He didn't need to listen to us; we were enlisted and he was an officer. One day he was bragging and showing off his prowess to all those who would watch and listen, and I saw an opening to get a point across.

I said to him, "With all that strength, I would imagine that you could curl a lot more weight than I could." He bit and laughingly took my challenge. I suggested we start with twenty-five pounds. He made a joke about how I might have trouble with that weight, so I volunteered to go first.

At that time I knew I could go as high as forty-five pounds, but it would be a strain. So I did twenty-five easily. The lieutenant struggled with twenty-five, and his laugh turned into a sullen quietness when I suggested that we go to thirty-five instead of thirty to preserve his strength. He declined with the comment that he always went up by five pounds and would prefer to do that. I agreed and curled thirty pounds. He huffed and puffed, but couldn't get the weight past his waist.

Having failed, he cussed me out and said I tricked him after he had done so many bench presses that his muscles were tired. I didn't respond. He *was* an officer, and he had been embarrassed enough.

I had hoped that after thinking about it, he would allow one of our instructors to work with him to achieve greater strength and a balanced workout. Unfortunately, he solved his problem another way. He quit coming to the gym. So much for the intelligence of all officers!

In handball (I've got to tell one handball story since I spent so much time playing handball), I had a captain come into the gym one day who had recently been sent to Greenland on TDY (temporary duty). He came into the gym and blurted out for everyone to hear, "Who was the best handball player here, before I arrived." Everyone in the weight room looked at me. I didn't say anything, but he headed straight toward me and announced, "I break two or three balls a game."

I said, "Okay."

He responded, "Are you man enough to go in the handball court with me?"

"Why not?"

"I'll be back tomorrow at two o'clock."

I told him that I would have a court reserved for us. To get ready for this human mountain, I played a series of games from one to two o'clock to be warmed up when he arrived.

He came in and took charge, announcing that he would serve first. I said, so he could hear me but the crowd in the gallery couldn't, the rules of the game and suggested we determine serve by lagging for the serve. Now that didn't set well with him and he said, "I outrank you." I replied, "Not in here you don't, lag."

He lagged. I lagged, and he won the serve. He snickered and as he was going to the service box, I said, "Doesn't it feel better to have won the serve?"

I think he realized at that point that I was trying to get under his skin. I had succeeded. On his first serve, he hit the ball so hard that it split. On a split ball, you get a redo. The number of balls you split or break doesn't help you at all.

He was big and strong, with one speed on his ball, but he didn't move real well. He generally won by intimidation. By this time I wasn't intimidated by anyone on the handball court. He broke four or five more balls, but I beat him handily in two straight games.

With the game over, I was stunned, surprised, and overwhelmed. With a great, big smile on his face, he came over, shook my hand, and said, "You're a player."

We never played again after that, but when we saw each other around the base, I saluted him properly and he always returned the salute. If he was with someone, he would tell them that he wanted them to meet me. Then he would proceed to tell them how I "kicked his butt." And then, there was always a big, hearty laugh.

Our base commander, Colonel Bryson Bailey, who was a pretty good athlete, had heard a lot of talk in his office about the handball being played on the base. He came over to the gym and talked with me about the game. He had played some and wanted to learn more about the game. The only way to learn it is to get into the game. He became a regular at the gym and progressed rapidly. We had a monthly tournament, and he began to enter them. After a few months, he improved enough to finish in second place.

After each tournament, they presented me with the small trophy as soon as the final game was played. Colonel Bailey asked the sergeant in charge to allow him to make the presentation in his office. That meant that I had to get dressed in a proper uniform and be at the headquarters building at a given time for the presentation.

After the presentation, Colonel Bailey asked me why he never saw me except in the gym. I told him that was what I do. He then said, "If you ever need anything, come by my office and see me."

I thought that was an awfully nice thing for him to say, but I couldn't imagine anything that could come up where I might be in that situation. I would learn that you should never say never, since it wasn't more than a week or so later that Major Goldman, a KC135 pilot on TDY and a former foot soldier at the Normandy landing in WWII, asked me if I would be interested in flying back to Missouri with his unit when its mission expired. I hadn't given it any thought, but after he introduced me to the idea, the idea of two weeks to visit with Beth would be great.

I inquired as to when they would be leaving and learned that it would be within ten days or so. We talked about it and I told him there wasn't enough time to get a leave approved. He suggested that I go over and talk with Colonel Bailey.

I thought about it and decided that since I had been invited to come by anytime, I would do it. That afternoon I went to the headquarters building and directly to the colonel's office. When I walked in, I was greeted by his secretary, an airman that I recognized from the gym, who was about to call the colonel. He walked out of his office with a major that I also recognized as the commander of the TDY wing that was getting ready to leave. As soon as he saw me, he asked the major to wait a minute and asked me what I was doing there. I quickly explained the purpose of my visit, and he turned to the major, who heard our entire conversation, and said, "Well?"

The major responded that he could probably get me on a C-24. Colonel Bailey surprised me when he said, "Major, Don doesn't want to fly on a C-24; he will fly back with you on a tanker."

The major responded that I would be scheduled to fly to Missouri on a tanker; he saluted the colonel and left.

The next day at about ten in the morning, a lieutenant from the administrative office came over to the gym and delivered my travel orders. I would be leaving on a plane in the middle of the pack, a KC135. The major's plane would be the last to leave. I arrived back in the states and spent two terrific weeks with Beth and then it was back to New Jersey to catch a plane back to Thule.

After I arrived at the MATS (Military Air Transport Service) in Trenton, New Jersey, while waiting for my boarding time, I met a young Filipino nurse who was headed for Thule and not feeling too comfortable about it. As we were going to spend the next several hours together, I attempted to calm her concerns as much as I could. We did become well acquainted in our time together and after we were back in Greenland, one evening I received a call from her. My barracks went crazy as the airman who answered the call yelled out, "Call for Rasmussen—it's a girl." By the time I got on the phone, everyone was stacked around trying to listen in.

I had nicknamed the nurse "Tiger," and she relayed a message to me that her CO (commanding officer) wanted to talk with me and would

THE AIR FORCE YEARS

have me picked up at the gym the next day. I agreed, but had no idea what he wanted.

The next day a hospital jeep pulled up in front of the gym and a corpsman came in to drive me to the hospital. The CO wanted to see if any arrangements could be made when the gym was closed for the nurses to come down and work out.

After visiting awhile, he was assured that I was of sufficient character, as Tiger had told him that I was, to supervise the nurses when they were in the gym. I want to mention that the nurses were the only women at the base among more than five thousand men. When I returned to the gym, I talked with my NCO (non-commissioned officer), then my CO, and both gave me the same instructions: "Work something out, because we want to keep the people happy that run the hospital."

We set it up to close the gym early on Monday and Thursday to allow the nurses time alone in the gym for exercise, the suntan booth, and showering. I was the only airman in the gym on those nights and if anything happened to any of the nurses, it would be my responsibility.

I was pleased with the ladies, and for several months, the program worked out well. The nurses tired of regular exercise, so we changed the program to an on-call basis. That worked out great as the sessions dwindled down to once a week, then every two weeks, and eventually once every month or so. I did have the opportunity to introduce Tiger to a friend of mine, Lieutenant Mike Maxwell. They eventually married, so the chance meeting on a trip back to Thule had a happy ending.

Shortly after I returned, our CO introduced me to a friend of his, who was also a lieutenant. They had been talking back and forth and wanted to know if I could do a thousand sit-ups without stopping. I told them that having never tried it, I had no idea if I could or not. I suggested they talk to Al Breckke. They had, and Breckke sent them on to me. I said I would think about it and excused myself to confront Breckke. He laughed and said that he knew he could do it, but wanted to see if I could.

I said, "Thanks a lot, as a matter of fact, if I do agree to do it, I want you to count."

He agreed so I went to my CO and told him to set the day and time. The time was set, a solid mat put in place, a crowd recruited to spur me on, and Breckke, along with two other airmen, counted. *If* they disagreed on the total, I would have to continue until the lowest number was satisfied, unless the two that reached a thousand did so on the same sit-up. I started, and it took the first one hundred to loosen me up, another hundred and fifty to hit the wall, and then it was downhill after that. When I hit a thousand, I didn't even pay attention to the call, because I wasn't thinking about what I was doing by then. After an additional ten to fifteen, all three counters were standing over me saying I could quit now.

The next day my abs were really sore, and I mentioned it to Al. Big mistake! He went over to the mat with me and said, "Do three hundred!" It wasn't a suggestion. I did three hundred, and he counted them. When I stopped and stood up, my abs didn't hurt anymore. I don't know if they didn't hurt because he was a pretty smart guy or they didn't hurt because I didn't want to have to do another three hundred! I looked at him and said, "Let's go to the chow hall." The whole experience seemed more invigorating as time passed, and I would look in the mirror and say, "I did it!"

When you live in such an isolated place, it is easy to get depressed, so to avoid the temptation, you attempt to fill your nonworking hours with activity that is beneficial at some level. I began reading when I had time off. I found that I enjoyed reading, as much as I didn't care for studying, except when I had to accomplish a goal.

I read *Day of Infamy, The Attack on Pearl Harbor,* and *To Hell and Back,* the story of Audie Murphy and his WWII exploits. I believe that time in Greenland caused me to think that maybe I wasn't really as dumb as I thought I was. I had to be away from my family for a long time to come to this realization. I came to understand my drive a little bit. It would be many, many years before I could overcome being verbally put down time and time again during my formative years.

I continued my schedule unabated until one day Colonel Bailey came to the gym to ask if I had the complete judo training. I told him that I could always use more. He asked, "Did you get to the point where you learned to give massages?" I answered yes. He said, "Good, what do you need to be able to give massages here at the gym?" I rattled off what I needed to do it right, not expecting to get everything and figuring I could do some compensating to get the job done.

He gave me a number to call the following morning and directed me to give the sergeant my name and tell him what I needed.

I followed the good colonel's advice and before noon, I had a couple of pillows, five one gallon bottles of alcohol, three gallons of wintergreen, a half-dozen sheets, and two bundles of towels. That, along with the seven foot table that I moved from the sun tanning area to a space just off the weight room that used to contain the boxing ring, and I was all set.

I was now in business, while on the job. I locked up all the alcohol and wintergreen and made a sign above the table stating, "MASSAGES - $2.00." During my slow times and in the evenings, I gave massages.

I had been working at it for just a couple of weeks, when this civilian came in and asked if I could help him. He went over his back problem with me and it sure sounded bad. I told him that I would work on that problem at the back end of my whole body massage to get him good and relaxed and that I would not do any harm, but I couldn't give him any guarantee. He said that he certainly understood that, and we got started. In about twenty minutes, I started on his lower thoracic vertebra and the lumbar region. It was like kneading solid concrete. After about fifteen minutes, I felt some slight movement in the lumbar vertebra. I continued to work and finished off with warming wintergreen.

He got up, walked around rather tentatively, then normally as he smiled at me, and said, "How much?" I pointed to the sign and said, "Two dollars." He handed me a ten-dollar bill and said, "Not enough. I feel better than I have in years. I'll be back next week and your services are ten dollars for me."

I didn't argue; I just took the money and was thrilled that he felt so good. There were times when this Air Force life wasn't so bad!

He came back every week as long as I was there and always left happy, and I got to the point where I was feeling guilty taking his money, but he insisted, so I didn't resist too much.

I also began giving haircuts for two dollars. Al Breckke was my first customer. He knew I had never done this before, so he told me that it would be for practice. I took over forty-five minutes cutting his hair. At one point he told me that he didn't want me to make a career out of cutting *his* hair, just one time! Although I didn't charge him for the haircut, a couple of weeks later he asked me to do it again. He was my best friend in Greenland, so I wasn't going to charge him for this one either. When I started, he said, "If you do as good a job this time as you did last time in much less time, I'm paying you for both haircuts." Never argue with a customer, particularly when he is bigger and a former judo instructor.

I had been working at developing my skills, when Colonel Bailey called to tell me that he wanted me at the gym at midnight. I arrived early to learn that we were going to be surprised by an IG (inspector general) inspection and the leader of the team, a major general, would be landing between midnight and two in the morning, and his first stop would be to the base gym for a massage.

He arrived a little after two, and I had the steam room ready for him, followed by a shower and then a massage. Afterward he and his aide left for the VIP quarters and I only had a short time before I was to report for KP duty, so I just went to the chow hall and got started. The day looked like it was going to be a long one since it was going on just a touch under twenty-four hours since I got up yesterday morning.

I was a little surprised when around eight o'clock the general, Colonel Bailey, and other ranking officers came into our chow hall to inspect the facility and its operation. The general looked my way and I pretended that I had never seen him before as I continued my work. In a very few minutes, his aide came to tell me that I was relieved of duty and instructed me to go back to the barracks and get some sleep. I followed orders. Wouldn't you know it, later the general came through inspecting the barracks, accompanied by my company commander. My CO skipped my room as they were checking the neatness of each room. He simply told the general that I was sleeping. I didn't know any of this had gone on until after the inspection was over and the general had left the base. I was advised by the CO that the general had requested that I not be assigned KP duty for the remainder of my tour. So I didn't check KP orders for the rest of my time in Greenland.

I did continue to do KP at the midnight chow hall when others were willing to pay me for substituting for them. The pay was good, and I had a good reputation for doing what I said I would do and as a result, no airman that I substituted for was ever written up for not doing his job.

Colonel Bailey was being rotated before I was and he was headed for Griffiss Air Force Base in Rome, New York. A day or so before he left, he sent his aide, another "bird" colonel, to ask me to accept an early rotation and accompany him to New York. I was pleasantly surprised by the invitation, but since new assignments coming out of Thule generally meant an assignment of your choice, if possible, I was counting on going back to Lake Charles Air Force Base, so I declined the invitation.

I was working to close that evening as I almost always did, and I got another shocker when Colonel Bailey walked in the gym when he was supposed to be at a going-away party at the officers club. He had excused himself from his party to come to see me in a last-ditch attempt to persuade me to attend college full time at Syracuse University. The university was only about forty-five miles from the air base.

The offer was tempting, but the tuition difference from McNeese could be devastating to my goals and a two- to three-hour drive each day would logistically make the whole concept unworkable in my judgment, so I turned him down. He was very gracious and as he expressed his disappointment, he wished me luck.

I had two other unusual situations develop while in Greenland. The first was a proposal from the commander of the Fifty-First Ordnance Company, representing himself, individually in conjunction with other senior officers. Major Theodore T. Giamario was the spokesman for this group of officers that wanted to have a portable handball court designed and constructed to be used by me touring the country and putting on exhibitions. He emphasized that I would be paid as a performer and would not have to put up any money myself. He and his group felt I would be a good draw and that we all would find the project very profitable.

Other than tournament finals and hoopla over particular challenges, I had not drawn any large crowds to watch me play, so I wasn't enthused by the idea, so I turned him down. I was focused on getting back to Lake Charles.

I was a junior at McNeese when I left for Greenland, and I was determined to finish my degree work there.

I didn't realize that Lake Charles Air Force Base had become Chennault AFB. When I put Lake Charles AFB on my form as my first choice, it was ignored and I was passed on to choice number two, which was also Lake Charles AFB, as was choice number three. Someone in operations decided that he would just send me somewhere else and found an opening for me at Laughlin AFB near Del Rio, Texas. That led to the most bizarre episode in my life to date. When I received my orders, I was destroyed emotionally as well as mentally. I went over to the section and hit a stone wall.

A sergeant that knew me from the gym was standing nearby as the discussion took place. He came over to the gym that evening and talked to me about the orders I received. He implied that the sergeant that I talked to wasn't happy being there and enjoyed making other people miserable too. He said that he would take care of it and would juggle things around to get me to Chennault AFB. The last thing he said as he left the gym was, "Don't worry."

How could I not worry? This was the beginning of a weird adventure that would last more than six months and have me listed as AWOL (Absent Without Leave), as well as, for the second time, get my pay records all messed up.

Within a week I had my new orders giving me time of departure and destination, which was Chennault AFB, Lake Charles, LA. It all looked good to me. I should have suspected something was out of kilter when I withdrew my travel pay. The paymaster tried to give me travel pay to Laughlin AFB in Texas. Since my orders rescinded his orders for me, he allowed me to withdraw less money, as the distance that I wouldn't be traveling was far greater than that which I would be traveling. Now, if you understand that, explain it to me!

My day of departure finally arrived, but my plane didn't. It would be three days of waiting. That sounds pretty cool in August with the balmy weather hovering between five and ten degrees below freezing. In the year that I spent in Greenland, we had one day when the temperature went charging above the freezing mark, hitting thirty-four degrees above zero for a short time. The problem was that everything was packed, and with nothing to do, nowhere to go, no mischief to get into, you become, for that period of seemingly endless time, a nonentity, and really, really bored! I spent my time in the library.

When the weather finally broke, several cargo planes came in before I saw that long-awaited MATS (Military Air Transport Service) plane arrive. I had gone to the terminal early, knowing that I had a long wait ahead of me, but I was tired of doing nothing at the base and I figured that the earlier I was prepared to load the better. Settling in my seat and looking out the window, I couldn't help but think that I was lucky I would never see this place again. After that logical, rational thought, I spent the flight south looking forward and conversely, reminiscing about the previous year. Some real conflicting thoughts, back and forth.

Once I hit the runway in New Jersey, the thoughts of Thule were behind me. I caught the first bus to Indianapolis, Indiana, where Beth was going to meet me.

Somewhere between Greenland and the states I came to think that my Chennault orders might be bogus, so instead of taking my full thirty days of leave and travel time, I decided we would go to Lake Charles early just in case there was a problem and I needed to get to Del Rio in a hurry. It was a good thing we did.

When I arrived and checked in, they weren't expecting me. I had a meeting with the sergeant in charge and discussed the entire situation with him and his suggestion was that I get to Del Rio as soon as possible. Instead, I talked with Captain Miller at the gym. We went through the whole thing again. This time I got a different response. He asked me to give him a day to work on it and to come back the following afternoon.

The next day when I arrived at the gym, Rene (Capt. Miller) sent me to see the base commander. I introduced myself to his secretary and was ushered into the CO's office. Approaching his desk I stood at attention and gave a sharp salute. He responded appropriately and offered me a seat. Once more I went through the entire story of what happened at Thule. He said his main concern was getting a personnel call through to the Pentagon. "You have quite a fan club here," he told me. I gave him a puzzled look. He laughed, a happy laugh, and then rattled off the name of Capt. Miller, Major Carmichel, the base chaplain, Sergeant Lucien, and a few others. "Within two hours yesterday afternoon, I received phone calls from more than ten officers and troops that you influenced before you were sent to Greenland, all wanting me to arrange to get you to say here."

He said, "I have one question, do you plan to stay in the Air Force after you graduate from college?"

I responded with a definite, "No, sir."

He smiled and said, "They were right, a couple of your recommendations said that you couldn't lie if your life depended on it. If you had told me yes, I would have pulled my support. Give me a few days."

A few days became a week, then two weeks. I was running out of time. Then the word came from Rene, "Get over to the CO's office right now. You have been assigned to this base, there isn't time to get everything squared away, but time will take care of everything. You have been authorized to sign in VOCO (Vocal Order Commanding Officer.)"

Yes, sir! I spent the next day getting myself officially signed in with no problems and began working the following night. I enrolled in school and settled into my old routine.

My first evening I was met by the base chaplain, who had an unofficial request of me. He said that we had a lot of officers on base that needed to get their bachelor's degree and either through too many years having passed since they were in school or reluctant to make a commitment, they needed guidance. After some clarifying discussion, I agreed to meet with any officer that I could help.

THE AIR FORCE YEARS

I did require a briefing from the chaplain or an appropriate office involved with the background of the gentleman I was to work with. I had to have some knowledge of the situation so that I would not be subject to being a know-it-all airman second leading an officer. The chaplain got my message and assured me that anyone sent to me would be fully aware of what I had accomplished in forwarding my education.

After a couple of months, I was notified to report to the pay master, who advised me that I owed Uncle Sam travel money, as I was authorized travel to Del Rio. I showed my withdrawal of funds from Thule, which showed that I only withdrew travel to Lake Charles. That was thus straightened out, or so I thought.

In communication about resolution of the finance situation with Laughlin AFB, there was the little matter that Laughlin had me listed as AWOL.

This could be easily resolved with a phone call from the base CO. It was at this point that I learned that the CO who authorized me to sign in VOCO had been RIFD during the last go around on promotions. I don't know what the letters stand for, but the meaning is very clear. He was passed over the last time permitted to retain his rank. He had two choices, retire or accept a reduction in rank and transfer to another base. In this case, he became an airman first class, somewhere, and he had to be found and state to the new CO that he did indeed authorize me to sign in VOCO. The former CO and now airman first was found and did verify that he had airman second class Donald A. Rasmussen sign to Chenault Air Force Base by Vocal Order of the Commanding Officer. (VOCO).

What an ordeal to go through because an overzealous sergeant tried to do me a favor. I was glad it was over.

The following spring Captain Miller informed me that Chennault AFB would be fielding a baseball team and I would be on it. I had no choice in the matter. He did tell me that I had nothing to worry about; he would handle the time I needed for practice and make sure I didn't miss any classes. With that established, he asked me, "How many hours are you carrying this semester?"

"Twenty-two"

"Twenty-two! Are you nuts?"

Before I could respond, he smiled and said, "Really?"

I nodded.

That spring of 1960, I had a few too many activities than I should have, but I couldn't figure anything to cut back on. My priority must be to my responsibility of my job assignment at the gym, then college followed by baseball, handball, and occasional exhibitions with judo, and when the college tennis team was going to be playing a match with a left-handed tennis player, I was asked to practice by a couple of the tennis players. For some reason, during breaks in the intramural action at the gym, I continued to get in some shooting with the basketball. I really don't know why, but I did.

As summer arrived, along with that beautiful weather mostly made up of high temperatures with high humidity, I cut back on my college workload to a more reasonable level of nine semester hours.

I didn't realize it at the time, but as I was entering the fall semester at McNeese and the last five months of my service in the Air Force, it had been five years earlier that I first stepped on a college campus as a freshman. The Air Force would have one more surprise for me that started out as a real annoyance.

Major Carmichael had communicated with the base adjutant general that in the case of a base alert, Airman Second Rasmussen would be used for night duty only. A month or so into the fall, we were hit with a surprise alert and I reported to the Air Police Augmentation Unit as assigned. I was escorted to the flight line and ordered to guard a specific B-47. I guarded that plane from dusk to dawn, without a break.

When the sun came up, I noticed that other guards were being relieved, while I remained on duty. Finally, I saw a jeep a distance away, so I went several strides from the plane I was guarding and began waving my carbine in the air. I had now been on guard duty going on twelve hours without a break of any kind. It was after eight o'clock when the jeep pulled up. The sergeant in the driver's seat asked, "What are you doing out here? This is not an assigned duty station."

"This is where I was assigned at approximately seven thirty last night, and I haven't seen a soul since that time."

He asked me where I would like to be dropped off. So as to make a specific point that I was ready to scalp someone, I directed the sergeant to take me to my CO's office. He said," Are you sure you want to do this?"

"I'm sure."

When I walked in and told the duty sergeant that I wanted to see Major Carmicheal, he literally jumped to accommodate me. The major met me with fire in his eyes. You see I was doing my student teaching and his son was in the class that I was teaching. When I told him the whole story of what occurred, he suggested that I get to school as soon as possible and see him when I returned to the base.

I headed for school, even though I would much rather have gone home and hit the sack. After concluding my morning at the school, I attended my two classes and drove back to the company headquarters to meet with the major.

He advised me that the assignment to the air police during alerts had been canceled. The sergeant that had put me on the flight line had been reprimanded and might face charges after the alert was completed. In the meantime, I had no assignment. He told me, "Each day through the conclusion of this alert, I want you to physically check in at the gym at your regular time. If the alert is still going, get some rest."

Well, that alert turned out to be the longest alert I experienced during my four years in the Air Force. It lasted over a month, so for that month, I was like a real college student. On Tuesday, the 27 of January 1961, I received my separation from the Air Force. On Friday of the same week, I received confirmation that I had completed my requirements for my bachelor of science degree with a major in physical education and a minor in social studies.

Thule Air Force Base

Chapter 15

SUBSTITUTE TEACHING AND THE NEW JERSEY FIASCO

Beth and I had often discussed the approaching completion of our college course work and qualifying for our bachelor's degrees, as well as our separation from the Air Force, which, when we checked the McNeese College fall calendar, we found that both events would occur during the same week toward the end of January 1961.

I had to make a determination regarding courses and extending our stay in Louisiana so that I could accept Coach Reed's invitation to play on the McNeese baseball team in the spring. I wasn't thinking about having the McNeese baseball letter on my resume, or where I would be able to play after the college season ended. My initial plan was to contact the Phillies scout that recruited me in 1955 and get into professional baseball, and I didn't need college baseball experience for that.

I hadn't talked with Beth about my thoughts, simply because they hadn't really been all put together with the time and unimaginable flurry of necessary activity that occurred in that final week.

We were wrapping up everything at the college, going through the process at the Air Base, selling our house trailer, and dealing with too many good-byes.

With everything completed and the car loaded, we headed toward Illinois. We had not really discussed anything beyond leaving

Louisiana and getting back to the Midwest. We each, in our own way, went through a withdrawal mini-depression and the realization that a significant part of our lives was over began to enter our thoughts. The past four years had provided a security that was important for us. I had been supporting myself since before my eighteenth birthday, and yet, I felt very inadequate going into civilian life.

It seemed that I had been going to college and serving in the Air Force all of my life and now I had nothing. And although Beth had been with me for more than four years, we had such a hectic life day in and day out that we really hadn't spent much time developing our relationship. We just needed each other to make it through.

Somewhere between Lake Charles and Danville, in my thoughts, I began to see Beth as a burden. Obviously, without the need to think rationally regarding external responsibilities of school and military, my head was in the process of really screwing me up.

Although we hadn't really planned anything, I couldn't resist going by EIU (Eastern Illinois University) on our way to Danville. Basically, I just wanted to see Dr. Carey, who was my landlord as well as a professor in the physical education department and head basketball coach at the school. I wanted him to know that I had completed my schooling. Why, I didn't really know. He was somewhat surprised that I also had completed four years of active duty military service.

After leaving EIU with an application for a job and an opportunity to complete a master's degree, a foggy, possible direction was in my hand. I frankly was not overly excited about the possibility, but it did, over the next month or so, become more of an intriguing idea.

We drove to Danville, and I left Beth with her parents and set out to find Judy. I think that seeing her was something that had been eating at me since I went to Greenland. I didn't really, conscientiously, have anything specific in mind, maybe I was hoping that we could put it together again, or I just needed to know that she was okay.

When I got to Chicago, the first thing on my mind was that I needed to get a job. My best option was to get an Illinois teaching certificate and register with as many school districts as I could to substitute teach for the rest of the school year.

I made copies of everything I sent to the state and headed to elementary school district 122 to talk with my former eighth grade teacher, Mr. Eugene Spizzirri, who was now a principal. My goal was to get an understanding as to whether I could use these documents to begin substitute teaching. After going over everything, he said that I could contact area school districts and individual schools to get on their substitute lists. He added me to his school's list and suggested that I go to the district office to become listed on the master list that would go to all the schools in the district.

While I was on my way to take care of getting listed as a district 122 substitute, Mr. Spizzirri called ahead. When I walked in, I was greeted with open arms. The secretary was effusive in letting me know that it wasn't often that former students came back that were qualified to teach. I met the superintendent briefly and was turned back over to the secretary. As we talked and she made copies of my papers, she mentioned the fact that I went to schools in three states, including Maryland.

I showed her my "certificate of service" that listed my dates of enlistment and release from active duty, and she could hardly contain herself. She was practically screeching as she said, "You were in the Air Force for four years, and you spent five and a half years in college—*all at the same time?* That's unbelievable."

She had recorded everything, and I hurried on my way, being somewhat embarrassed by her reaction to my combination of military service and education circumstances.

So as not to create any confusion or problem with other districts, I kept quiet about my military service as I went around the area signing up as a substitute in other districts. The few times that the question of my credits from the University of Maryland came up, I merely commented that that was correct, or simple replied, "Yes, ma'am."

The first couple of weeks I received sporadic calls to substitute, but I was in greater demand with each passing week. By the first of March,

I was averaging four-plus days a week. Depending on the school, a day of substituting earned between seventeen and eighteen dollars a day. I was earning between eighty-five and ninety dollars a week when I worked five days.

In late March I was approached by Miss Lucas, the superintendent of Worth Elementary School District, to work full time for the remainder of the school year. A teacher had to resign for health reasons and rather than have a succession of substitutes, the school board had authorized Miss Lucas to offer me the job. It meant a good increase in pay to what averaged about twenty-five dollars a day (I was still thinking like a sub) through the last day of the school year.

Getting to meet the other teachers in the school on a more personal basis as an equal, albeit a first-year teacher, was an enlightening experience. Attending teacher meetings, even though I never said a word, gave me further knowledge into the workings of a faculty.

It was during this time, even though I had been saving as much money as possible in preparation for attending EIU as a graduate assistant while securing my master's degree, that I was offered a summer job as a YMCA counselor with the Southwest Suburban YMCA as an assistant to Mrs. Dare Porter.

Beth had come to Chicago for Bob's funeral, and we got an apartment shortly thereafter. She had taken a job working at a candy store and the future was bright, since we were both focused on simply making it through the summer before going to Charleston in the fall. While I would be attending school, Beth had a job teaching third grade in Mattoon, just sixteen miles west of Charleston.

1961 YMCA Announcement

NEW JERSEY

Circumstances came together, engineered by Dad, that totally disrupted our plans and led Beth and I to go to New Jersey. This devastating part of my life must be laid out as a whole rather than be segregated as jobs, school, and baseball.

When I graduated from high school, I had one goal that had been with me for as long as I could remember. I had no backup plan. My plan, one might say dream, was to play professional baseball. In July of 1955, a scout for the Philadelphia Phillies talked to me and had a spot for me in their organization. He offered me a contract, but I had to get Dad's signature on the contract. Dad knew that baseball was what I wanted to do, but after Bill had told him a story of the Tigers offering him a contract in 1950, and Bill turned them down in order to go to college, playing baseball was out of bounds for me, I just didn't know it.

After I talked to the scout and he laid out what had to happen, I was on cloud nine when I went home and asked Dad to sign. He said, "No, end of discussion."

I tried to talk with him, but all he would say was that, "All of my boys will go to college." Without rehashing that ugly scene, I went to college and the day I stepped on campus, I learned from Dad that I was on my own financially.

The end result of that was I ended up in the Air Force and put myself and my wife through college. During those five years and five months from the day I stepped on the campus at Northern Illinois University, I was totally independent from my family that I had longed to be a part of all my life but never was.

Dad had never cared about my jobs, how I got them, what I did, or what I made. The important thing was that from the time I made enough to pay my way, it didn't cost him anything.

While substitute teaching, I was playing baseball and one particular game was attended by a couple of scouts. After the game, I overheard them talking about me, but since the Phillies scout had told me in February that at seventeen I was a prospect and at twenty-three, I wasn't, I threw his card away and had since forgotten his name, even though I had carried his card with me for over five and a half years and talked with him briefly that past February.

I thought I recognized his voice when one of them said to the other as I was the last player in the area, "There's the best player on the field today."

A few days after I overheard their conversation, Dad got hold of me and said that Bill had called and that he had lined up some jobs for Beth and me for the summer. I told him that Beth and I had jobs that would get us through the summer and Beth had signed a teaching contract in Mattoon, so we didn't want to leave, and besides, I was having more fun playing baseball than I had had since 1955.

Bill had told him that these jobs wouldn't be available very long and we needed to get going before they were filled.

"Why would Bill do that?"

"I told him that you were just killing time."

"I don't consider what I am doing as 'killing time.' I have been taking care of myself for a long time now, and I don't need Bill's help."

That went right over his head and he responded, "I'll talk to him about baseball."

Then he hit me with the clincher, "Look, the fact of the matter is Bill is having a difficult time dealing with Bob's death, and he needs family to help him through his depression."

"I don't know what I could do?"

"Just be there for him. You will know what to do when the time arises."

How could I say no? I had spent my whole life trying to be a part of and be accepted as a part of my family. Maybe this was the moment.

I agreed to go.

I couldn't leave the coach high and dry, so I told Dad that I would have to play one more game. He wasn't happy about it, but he didn't press the issue.

Dad and I hadn't talked much about baseball since 1955 and as far as I knew, he didn't even know that I was playing that summer, or that I had played last year for that matter. Although I didn't think about it at the time, he had to have talked with someone to know when and where I was playing. Have I mentioned that I was pretty naive and I trusted Dad?

When the game day arrived, Dad was there to see the game. This was the first game he came to see me play since he saw me play parts of a couple of games back in 1955.

As usual I was in the leadoff position in the lineup. Batting left-handed, I hit a pop fly down the left field line in the first inning, which dropped fair. I would have normally been running from the crack of the bat, but I just stood in the batter's box. The guys on the bench began to yell at me and I ran, belatedly, to first base. I was easily safe, but it should have been a double. Fortunately, no harm done. I stole second on the first pitch to the next batter. It wasn't much of a game; I ended up with two hits, a walk, and a strike out. I stole two bases, scored two runs, and drove in one, but the most important thing, Mom showed up in the early innings and stood on the third base side of the field. Dad was on the first base side of the field. Dad would disrupt me between innings, and then Mom began doing the same thing, alternating innings. This was the first time my mother had *ever* seen me play baseball.

They were driving me crazy and to say that they were making it difficult for me to concentrate on the game would be a gross understatement.

In my last at-bat, I struck out and then got myself thrown out of the game. This was the first and only time an umpire ever ejected me from a game and it was well deserved.

I took a called third strike on a fastball knee high on the outside corner of the plate (a good pitch). I never took a two-strike pitch near the plate. I would either foul it off or strike out swinging. It was a good strike and the umpire made a good call. I was upset with myself and took it out on the ump. I didn't question the call, just his eyesight, as I offered him my glasses.

After the game I apologized to the umpire, approaching him with a big grin on my face so not to allow him to think I might be a threat. He, very kindly, accepted my apology and I went on my way.

Mom and Dad had left when I went over to see the umpire and I began to relax. I hung around the field for a few minutes until I thought they had enough time to leave.

When I headed for my car, Dad was standing there waiting for me. Mom had left.

As soon as I arrived, Dad asked me when I would be leaving for New Jersey. I didn't respond immediately so he filled the air with the one thing he knew I was waiting to hear. "Bill has lined up a team for you to play with."

I was still trying to become an accepted part of the family, even though I wasn't conscious of my motivation. I said, "We'll be leaving in the morning." With that he turned and headed for his car.

Beth and I had an early breakfast, packed our meager belongings, including my spikes, glove, and the rest of my workout clothes, and began our trip to New Jersey. We weren't in a big hurry, as I knew it would take us two days to get there unless we wanted to arrive late in the evening.

We arrived the afternoon of the second day and Bill was waiting for us. After initial greetings, I got right to the important things. I asked about baseball.

Nothing had changed as he lit into me about forgetting about baseball in a non-conversational voice. I could feel anger in his voice as he continued to expound and became unglued as he yelled about me growing up. It was not exactly the rant he used on me in 1951 when the family arrived in Greencastle and I expected to see him playing for the

DePauw baseball team, but it was close. I should have figured out that he wasn't on the team and never did play for the school, or we would have heard about it back then.

After he ran out of steam on his baseball tirade, I asked him about the jobs that he had gotten for us. He handed me a clipping from a newspaper that was announcing a meeting at a nearby Holiday Inn for teachers wanting to sell World Book encyclopedias.

I was incredulous, speechless, and felt kind of numb. Bill filled the void by building up the opportunity to make good money by applying ourselves during the few days of training. If he were grieving over the loss of our brother, it sure wasn't showing in any way.

We were here. We had given up our summer jobs, so we attempted to make the best of things for a few days by going to the World Book training. The training held in one of their larger conference rooms was well attended the first day and cut in half the second day. We stuck it out for three days and then were turned loose on the populace, with leads.

Beth and I were not well suited for this type of work and it showed up quickly on our first and only day as sales representatives. As we contemplated our future in the Garden State, it dawned on us that we not only didn't have the "good jobs" that Dad had told us that Bill had waiting for us, we were sharing a non-job.

We were obviously "not the brightest stars in the sky" for getting ourselves into this situation, so we decided that we would go back to Bill's house, pack up our belongings, and head back to Chicago. Back there, I could at least play some baseball. When we made the announcement to Bill, he immediately volunteered to hire us in his factory.

I really didn't make any connection between Dad's rush to get us on our way to New Jersey, the conversation I had overheard between the two baseball scouts, and Bill's attitude and tirade, much less the differences between Dad's story and Bill's presenting us with the news of "World Book Encyclopedia."

We had been had! But why? Beth and I gave up jobs that would take us through the summer, we were living on our own, and not impacting the lives of Mom, Dad, and Bill in any way. Dad's reasoning had gone out the window the minute we had our first exchange with Bill. This was not a grieving man.

Bill obviously didn't want us to leave. We agreed and accepted the minimum wage jobs. We went in the next day with him and were put on the pay roll of Ad-aid, Inc. On the way into the factory, he described the kind of people we would be working with and encouraged us not to make fun of them, because they were just line workers and generally not very bright.

He really didn't need to be concerned; we both knew how to work with people and did just fine. The work was not challenging in any way and became real boring. In a couple of weeks, Beth was moved to operating the collating machine, and I was running the assembly line.

There was some grumbling among the troops, but that soon died down when Beth and I continued to treat them respectfully as equals. Things went along in a pretty routine manner for a couple of weeks.

I was called into the office to help Bill and the other owners solve a packaging problem.

One of the gentlemen advised me that Bill had told them I was good with "spacial relations." I had no clue what that meant, but I went along to see where we were headed. They were working with a complex packaging problem that had to be put on the line and produce over five hundred packages a day to keep from losing money on the project. They showed it to me and explained the dilemma that had to be solved.

I studied the shapes, sizes, and number of pieces that had to be quickly and precisely assembled. It was apparent that I would have to handle the elements of the project to determine the possible means of assembly, and I couldn't do it with three men who were superior to me in the company offering opinions as I was doing the organization.

I asked them to leave me with the project for a period of time and I could figure it out.

"How much time will you need? This is a priority job."

"I'll need fifteen to twenty minutes."

"Oh, okay!"

They all left and I began moving the pieces around and when satisfied, I set them up in an assembly line formation as they would be placed in the shipping box.

In a little over fifteen minutes, I opened the door and invited them in to demonstrate the line for them. The first question one of them asked was, "Why did we need to leave for you to do this set-up?"

I told them, "With three men commenting and recommending various alternatives, what I did here could have taken over an hour."

They all laughed, and then I demonstrated the line. "Can you knock out five hundred a day with this approach?"

"I can if I can pick my line members and run the line with my rules that will get maximum effort from the troops."

"What are your rules?"

"No questions, yes or no."

They looked at each other back and forth and finally, Bill said, "Yes."

"I will get it set up, pick my guys, and start the line this afternoon."

I selected the two that would help me set the line and had three more prepared to report to the assembly area after lunch. That afternoon we kicked out a little over two hundred and fifty. As we drove home, Bill was pleased and asked me if I was tired.

When I said no, he asked if I would like to help him with a project. Always trying to please, I said yes.

After dinner, we walked out front and he explained a flooding problem that he had, and he wanted to dig a hole deeper than the basement that would gather water before it could reach the house. He had located the spot and said, while you dig, I will go into the mountains and gather some stones to fill it with.

Sounded good to me. As he drove off, I went into the house, got Beth, and together, we began digging. Obviously, I did the heaviest part of the digging, but Beth was a big help.

When Bill returned, I took a break and helped him unload rocks. We piled them far enough from the hole so they wouldn't get covered up with dirt.

Over the weekend, while I was taking a break from digging, Bill started asking me about judo. I answered his questions and then he made a statement to the effect that I couldn't throw him. I told him that I didn't want to.

He decided he would rush me. He really didn't give me any choice. As he got to me, I took him down as easily as I could. It wasn't easy enough, as he ended up with three cracked ribs.

Physically, that was the end of it. He never mentioned judo or tried to push me again. Of that I am glad. I never brought it up to him, and I am very pleased that no one ever tried me again after that.

Since I had pushed back in the eighth grade and established respect for myself, I have never started a fight, but when pushed, I have never lost a fight. I am glad it is over. I like being a good guy.

Back at Ad-Aid, the project went well. On the first full day of the line working, we exceeded our goal by better than fifty percent packaging over seven hundred and fifty for the day. The key to our success was five minutes, ten minutes, and five minutes. The mental attitude, or mindset, of these workers was the next break. When we started in the morning, I advised the whole team that if we exceeded one hundred and seventy-five units by the time the first break horn went off, they would get an extra five minutes on their morning break. At noon they would get ten minutes additional lunch break for another one hundred and seventy-five units. The same applied to the afternoon.

After the afternoon break, they needed another one hundred and seventy-five for us to keep the schedule the same for the next day. They always exceeded the goals by more than ten units. When we reached a break time or lunch, I would total up the numbers and announce to them that they should ignore the end of the break period and take the extra time. They always responded. It was my respect for them that made it work.

When we finished, each and every one that worked on that line asked me to pick them if we ever needed another special project.

For some of our time in New Jersey, we stayed at the home of Mr. and Mrs. Justin McDonnell, Bill's in-laws, while they went on vacation.

They left us with everything that we needed or could possibly need when they headed out for a couple of weeks. Beth and I replaced all the food we used and kept the home as we would keep our own. We were surprised when they came home a day early and were preparing a meal for us on the grill.

Beth was somewhat embarrassed that she hadn't made the bed that morning, as she planned to wash the sheets that evening since we didn't know what time they would be coming home the next day.

They were more than pleased to see everything in order, and Mr. McDonnell made a comment to me such as I had never heard in my life. In the middle of conversation, he said, "I wish Bill had a little bit of you in him."

With the idealized view I had of Bill, this really came at me from left field. I couldn't think of anything to say except, "Thank you."

That was the most memorable moment of our stay in New Jersey.

When the summer was over, after Bill had loaded our car up with several years' worth of Westinghouse light bulbs that he had received from Westinghouse when he left the company, Beth and I headed back to school, me at grad school and Beth teaching.

On the trip home, we discussed this experience in our life and asked each other, "Why?"

Bill knew we were coming, but had no jobs and no baseball team for me to play with.

Was the whole thing made up by Dad?

If so, why?

When did Bill learn that we were coming?

Had he called Dad and asked that we drive out to New Jersey, or had he called him while we were driving to New Jersey?

Regardless of the answers to these questions, it seems to me that the whole experience we had was tied to baseball. In 1955 Dad wouldn't sign for me to play. In 1956 he let me know that by the time I could sign my own contract, "they won't want you." In 1961, after overhearing positive comments about my play, he showed up in a couple of days with a scheme to get me out of Chicago.

After these many years while putting the outline for this book together, I thought about the irrationality of us quitting our jobs and leaving Chicago for a couple of months in New Jersey.

What could the rationale have been for Dad and Mom to team up and get me out of Chicago?

The first thing I realized was that they didn't know my baseball schedule. They had to have talked to someone. The only people that would have known my schedule were my coach Bob Hunt and maybe the two scouts that I overheard talking about me and my teammates, none of them were known to my parents with the exception of Bob Hunt. Bob either called Dad or gave Dad's phone number to the scouts.

It would not take much of a leap to realize that had I not gone to New Jersey, I would have had a second shot at professional baseball.

Did I mention that sometimes I am not too quick on the uptake? It only took me fifty years and this book to allow myself to connect the dots.

Would I have taken a pass on my master's degree to play professional baseball? You know I would have.

Chapter 16

NEW AND DIFFERENT CAREERS

After graduating with my master of science in education degree at age twenty-four in August of 1962, I began a teaching career that really wasn't my cup of tea.

Schools are not set up to provide a challenging incentive to succeed as an individual, like the business community is, so I taught because I enjoyed helping young people. That reason alone, however, is a discouraging atmosphere because few teachers are so motivated by their discipline that most of them are going through the motions from about their third or fourth year of teaching until they retire.

I needed more. When able to find a baseball team I could play with, I always found that challenging and exciting. Sometimes I found the necessary challenge in studying and going back to school, sometimes on my own—such as nutrition and the Kennedy assassination.

From January of 1963 through 1966, I was a teacher-coach at the Intermountain Indian School in Brigham City, Utah. These kids were enjoyable to work with. Most of them had never seen a town beyond the huge Navajo reservation that extended in all directions from the four-corner area where Utah, Colorado, New Mexico, and Arizona meet. Most of the reservation extends throughout northeastern Arizona.

Every fall we bussed a couple thousand young people from their homes on the reservation to Brigham City in the northern portion of Utah. Their parents were generally cooperative with the program because it meant that their kids would get three meals a day.

We knew one young lady who became very distraught and wouldn't talk about the reasons or what the problem might be. I invited her to our home for dinner, and she very rapidly became an unofficial temporary adopted daughter. She and Beth hit it off and soon she was discussing life on the reservation with us. Still, she remained more withdrawn than she was when she first entered my classroom.

It seemed like forever, but eventually we saw the smile come back to her face. She asked to speak with me one day during school, so I took her to an empty office and she started out telling me a story of her family, but suddenly began to become visibly quieter and withdrawn all over again. I asked her if she wanted to finish at another time, because I could see that she was really hurting. Her name was Edith Ann Yazzie.

At this time Beth was pregnant with our second child, and we had discussed naming a baby girl after Edith Ann if that was what we had. I decided that this might be a good time to tell Edith what our plans were. At a convenient time during our talk, I let her know what we planned to do. It lifted her spirits and, though difficult, with tears in her eyes, she told me about her four-year-old brother had died of malnutrition on the reservation.

As soon as she got it out, I was tearing up, yet I could see she was feeling some relief.

After that she began being like her old self, little by little.

Working with my basketball team was an interesting experience.

These boys, on the reservation, ran every day of their lives as a part of their religious beliefs. We had so many boys that wanted to go out for the basketball team that we would put them on buses and the drivers would take them out five miles and the first one hundred to make it back to the campus could try out for the two teams.

Those that didn't make it were not very upset; at least they got a run in with some different scenery to enjoy. It seemed to me that most, if not all, the Navajo enjoyed nature. I coached the junior high school team, and we ended the season with a record of 11-1.

In addition to coaching, I taught English, health and hygiene, and physical education classes.

NEW AND DIFFERENT CAREERS

One of the most interesting phys. ed. classes I taught was archery. The kids were really eager to learn how to shoot a bow and arrow. Their intensity over the sport spurred us on to really dive into the activity.

Our school track team was naturally outstanding due to all the running the boys did on the reservation. We had one boy, Harry Chee, that ran the mile in just over four minutes the first time he ever ran a timed mile. His coach, Hal Reeder, made arrangements for him to run as an exhibition runner in a couple of Utah state track meets. He acquitted himself very well.

I seldom had any problems with students. They were generally pretty docile. I had one basketball player that decided to get in my face one day, and all he could to think of to say was, "I hate you, white-eye!"

I looked him right in the eye and said very slowly and in a controlled and even voice, "Hoskie, it is okay for you to hate me, but not okay for you to hate me for being a 'white-eye.' Hate me for what I make you do to become a better basketball player."

He thought about that for a couple of seconds and said, "Okay." Then he went back to work on the court. I don't know the dynamics of the Navajo culture, but after that, he smiled at me a lot, and the rest of the team settled down into a team that practiced well.

I was able to maintain an interest in teaching these young Navajo, so long as the BIA (Bureau of Indian Affairs) didn't bug me too much. Their budgeting process was way beyond my scope of reasoning. It was important for each department to spend all of their money each year and ask for more the following year. I could only imagine the cost of government if every part of the government did that.

It was standard for the head of the physical education department to order a hundred basketballs each year. The excess was used to barter with other departments. I didn't like it and it was something I could not live with indefinitely.

I had other jobs going on the side, and after three years, I couldn't deal with the dishonesty that was standard operating procedure at the Indian School any longer, so I became a full-time securities dealer in Salt Lake City with Alexander Hamilton Management Company, selling mutual funds and life insurance. It wasn't long afterward that I became the top life insurance representative for the company in the state of Utah.

As I was striving to get a handle on this business, Dad came down to Salt Lake City to see me. He was carrying a message from Bill. Bill was doing radio and assured Dad that with the spread of FM in cars, radio was the place to be, and I would really like it. You would think that after the New Jersey fiasco, I wouldn't have anything to do with any of their ideas. I would occasionally think of that time and wonder why, why would they conspire to get me to go to New Jersey under the guise of Bill needing family, when Bill could have cared less?

One day I would figure it out and get an answer.

In the meantime, I guess I was still that little kid trying to please Dad and in some distorted way, Bill.

I looked in the Salt Lake City Desert News classifieds and to my surprise, a new radio broadcast school was opening in Salt Lake City. I became their first student.

After completing the program, getting my FCC license, and searching the area, Beth and I decided it was time to get back to Illinois, where I knew the lay of the land better and could get a decent radio job.

Within a week, I was a disc jockey and news director at WITY in Danville,

Illinois. I really enjoyed the work, but the hours were beginning to get to me. I was on call twenty-four hours a day, seven days a week. Working ten hours a day and twelve on weekends was just a disaster of a schedule for a hundred dollars a week.

After three months, I requested a day off. It was granted on the basis that I would let the station know where I was when I wasn't at home. That night we went out to dinner with one of our announcers, Ted Bare and his wife. We were no sooner seated than I got a call that there was a drowning behind the Lakeview hospital. Ted said that he would go with me and we would make it back as soon as possible. We jumped in my car and headed for town. On the way in, I received a call on my two-way.

There had just been a second drowning over at the park, and we were to get over there as soon as possible after the story at Lakeview. We covered and called in both drownings and headed back to pick up the ladies. On the way to the restaurant, I had another call for another drowning. That was three drownings in one night.

I dropped Ted off at the restaurant and picked up Beth. I took her home before heading out to the third drowning. They were still searching for the body when I arrived.

I put a story together, called it in, and headed for home a little before midnight to get a few hours of sleep before reporting back to work in the morning.

This was an interesting and exciting field, but there had to be better situations, and I needed time to find one. To give me breathing space, I took a job as a teacher in a nearby town that fall.

Every school has its own peculiar personality and tone. This one was no different. I came in as a teacher and coach. The principal saw in my records that I was far more academically qualified than he was as an administrator. I had planned a one-year hiatus from full-time radio to support my family while I searched for a more appropriate radio position. I gave no indication that I was planning anything long term with the school district. The principal spent the entire year in a panic that I was going to make a move on his position.

My students made the whole year worthwhile. I had the best, most curious, talented, and interesting kids to work with. My girls were all too young to be in public school, but they became the future cheerleaders for my basketball team. Everyone adored them, particularly our cheerleaders.

In the spring, I submitted my letter of resignation, as I found one of the most successful small market radio stations in the country seeking an account executive (advertising salesman). I never could get used to the self-aggrandizement titles that corporations, large and small, give to the personnel of their businesses. I was also a sports broadcaster. I did play-by-play descriptions of athletic events. I was surprised at how rapidly I became not only good at my presentation, but innovative and expansive.

I found a way to expand my play-by-play experience and increase my income by making more money for the stations. I sold rodeos and created a community "Wild West Days" in a northeastern community in Missouri.

With no one on staff that had ever broadcast a rodeo, a staged bank robbery, or an entire town celebration live, while admitting that I was among the very same under-exposed group, I stepped up to do the broadcasts.

The first rodeo I did the play-by-play of was in Monroe City, Missouri. I had a go-fer that hunted up interviews for me and I did the action in the arena, sometimes using verbiage that I didn't know I had. The broadcast was very well accepted and the advertising I sold was a real plus.

That experience was so beneficial that I expanded the scene by working with the chamber of commerce in Edina for a full-blown "Wild West Days." The mic work and the financial haul both made the Monroe City experience look like small potatoes.

When possible, I relaxed by going to a nearby football field and kicking a football. It was just for fun, but some out of town students at Moberly Junior College suggested that I could kick professionally. I blew them off, but continued kicking, usually once a week. One day a student came out to watch me and when I took a break, he not only discussed professional football with me but also had the address and phone numbers of a couple of Continental Football League teams that he had talked with about me.

One was in Tulsa and the other in Omaha. I randomly called the Omaha Mustang number and received an invitation to their training camp. I had vacation time coming, so I accepted the invitation and made plans to go to Omaha. It was a pretty cool setup. We lived in the dorm at Creighton University and practiced at Boy's Town. This was a real interesting experience. After the first practice, I was introduced to a gentleman who went over the contract with me and told me what I would be paid. "No negotiation here, take it or leave it. If you take it and you're not from the area, you need to get a job."

Based on the salary, that was obvious. I was just up there for the experience, not seriously thinking of a career in football. I held off signing the contract for several days and just enjoyed the atmosphere. I particularly liked the evenings that were filled with talk of football and everyone's aspirations. The guys got a bang out of me, primarily because I was eight or nine years older than most of them. A couple of the guys that I tended to hang with were both hoping to catch on with an NFL team. At different times they each asked me, "How does an old guy like you stay in the shape you're in?"

I couldn't convince them that I wasn't "that old."

Everyone's perspective gets twisted around in this atmosphere. One day during an afternoon practice session, I noticed this gentleman standing down from the usual crowd that gathered at our practices. He waved me over and introduced me to his ten-year-old daughter and asked if he could take a picture of me with her. I suggested that if she wanted to have her picture taken with a football player, I could get one of the bigger guys to come over.

In all seriousness, he looked at me and said, "You mean they come bigger than you?" Those pads do wonders,

It was all I could do to keep from laughing, so I quietly went over and put my arm over the little girl's shoulder and suggested that he take two pictures, one of us being serious and the other smiling. When I ran back on the field, I looked back and that little girl had a grin on her face from ear to ear. Now, that made me feel good and the whole experience worthwhile.

After about ten days, I had to think about getting back to a real job, so I turned in my uniform and headed back to Missouri.

Although it was not a real job, I just had to throw it in here since it completed three levels of football that, just goofing off, I experienced. I wouldn't trade any one of the three for anything. I left thinking that I was in the right place—behind the microphone.

The following fall one of my advertisers stopped to visit with me. He was a vice president of Pay Way Feeds in Kansas City and a social friend of Ewing Kaufman, the owner of the Kansas City Royals. Dean, the advertising contact, wanted a tape of me doing play-by-play to demonstrate to Kaufman that I should be his Royals announcer. I sent him a couple of different tapes and within a short time, he called me and invited Beth and I to come to Kansas City to attend a Chiefs vs. Boston Patriots football game that just happened to be on our anniversary. We had a delightful time, but also learned that Kaufman wouldn't listen to any tapes made by people that hadn't played professional baseball. That news was a real downer.

With the realization that the big boys would only deal with big boys, and I wasn't getting any younger, I began looking at school superintendent positions in Illinois.

I contacted Eastern Illinois University and put my name on the lists of available principals and superintendents. As openings became available, I would be notified. When one was in driving distance, I would respond and arrange an interview time with the board of education.

The first school I interviewed with hired me on the spot. I thought that they must be desperate, but it was a good financial situation for me.

I started at the beginning of the summer and found that we had no budget prepared, several teaching vacancies, and the district had been out of compliance and not received state aid for several years. That would be the first thing to be addressed, along with the budget. I knew that the teaching situation would resolve itself before the first day of school, but the others should have been in place before the end of the previous school year.

This situation was one of the strangest in the state of Illinois. Instead of a community school district, the community had a high school district and an elementary school district that each had their own school board of seven members. They combined as much as possible and generally had joint school board meetings.

For the superintendent, this was the worst kind of nightmare. Two agendas, two budgets, and fourteen board members trying to establish their identity as a leader of the community.

The school year got off on a high note. In the first five minutes of the first day, two of the boys got into a fight right in the main entrance of the school. I walked out of my office and the students separated to give me a direct path to the two fighters; I stepped between them, grabbed them by the collars of their shirts and pulled them together in front of my face, smiled, and said, "Do you want to walk to my office, or do you want me to drag you?"

They both chose to walk. Surprisingly, that was the last fight in the school for the year.

We did have one altercation later in the year, but that was outside of the building. Our basketball team had been working hard to get off to a good start for the year and on the day of its first game, we had some vandalism done to a door of our school. It occurred in the morning before school, and it was significant enough that I had to put a stop to it immediately.

I called an all-school assembly. This was probably the shortest assembly on record. I had called the school we were going to play that night and advised the superintendent that we may forfeit the first game of the season, and why.

When all students were seated, I informed the entire school that the vandalism of that morning would not be a part of our school. I then made a straight-out statement: "Those students that committed this act of vandalism will report to my office by one o'clock this afternoon. I do not want to hear who did it. I will have the guilty persons come to my office in person."

Now, I will tell you that this brought a lot of smiles, a few snickers, and some out right laughter. Then I concluded the assembly with this statement: " I have put Astoria on notice that if the students who committed this act of violence against their fellow students do not appear in my office by one o'clock this afternoon, I will be calling him back to forfeit tonight's basketball game."

I was in a win-win situation for our school. The students had learned that when I said something, I meant it. The second thing in my favor was that the community waited all year to see their team play.

At twelve forty-five, two boys walked into my office and confessed to vandalizing the school that morning. I thanked them for coming in and asked them to sit down for a moment. With them in the office, I called Astoria and advised them that we would be there for the game.

When I arrived for the away game that evening, I was met by our school board president, who congratulated me for pulling of the bluff of the decade. I looked him in the eye and said, "I don't bluff! I will be meeting with those boys and their parents next week, and they will make restitution and a pledge to work hard on their studies for the rest of the year. I don't think the parents will object to that one bit."

They made restitution, and they didn't complain. Talking to the parents, I made a recommendation that the boys be required to work and pay them back for their support. I also waived all suspensions for the boys, based on their behavior for the remainder of the year. All in all it worked out pretty well, except, we lost the game.

After setting up a responsible financial program and budget guidance that was lacking when I arrived, the districts were back on track.

I was surprised to learn that just a few years after I left, the school was consolidated out of existence. It saddened me to hear that the heart of the community had been torn from its midst, but at the same time, I was happy for the students that would grow up and attend a larger school. Those small rural high school graduating classes of ten and fewer students simply don't have the ability to provide the opportunities that larger schools can.

I was motivated to continue in educational administration and treat radio as an avocation when I left the small town environment. I landed in east central Illinois with a junior-senior high school principal job and as a play-by-play announcer for the school.

As all schools go, this one seemed to be a slice above the smaller schools that constantly had to struggle to survive.

From the outside looking in, many known and existing problems are shielded from new administrators until after the contract had been signed. The Casey-Westfield school district had a serious drug problem that had been swept under the rug for some period of time. Denial is not a solution. The summer before I arrived, a young former student was run over repeatedly on Route 49 just south of town. During the school year, a student overdosed in school. When it happened, a male teacher and I lifted her into the backseat of a car, and as my secretary called ahead, we drove her to the local doctor's office, as no hospital was located in town. While this was happening, my secretary called the girl's mother and told her what happened and that she should get over to the doctor's office right away.

By the time she arrived, the girl was being treated. I was concerned about the young lady's life when her mother came screaming into the building that she was going to have me run out of town and that I had no right to say that her daughter had overdosed on drugs, when she knew perfectly well that her daughter would never, in a hundred years, touch those vile things. As she was ranting, I just stood in front of her and respectfully listened.

Finely, after what seemed like forever, the doctor came out of the treatment room, looked at the now silent woman and said, "Mrs. ——-, instead of screaming at Mr. Rasmussen, you should be thanking him. He saved your daughter's life, even though I didn't know it until a few minutes ago when her breathing began to settle down." I felt sorry for the lady, a respected bank officer, as she crumbled into my and the doctor's arms.

When I knew the girl would survive, I headed home, since it was now well after six o'clock in the evening. My wife probably would be wondering where I had been.

During the spring we learned that another girl was leaving school at noon and not returning for the remainder of the day. This was becoming a regular practice, so I called the parents to make them aware of the situation. At first, they resisted all contact with the school. I knew we had a serious problem on our hands, so I began talking with the girl in my office in the morning. I was getting nowhere with her after a week or so when I received a call from her dad, requesting a conference.

His wife wouldn't come with him, because she was so ashamed of what her daughter was doing. I said that I was glad he knew, because I hadn't gotten anywhere or learned anything from her in several days of visiting with her in my office.

It seemed that she had gotten involved with a group of older girls that were picking her up and taking her to various places and having different kinds of sexual activities.

The next morning when I had her come to my office, I suggested to her that we take a walk around the track so that if she wished to talk with me, she could do so without having to look at me across that big desk. She smiled and agreed to the walk, not any discussion. When we started walking, I assured her that all I wanted to do was help her. I pledged to her that anything said to me would be in strict confidence, unless it broke the law, in which case I would do anything in my power to protect her. It was a big risk that I was taking, but it paid off.

Her dad was talking with the police, and my concern was more with her well-being and putting her in a state of mind that she would stay in school and enjoy the rest of her youth as best she might. Within a week she was talking freely with me and staying in school all day. I kept her confidence, and after things settled down with her, her dad had scheduled the family to go for some counseling. The whole episode turned out far better than I expected it would.

During the year I also did play-by-play of the school's football games. It provided me with a nice diversion and kept my interest on things other than the responsibility that goes along with managing and scheduling the activities of a few hundred people day in and day out.

I had a satisfying school year that came to an unhappy ending as the superintendent was fired and decided to take me down with him. I thought I had found a home, but alas, the banker, who now had control of the board, knew that I would not allow him to actually run the school.

To add insult to injury, as well as violate the law, he had his board of education not pay me for the last month of my contract. I walked away and never looked back. Small people with small minds and overblown egos can't be reasoned with.

I decided to take another fling at being a small town superintendent of schools, and since the word traveled within the world of school administrators, I had a solid reputation of being a financial problem solver, a disciplinarian, and an understanding of the roll of a superintendent and a school board.

In small districts, the most difficult job for a school superintendent is to educate the school board of its function.

After leaving Casey, I ended up at Wellington, Illinois, where the financial situation was precarious, at best, with a faculty that wanted more money that simply didn't exist.

The school district functioning on a day-to-day basis was far more conventional than either of my previous school districts. The students came primarily from well-grounded and interested families. The buildings were another story, and the district had been dodging needed repairs for far too long.

I started moving us toward state of Illinois compliance by addressing the necessary safety issues first. The financing was the biggest concern.

Wellington was, to my understanding, the last community in Illinois still to have its eighty acres set aside for education that was owned by the citizens. This land was leased and administered by three elected officials that every three to five years issued checks to every person in the district from the farm profits since the last distribution. Each check would be for two or three dollars.

I discussed selling the land and using the money to move toward complete compliance with the state of Illinois building and safety requirements. The basic position of the board was that it couldn't be done.

When I asked, formally (to get it on record), the board unanimously agreed that it would back such a move.

That was all I needed. I contacted the county superintendent, and we started the process. Two months later I was able to advise the board that the county superintendent would work with the board in calling an election to sell the land. With the actual prospect now facing it, the board was not quite as enthused as it was initially, but when I told the members that the cost of farmland was on the rise, which it was, they were more accepting. The process would take some time and in the economic picture, it wasn't looking very bright as inflation was really taking hold. This was the seventies era of malaise.

When we started talking about the advantages to the school board and the community of selling the property, farmland had risen to $400 an acre. It was predicted that a $1,000 an acre might be in sight within months. The school board wanted to pass a resolution prohibiting the sale of the land for less than a $1,000 an acre. Fortunately, I was able to convince them not to take such action, as that would tip off any local buyers that the land would be sold when it reaches that value.

They would be far better off to advise the superintendent informally not to pull the trigger on the sale until such time as that level was met, which is what they did. We had everything in place and waited and watched as the value continued to rise. Over time the price did indeed reach the $1,000 an acre mark. I was given authority to sell. I talked to the adviser I was using at the bank, and he suggested that I hold on a while. I had followed his recommendations up until then and decided to continue to. He suggested that we talk every day, as things could move quickly when it topped out, which he expected to happen between $1,200 and 1,400 an acre. We talked and when the price hit $1,200 an acre, I gave him the order to sell. He contacted some buyers that he had lined up and started accepting bids with a floor of $1,200 an acre. When the final bid came in, we just barely hit six figures on the sale.

We met with the buyer, who happened to be the local farmer that was leasing the land, and the banker and lawyers finalized the deal. The board was ecstatic and congratulated me on a job well done.

Within a week, the price of central Illinois farmland went to over $1,300 an acre and I began getting calls from board members that were very hostile. I should have waited was the consensus for the seven members of the school board. Within a matter of a month, the price dropped to near a $1,000 and continued going south until it reached a point near the $400 an acre it was at when we started the process. I never heard a word from anyone on the board as the slide continued.

Although the sale was finalized, I kept in touch with the bank, as we had not received the money. After a month I had a meeting with the buyer and advised him that the school board, through their attorney, was going to demand payment or request the county superintendent to file a suit demanding late charges and a reasonable interest charge for every day the full payment had not been paid.

I pointed out to him that as a member of the community, when word got out that he was stalling, it would have a negative effect on his reputation. He asked me how much the school was losing per day. When I told him, he had a startled look on his face and said, "*Really?*"

We met the next morning, and in my presence, he paid his bill and then invited me out for coffee.

As the end of the school year was approaching and the verification of all graduating seniors' diplomas were being signed by the school board president and myself, the president told me to keep one boy's diploma out of those to be awarded. The reason was that that boy had dated his daughter all through high school and dumped her a few weeks earlier.

The requirements to graduate had been met and there was no way he, or I for that matter, could withhold the diploma. He tried persuasion, which didn't work, so he ordered me. That didn't work either.

The only course that was left was to remove me from my position, which the whole board did. I stayed through graduation and presented all students their diplomas.

When I left after the graduation, I carried with me an additional year's salary.

Do to health reasons, I didn't seek another job, and Beth took a teaching job to get the family through a very tough time.

Chapter 17

EXPERIMENTATION – A NEW BUSINESS and MY FINAL JOB IN EDUCATION

I had to find a way to make a living for my family that wouldn't make things worse as I worked through what was probably the most difficult time in my life. I never gave any thought to anything other than coming out of the physical, psychological, and mental depression that encompassed my every waking moment.

Not knowing what lie ahead, Beth and I agreed that it would be wise to take the extra year pay that I had received from the Wellington school district and put it in a house in a town that we would like to be in.

A few years earlier, I had been hired to be the announcer for a country music concert featuring Porter Wagoner and Dolly Parton. Of course, I met the band and band members, as they were the warm-up for Porter. When I brought Porter on stage, I was going to have considerable time during his initial presentation, at which time I would bring Dolly out on stage.

Dolly had been singing with Porter for about five years and had an enthusiasm for what she was doing that was just electrifying. She came in from the bus early and we visited for over a half an hour before she went on stage. The show was a great big hit.

After we bought a home in Villa Grove, I began working on learning about the business. I traveled to Nashville and met with people in the industry, getting tips on how to get started. It is a tough business that, in the long run, turned out to be more demanding than my energy level could handle.

While licking my wounds from country music promotion, I met Mr. Herb Price in a coffee shop in Campaign. As we talked, he picked up on the fact that I wasn't as healthy as I should be, and we began discussing nutrition and its importance to our health. The more we talked, the more I realized that I knew more about the subject than he did.

Before we finished our coffee, I had agreed to try a basic program. A month later Beth and I had a business that would be both satisfying and profitable.

I had begun the nutritional supplement program in the middle of February 1975. By April 1 I was investigating school administration jobs. Before the end of the month, I had agreed to move to East Peoria and serve as the junior high school principal in District 50 located between East Peoria and Washington beginning in September.

From April through August, I continued my second experiment both personally and as a business. As a Shaklee distributor, I began making a profit and contributed to the family financial base for us to not only continue to exist, but to also begin moving forward. Through thick and thin, I would remain involved with Shaklee well into my retirement.

The school had problems with discipline and overall control of the student body. When we discussed the situation and I laid out means of controlling the educational atmosphere and reestablishing an emphasis on academics, Superintendent Bill Toler was enthusiastic, and the board, although somewhat less so, was cooperative. We were one of five feeder schools to Washington High School and of the five, we were the largest, and on average academic testing, we were ranked number five. In my judgment, that was totally not acceptable.

The first thing to accomplish was to relieve all teachers of the responsibility of administering corporal punishment and introduce the ancient concept of suspension from school accompanied by a required meeting between parents and principal. This information was released through the local newspaper prior to the date of the beginning of school.

On the morning of the first day of school, I strolled around the school property greeting students and welcoming them back to school. In the process, I noticed a baseball bat sitting in some weeds, so I picked it up with the intent of throwing it away when I got near a dumpster. The bat had been split and had a flat side to the barrel so it wasn't much good; the only problem was that I didn't come upon a dumpster, so I carried the bat inside with me as the bell rang.

We had four large doors for the students to enter at the main entrance to the building. As I stood there, standing tall with my arms folded, holding a flat-sided baseball bat between the first two fingers of my left hand, swinging, slowly from side to side, the student body came bursting through all four doors. You would have thought there was a thick glass wall five feet into the building that could only be penetrated if you were walking slowly, because that was what everyone was doing as they walked by me, respectfully.

I would like to say that that attitude lasted all year, but I'd be lying. Later that morning I had my first encounter with a negative leader of the class.

A teacher sent a student to my office for disrupting class. He was not a bad kid, but he had status among his peers that he was maintaining. He knew that he was going to receive corporal punishment and asked when he came into my office with kind of a half-smile along with a touch of concern on his face, "How many swats am I going to get, fifteen, twenty, what?"

I asked him to sit down for a minute and we talked about such things as the purpose of his being in school. I must admit, he wasn't much interested. During this conversation I informed him that I found fifteen or more swats offensive, so I was going to give him three. The smile on his face was a thing of beauty as he got up and bent over, and said, "Let's get it over with."

As he got in this rather strange position, with his hands on his ankles, his head down, and his butt sticking up in the air, I questioned him as to what he was doing and he said he was "taking the position."

I said, "No, that is not the position."

He looked at me in a puzzled way with a little concern in his eyes. I showed him how to stand to receive his punishment. Bend over slightly, it keeps the muscle and fat in your butt further away from the bones that support your legs, making it safer.

"Now, with your arms by your side, lift your hands up about twelve to fourteen inches in front of your hips."

He looked at me and asked, "What is this for?"

"Someone has to catch your butt when it comes flying through."

The smile was gone and for the first time since he came into the office, I felt that he would rather be somewhere else.

I administered a swat that was very fast and strong.

He stood up and I could see the tears that he was fighting to hold back, welling up in his eyes. I told him that he had a decision to make, and I explained the decision to him.

"I always make the first swat 'the light one.' Now you can choose between two harder swats than the first one, or, you can let me put them in the bank for you for your next trip to my office for disrupting class or being disrespectful to your teacher. It's your choice, but before you make that choice, remember that your next trip will be five swats and no banking chance. Understand.?"

To my surprise, he began to cry and said, "Thank you, put them in the bank. I won't be back."

Before the year was over, he had improved his attitude, his classwork, and, I could tell, he felt good about himself. He also got the word around pretty good without telling any of the other students the specifics about the time he spent with me.

After that I ended up, over a four-year period at District 50, giving three boys swats.

Suspensions were another thing to deal with. These had not been experienced by anyone that was currently a student in the school. I am sure that in many a household kids were told that, "If I have to take time off work to come to school because you got suspended, you will be in such trouble that you will wish that it never happened."

EXPERIMENTATION – A NEW BUSINESS AND MY FINAL JOB IN EDUCATION

Since I involved parents with the suspensions, which was necessary, the serious misbehavior of students created embarrassment in the family and an initial "my son (daughter) wouldn't do anything like that." Generally, once I sat down with the parent and they realized that I didn't have horns and was concerned with not only the immediate, but also the long-term success of their child, we came to an understanding. Once we had an agreement of the need for an improvement in certain behavior, we could resolve the immediate problem so that I could waive the last two days of the suspension. This always pleased the parent simply because they would rather have the kid in school than roaming the streets while they were at work.

The way I worked with parents brought me support from most homes, which in turn caused the students to feel better about school and the teachers were thrilled to be able to concentrate on their subject matter.

No matter how hard you work to create an atmosphere, when a void is created in the routine of working adults, that void must be filled with something.

District 50 was a non-union school district, one of a very few in Illinois in the mid-1970s. With a better-behaved student body, rising test scores, and annually passing another smaller school in the five schools that sent students to Washington High School, the teachers needed something to be unhappy about. I think this is just natural human behavior.

A couple of the teachers began to organize for a union vote. We, the administration, held several meetings with them to attempt to figure out their motivation. At a junior high teachers meeting, I tried to determine that through civil conversation without the canned propaganda that was being fed to the teachers through the state of Illinois branch of the National Education Association.

We had been going at it for over an hour, when my math teacher blurted out, "We want power."

He was angry and really became livid after his outburst. He kept ranting and when he would take a breath, I would say something like, "Now we have a point where we can begin a civil discussion."

That would set him off again. This went on for a while, so I simply concluded the meeting. I had been familiar with irrational behavior, and he was way out in irrational, non- logical la-la land.

One of my friendly teachers, who was basically harassed into supporting the group, called me that evening and thanked me for calling the meeting adjourned. She told me that she didn't know what they were doing or why.

I continued to treat the junior high leaders of the movement as I always had, with respect, but they seemed to have developed a real hatred toward me. We were never able to get the union movement leaders to sit down and discuss their rationale behind the movement. Of course the prime purpose of unionizing was never mentioned, that being salaries.

After a year of agitating and just playing the helpless used and abused teachers, they got their union rules, which all concerned had to abide by.

When we started my third year at the school, we were well versed in the rules. The one that I knew was going to cause problems was the length of the school day. Sure enough, the social studies teacher came to see me about leaving an hour early to take care of some business as she often had done in the past. I explained that we all have to live under the agreed upon rules or I could have a union official create an issue unnecessarily. I turned her request down.

Many of the courtesies we extended to our faculty were not permitted under the union contract. We were basically hamstrung from making compassionate decisions in favor of our good and formally loyal staff.

The math teacher, who became the union spokesman, wanted to renegotiate the union contract. We declined, which was well within our rights, even though we would have preferred to sit down and work things out on a local basis as the cooperative coworkers we were.

The long and the short of it was that the teachers called for a union recall vote and voted themselves out of the union.

It took a long time for the math teacher to come around, but generally we were back to working as a team to educate kids. In my fourth year, after things got back to normal, we pulled together and became number two on the list of feeder schools to Washington High School. This was an academic achievement that members of the school board told me they never thought we could rise to. The top feeder school was a small private school with an average graduating class of twelve to fifteen students. Our graduating classes averaged between and 160 to175 in an all-inclusive district. To move from fifth to second in just four years was an outstanding feat for the school district.

Were it not for the creation of ESPN, I could have spent the remainder of my career at District 50.

Chapter 18

OWNERSHIP OF ESPN

I was entering my fourth year as the junior high school principal in District 50 and having established a solid record within the community, I was looking forward to a long and stable career in education for the first time since completing my degrees.

On Thursday evening, September 14, 1978 I received a call from Dad. Bill was in town and wanted to drive down to Peoria to visit with me. I suggested that they come the following evening, but Bill and his son Scott had to leave Friday evening, so it would be better if they could come down earlier in the day. I finally agreed to meet with them when they got to East Peoria. I would have Beth call me when they arrived and have arrangements made to leave school as soon as possible.

As soon as I hung up and told Beth that Bill and Scott were coming down to see me the next day, her immediate response was, "Bill wants money!"

I accepted her skepticism on the basis that in two months and two days, we would be celebrating our twenty-second wedding anniversary and this would be the first time in those twenty-two years that Bill had stepped foot in our house.

They arrived in the early afternoon and when I got home, everyone was in the backyard enjoying the pleasant fall day. Dad started the conversation with the enthusiasm he and Sis had for Bill's project.

Bill laid out the progress that had been made in raising funds and the fact that they had gotten things to the point where he wanted to bring the family in on it, as he saw this as an opportunity to fulfill Dad's dream of having a family business. For most of an hour, I listened and asked questions. The point that puzzled me the most was that this was going to take a lot more than the money Sis, Dad, and I could provide.

Bill stated that they had some big companies that were putting together proposals to provide the big money needed to get the network on the air.

I asked, "Who are these companies?"

Bill replied, "We have confidentiality agreements with them until all the paper work is completed."

"In general terms, how much money are you talking to these companies about?"

"Enough to get the job done. Look, Dad and Sis are in as part of this to have a family business. We are offering you a chance to be a part of it. If you want to, great, if not that's fine too. All we're talking about here is a little bridge money to fill a gap until the companies and their lawyers complete their paperwork."

I told him that I would like to participate, but I had a family to support, as well as the house, so I didn't have any money just lying around.

"Could you get ten thousand this weekend?"

"Probably."

The discussion turned to me becoming a part of the company when my contract ran out in the spring. Everyone seemed to think it was a good idea. When that was resolved, Bill said that he and Scott had to get back to Chicago and catch a plane to Connecticut. For the first time in forever, I felt like a part of the family.

As they were leaving, Bill stayed back a bit to give me a final word. "If you can't get the money to us by noon Monday, forget it." I took this to mean that they had a major bill that had to be paid before the end of the workday Monday.

If I could raise ten thousand dollars, I would own two percent of the company, the same as Dad. Sis gave Bill fifteen thousand, so she owned three percent.

The material he left with me was very inviting. I had two prospects that could possibly get me the money by Monday. I went to see

Herb first and he was the most capable, financially. My backup gentleman was an engineer from Caterpillar who became a friend through his daughter that managed to get in trouble regularly, with one of my daughters. They were good and decent parents that believed in being involved with their children. He also was very much up on the satellite development, so when I presented it to him, we quickly agreed that he would give me the ten grand, five for him and five for me. He said that it might take some time, but it would be a help for their retirement.

I insisted that I give him a receipt for my own piece of mind. He said that it wasn't necessary. He felt that he knew my character and would trust me with anything. I gave him a handwritten receipt anyway. Our agreement was simple: anything I received would be split equally.

When I got up on Monday morning, September 18, I called Bill and told him that I had the money to wire to him and all I needed was the wiring instructions for the bank. As I said it, I heard very loud noises in the background like a couple of people dancing and whopping it up. Bill had to ask them to quiet down so he could give me the information. I got the numbers and read them back to him. I could still hear unbridled joy in the background. I knew at that moment that the money I sent was more than bridge money. I was sure that the money was going to be used that afternoon to secure the transponder on Satcom I.

Bill continues to this day to insist that the family money was mere bridge money.

> *In the middle of January of 1981, after I resigned from ESPN, Scott met me in the parking lot of Enterprise Radio and said to me, "You know that if it weren't for you, there would be no ESPN.*

So, between the background celebration on September 18, 1978 when I wired the money to Bill and Scott's statement above, we know, unequivocally, that I provided the final and most important piece of funding that secured the transponder on Satcom I, the first asset of ESPN, and it was the critical asset that allowed the network to proceed.

In May of 2007, almost thirty years after we agreed to help Bill fulfill dad's dream, Rosa Gatti, a long-time vice president of ESPN and the last person I spoke with the day I resigned, asked me, "Why don't you consider yourself a founder of ESPN, you made it happen as much as Bill did by giving him the money for the down payment on the transponder and did far more than Bill to build the network. We consider you a founder."

Scott, Don Jr., Bill

Scott, Dad, and Bill
Don sitting next to Mom

401 Illini Dr. East Peoria, Illinois, September 15, 1978

These are the only pictures taken the day Dad, Sis (not pictured), and Don committed to providing $35,000 to secure the transponder on Satcom I.

Bill was obviously less concerned about Dad's dream of having a family business than he was of just getting the money to keep the network going. As he scrambled to find interim financing, it was also clear that he misled Sis, Dad, and I about the big companies that were setting up funding for the network.

To Bill's credit, he lined up interim financing through KS Sweet Company in King of Prussia, Pennsylvania, as well as a viable business plan and a route to find a company that would commit ten million dollars to build ESPN (Bill's figure as stated to me).

In spite of the fact, that was now obvious, that Bill had used less-than-honest techniques to entice us to collectively provide him with the funds that allowed him to go forward, looking down the road, I could see positive things for the future. This feeling was enhanced when Bill began showing up periodically to update me on my roll once the school year was over. He would show me different sides of his personality during these visits. He would emphasize the importance of building a subscriber base for the network and inquire as to my studying of the structure of the cable systems countrywide. Another time he would make it perfectly clear to me that I had better not be thinking about being a talent on the network just because I had a background in radio, stating, "You will never be seen on ESPN!" This became a recurring statement, with an edge on his voice for emphasis.

This was not often enough to be a disturbing trend at the visits, perhaps four or five times over the period between September of 1978 and May 1979.

Before we step into the murky waters, it is important that we meet a couple of people that become an integral part of ESPN.

Mr. Stuart Evey, vice president of Diversified Operations Division at Getty Oil, was introduced to the concept of ESP-TV by J. B. Doherty of KS Sweet Associates, the company that was providing ESP-TV with interim financing as well as having developed the business plan and seeking long-term big money in the ten million range. Mr. Evey convinced the Getty board that ESP-TV, which became ESPN, was a viable business to become involved with.

Having met with Bill in the middle of December 1978, by the end of January 1979, Getty Oil had committed to and paid ESPN $5 million with much more to follow. What followed was Getty Oil buying 85 percent of ESPN, leaving 15 percent to the individual investors.

Stu reorganized the network stock from three hundred shares to five thousand shares of stock, but more importantly studied, learned, and gradually took control of the company. With 85 percent of the stock, that only made sense. He would become the man in charge of overseeing ESPN.

Stu selected Chet Simmons to become president of ESPN. Chet had been a long-time sports director of NBC, who was in contract negotiation with that network for a new contract when he was contacted by Stu. Chet, a brilliant man, would build ESPN in very few years.

Now, we step into the murky waters. With the hiring of Chet, Bill became the CEO, pretty much in name only.

Two days after the launch of ESPN on September 7, 1979, Stu and Chet had a breakfast meeting with Bill.

As Stu related to me in June of 2008, the purpose of the meeting was to muzzle "a loose cannon." Stu, having realized that because Bill had done such a good job of making himself readily visible to the media and cable industry that firing him would create a public relations hit that would be more expensive than simply giving Bill his salary, a desk, and nothing to do, decided that would be the best course for the network.

Working in East Peoria, I didn't learn of this meeting until Bill's book came out in November of 1983, more than four years after the meeting.

During the one year and one month before he left ESPN, he regularly called to get updates on my activity and cable systems that I was working on. If I reported that I had signed systems X, Y, and Z, he would go over to the affiliate office to see if they had been recorded. Ultimately, the vice president of the division, Jim Cavazzini, would call me about Bill interfering with our work.

I would point out to him that Bill was the CEO of the company, and then ask him how I should handle the situation? Frankly, I was frustrated but had no recourse since Bill was in the position of ultimate responsibility.

He would not have any suggestion for me to help him.

When his book *Sports Junkies Rejoice* came out, I first learned of the above meeting and that he had me leaving ESPN in January of 1980 rather than 1981.

After reading the book, I pointed out to him that that he had me leaving the network a year before I did.

His response was, "I hadn't noticed, it must have been a typo. There is nothing I can do about it now, but when we have the next printing, I will see to it that a correction is made." He has had at least two releases of his book since then and the rather significant mistake remains. With all that I have learned over the years, I am convinced that the "typo" was not accidental. The mistake was executed to accomplish two things for Bill. One was to minimize my contribution to the network, which was substantial, and two was to have me leaving ESPN before he did, which was ridiculous. Bill's literal cutting of my tenure at ESPN had been accepted by other writers over the years.

Bill called me on September 14, 1979, five days after his wings had been clipped by Stu, and ordered me to a "family" meeting that evening at seven o'clock in the O'Hare Airport Hilton.

I advised him that I had commitments up through five o'clock and I couldn't make it to Chicago in two hours or less after eating a bit of dinner.

Well, as Bill would often do, he began yelling that he was the CEO of ESPN and that this meeting had to do with ESPN, and I had better be there, and on time.

As always, I capitulated, although the meeting was about our stock holdings in the company, which was different than being an employee of the company. He was not the CEO of our securities, although he acted as though he was.

The discussions that took place during the meeting are paraphrased.

In retrospect, it was at this meeting that all pretense of fulfilling Dad's dream of a "family business" evaporated into thin air.

Bill was in a belligerent mood when I arrived. Mom and Dad were there, with Dad speaking for Sis. Bill presented us with a sales agreement to sign for when he could sell our stock. His assumption was that he could sell the stock and provide us each with a million dollars. The first thing I wanted to know was, "Is there a buyer?"

"No." He just wanted us to be prepared when he got a buyer.

I then made a statement to the effect that when we got a buyer, it would be the time to make that determination.

He then went into a long dissertation about how he had traded away some of his shares to keep the momentum moving forward in the development of ESPN and he now had fewer shares than we did and he just didn't think that that was right.

I said, "When you consider that each of us put more money into the company than you did—"

Bill jumped in with, "Ed (Eagan), Scott, and I each put seventy-five thousand into the company."

I knew that Bill was lying through his teeth, when I looked at Dad, I could see that he was buying Bill's rant hook, line, and sinker.

About this time, the phone rang. Bill answered it. On the other end of the line, Scott was telling Bill that the meeting he was having with Stu Evey was over and Scott had just quit ESPN. Bill was visibly shaken, for just a second. In an instant, he was back at it, after advising us that Scott was leaving the company.

I wanted to get a definitive clarification on the total of the $225,000 that Bill, Scott, and Ed had contributed. So as not to trigger another rancorous outburst, I asked about the $9,000 that he often was quoted as using to start the company. He smiled and said, "That was just for public consumption."

I knew that his statement regarding the $75,000 each invested was a flat out lie, but now he was now telling me that the $9,000 was made up too. I knew now that ESPN was started on "bluff, bluster, and BS," as well as a wing and a prayer.

There was no doubt in my mind that Bill was really reaching for something, I just didn't know what or why. The meeting was successful for Bill in that Dad signed for him and Sis. I told Bill that I needed more time to think about it.

He tried one more time, without the condemning, harsh voice, to bring me around before I was to leave for Peoria. This time around, I got tears and pleading from Mom, urging me to get along with Bill.

Once again, I was the one out of step. Bill demanded and got Dad to sign over an unknown percentage of his and Sis's investment in ESPN. I was balking and attempting to stand up to the rest of the family. We, the first true investors in the network, were targets of "The Founder" (Bill's words) of the company to take as much of that investment as he could get away with. The family business was dead.

As I left Chicago, I didn't realize that I was the only family member working at ESPN. Bill had a salary, a desk, a company car, and nothing more. Ironically, this night concluded the first year of the family involvement in ESPN, as the next day would have been our brother Bob's forty-third birthday, and it was on his birthday that we had a friendly gathering in my backyard that resulted in the initial funding of ESPN.

It is important to note the financial efforts put forth to create ESPN: Bill $9,000 (split between Scott, Ed, and himself), Vivien, Dad, and myself, KS Sweet carrying the ball on financing until Stu Evey, in the name of Getty Oil Company, stepped up to the plate and made ESPN happen.

The whole picture, financially, looks pretty reasonable as to the contributions made toward the creation of the network:

1. The Minority Shareholders, and the number of shares of common stock of ESPN presently owned by each of them, are:

Vivian J. Rasmussen	150 shares
William A. Rasmussen	100 shares
Donald Rasmussen	100 shares
William F. Rasmussen	49 shares
Scott W. Rasmussen	49 shares
Edward A. Eagan, Jr.	25 shares
Communications Investors	225 shares

Getty Oil Company (Stu Evey) 4,250 shares

The above chart was sent to me by Bill in October of 1981, which lists the minority shareholders that have been brought together through various means to accomplish the impossible.

In the original deal that was put together, Getty Oil Company held control of our shares in ESPN, until all monies the network owed Getty were paid back. That wasn't going to happen any time soon. Stu Evey wasn't going to cut Bill any slack on the terms he had agreed to, so the money, that we didn't have, that Bill was paying to KS Sweet and later a law firm called Skadden & Arps to pry the shares loose from Getty was completely useless.

By October of 1981, we were all gone from ESPN, and the company was still struggling to get in the black. It wouldn't take a rocket science to figure out that the time wasn't right for Getty Oil to release our stock.

When Bill had finally convinced me that I couldn't wait any longer to leave ESPN because Chet Simmons was going to fire me, he hired me to work for Enterprise Radio.

When it was obvious that Enterprise Radio was going to go belly-up, Bill mustered all his courage and dropped a pink slip to me in the nearest mailbox. He knew that as soon as I received the pink slip, I would call him. He instructed his receptionist not to accept calls from me.

The corporate world really and truly blows me away. It seems to me that amoebas group together to form organisms whose sole purpose is to extract rectangular pieces of paper from unsuspecting billfolds that they feed on. With no sense of right or wrong, honesty or dishonesty, ethics or unethical meanings, these gooey, slimy creatures go through their life cycle jumping at or creating another group or individuals to suck dry. As they grow old and less powerful, these organisms are replaced by newer slime, but they don't mind. They got theirs.

Between the meeting and the above developments, I had the greatest job in the world working day in and day out building the subscriber base for ESPN. Although I never worked less than ten to twelve hours a day, it was a whole new experience every day.

The only negative was the calls from the CEO of the company to discuss my investment and family cohesion, which was necessary to move my financial interest to him. The most difficult call came less than a week after the Chicago meeting. He asked what I was going to do about signing the agreement.

I told him that I didn't know, it seemed pretty one sided to me and I had my partner to think of. You know, right is right, and I wanted to do what wass right by everyone. At one point in the discussion, in regard to the one-sided aspect of the agreement, I said, "Based on my reading of this, if it sells for ten thousand a share, my one hundred shares would sell for one million and we would receive the full amount, but if it sells for fortythousand a share, we would get one million and you would get three million. With the three of us collectively getting three million to split and you would walk away with nine million. That really doesn't sound very family oriented to me."

He assured me that it wouldn't sell for forty thousand a share.

"If I sign, I get ten dollars and other valuable consideration. What's 'other valuable consideration?'"

"You're job!"

"You're telling me that if I don't sign the agreement, you're going to fire me?"

"You said it."

He made no further statement, as he knew he had me concerned, so he wrapped up the call and hung up.

Knowledge is power. He knew that he didn't have the power or authority to fire me, but I didn't. As I stressed over the right and wrong of it, because of the basic indoctrination I grew up with, he felt sure that I would come around.

I discussed the situation with Beth, because I strongly felt that he had me over a barrel. Since the job meant more to me than money, I capitulated and signed. I felt that the pressure he brought to bear on me was illegal. I knew that I could never sue my brother and since it was not a violent type of crime, I wouldn't know how to go about protecting myself anyway.

So I signed my authority to control my shares in ESPN to keep peace in the family and get Bill off my back.

```
            TOTAL MINORITY POSITION

               ESPN 750 Shares

 On 8/16/79 distribution should have been:      It was:
                                     1             2
 Robert Chamberlain                  15            15
 Robert Bray                         37            37
 W.A. Rasmussen                      15           100
 D.A. Rasmussen                      15           100
 V.J. Rasmussen                      23           150
 Communication Investers            225           225
 W.F. Rasmussen                     168            49
 S.W. Rasmussen                     168            49
 E.A. Eagen                          84            25
```

Within a month of receiving the above assignment of our shares, we received this one, which Bill was trying to convince us that the proper distribution was supposed to be column number one.

One day we met in Las Vegas, and he proposed that we should put all our shares in one pot and divide them up with him getting the most, Scott getting the second most, me third, and Dad and Sis the least. This would be based on the value of our contributions to the success of the network. I told him that I thought he was out of his gourd. First, Dad would never go for it, and second, neither would I.

After I was back in my office in East Peoria, I got a phone call from Dad. He was furious. "Where did you ever come up with such a bonehead idea?"

I asked, "What are you talking about?"

"Bill told me about your idea in assigning shares according to how much each of us has done for the company."

I virtually jumped through the phone at him. "You have *got* to be kidding me! That was Bill's idea, and I said no. And I also told him that you wouldn't go for it either."

I got the now standard response, "Bill doesn't lie; now, *you* stop it."

There was no sense trying to talk with him about this entire issue. I tried to be accommodating, but there was no way that Dad was ever going to see the light.

I received regular calls regarding the fact that he had once again saved my job. These calls constantly kept me in a state of anxiety that was totally uncalled for, as I learned after I resigned. I was never in danger of being fired. Bill was not happy that I was doing well and had to keep doubt in my head. He was very good at doing that.

After he resigned in September of 1980, he made sure to let me know that he still had a lot of contacts at ESPN and would hear if there were any more rumblings about my status.

From the first of October through the end of December, I had two or three of these heroic calls letting me know that all the Rasmussens would be purged from the company. In one of these calls, I suggested that I would just call Chet and discuss my demise with him and get it over with.

He, very calmly, asked me not to do that because he had an agreement with Evey and Simmons that he would not interfere with any ESPN employees. If I talked to Simmons about my impending separation from the company, it would cost him a lot of money.

Now, let me tell you, I am either extremely naive or "dumber than a brick," because I bought his line and believed him, as I always did, to my detriment.

A couple more decades would have to pass before I would be able to even begin to overcome the indoctrination of my childhood. In my mind, the belief that within "the family," Bill was always right and Don was always wrong, no exceptions, was true.

In 2012 Scott Rasmussen wrote a book, *The People's Money*.

Within the covers of that fine piece of work are these lines:

"The simplest way to get people to make bad decisions is to give them bad information. That's how con men work."

Don at ESPN booth

Chapter 19

ESPN JOB

When I left School District 50 in June of 1979, I began the process of joining ESPN as an employee. When I completed that process and began working on July 1, I became the first and only independent investor/employee in the history of the company. I had previously carried out two projects for the company on a pro-bono basis. The first, in response to a call from Bill, was to attend as much of the Illinois-Indiana cable convention in Indianapolis as I could. I got up early Saturday morning and drove from East Peoria to Indianapolis. I was to meet cable operators and get a reading on the feel for the coming September launch of the network.

I had been studying the makeup of the industry since October of the previous year in preparation of selling the network signal to cable operators throughout the country. Knowing the approximate size of the convention if it were to be well attended, I suggested that I go down the night before. That idea was rejected even though the convention was scheduled for Friday and Saturday.

The result was that I arrived as the last of the conventioneers were preparing to leave. I was able to visit with the managers of the Missouri systems in Sikeston and Caruthersville. Both gave me a favorable response, based on the commitments of a September launch and the Getty Oil company maintaining its involvement. As I gathered their business cards, I gave them an approximate time that I would be calling them that summer after I became an employee. I had driven over four hundred miles, round trip, for two contacts and business cards that would not take fruition until after July 1.

The second involvement was the National Cable Television Association held in May of 1979. It was the coming-out party for ESPN, and Bill said it was important for me to be there. This time ESPN picked up my expenses, and I used some of my vacation time from the school to spend the four or five days that we were working. The overall results were far greater than my first effort back in April. My schedule was full every day. I would open our booth by eight o'clock in the morning and work the booth until after six in the evening (with a half-hour break for lunch), then I headed for the hospitality suite where I met and discussed the network with cable operators. My evening nourishment was the hors d'oeuvres in the hospitality suite and once again, my main objective was to collect business cards on which I put notes on the back for future reference. A little before ten o'clock, I would be given show tickets and introduced to the guests I was to take to the show. After completing that show, I was directed to take another group to the late show. All of our guests were potential network advertisers or cable system operators. After that show, I would head for my room and crash.

The first sports celebrity host in our hospitality suite was golfer Bob Murphy. Having sports celebrities at national and regional conventions would become a standard operation procedure for ESPN.

I got to bed around three in the morning with a wakeup call to get me up at six, so I could shower, shave, dress, and get some breakfast, which became my largest meal of the day. Then I would head for the convention floor to prepare the booth for the morning opening.

I carried out these duties each and every day of the convention. I was surviving on adrenalin and about three hours of sleep per day. It was an exciting and fulfilling time. When I left Las Vegas on the non-stop flight to Chicago, I was sound asleep before the plane left the ground, and a flight attendant woke me when we were ready to deplane.

When I returned to East Peoria, I put all the cards I had gathered on a desk I had set up in my basement that would serve as my office when the school year was completed.

Leaving District 50 was a bittersweet experience. For the first time in my career as a school administrator, I was saddened to leave a school. My staff over the four years I was the principal of the school was outstanding. The school board was knowledgeable, efficient, and most pleasant to work with. The superintendent that hired me, Mr. Bill Toler, had been forced to retire midway through my tenure with severe health problems. Along with Eugene Spizzirri, these were the two greatest educators that I could have been associated with.

Several parents made contact with me expressing gratitude for the job I did for their kids. Even those parents that were upset with me turned out to be primarily upset with me for leaving.

The first order of the day was to get to Plainville, Connecticut, and fill out the paperwork, meet the vice president of affiliate relations, Ron Newman, and get briefed on the status of the department. The United Cable System in Plainville was the temporary headquarters of ESPN. Before going to Plainville, we met Bill at his condo in Avon, which was in a condominium community with a country club plus other amenities. I was quite impressed. He and Scott were each driving a new Cadillac.

I couldn't help but think how far they had come in just four short years since I had last visited them in Enfield, Connecticut, when I was asked by Bill to build a stockade fence to enclose their backyard since he was putting up an above ground swimming pool. Scott was graduating from high school and Mickey was teaching school too, as she related to me, to pay off some debts.

It was on that 1974 trip that I learned that Bill's eleven-year-old daughter, Lynn, didn't know that she had an Uncle Don or any cousins, much less four. Lynn was just two months older than my oldest daughter Alene.

Due to my upbringing, I was to look up to Bill and his superiority over me. I would do anything for him and I thought, at the time, that was what younger brothers were to do. Despite that, it just didn't seem right to me that an eleven-year-old niece didn't know that she had an uncle. Since Bob died in 1961, I am Lynn's only uncle.

All that was past history now in 1979, as I was embarking on a new adventure to build a cable TV network in the field. I would do this from the basement of my home along with attending and securing cable systems for ESPN at state, regional, and national meetings and conventions.

Ron Newman basically gave me free reign to work from the East to the West Coast in search of cable systems. At that time several systems had made promises, but not many had signed up. Bill had promised advertisers that ESPN would have four million subscribers by the time the network went on the air on September 7 of 1979.

I asked Ron what approximate number he expected from my office. He made no specific goal or quota for me, but suggested that two million would be nice. I took that as a matter of fact.

I completed my paperwork and was briefed on various contact people I would need to use and given a boatload of reading material as well as a stack of contracts.

I had been a part of the company since September 18 of the previous year when I provided the final piece of funding to secure the transponder on Satcom 1.

With that completed, I had one major piece of business to take care of before I left Connecticut. I had to drive up to Maine and conduct a couple of meetings for some ladies in our Shaklee organization. All went well and since we had time before I went to work on July 1 for ESPN, we did some sightseeing with the kids. I had no idea if I could ever bring them out east again.

When I arrived home, I contacted the phone company to complete the connection of my phone system. We had ordered the outside work to be done prior to our arrival back in East Peoria.

My first day on the job was interesting. Virtually everyone I called had a positive attitude and I signed up some systems.

In less than a year Bill had done a marvelous job of establishing the Rasmussen name in the cable industry and I was going to take full advantage to build the network. The parade of contracts each week in July and August was consistent but far short of the two million subscribers Ron Newman had said it would be nice to develop.

My workday was pretty consistent. I worked the phone starting at eight o'clock in the morning calling cable systems on the East Coast and then would shift to the Midwest and finally to the West Coast around six o'clock in the evening. After dinner I would go back to my desk and prepare contracts to be put in the mail. When that project was completed, Beth would take them to the post office to mail as I developed my call list for the next day.

With the individual participation of Illinois General Electric cable systems and Heritage Systems in Iowa providing substantial numbers along with numerous individually owned systems throughout the country, I was able to bring around over half a million to the table for the night of the launch on September 7th. Not all of them were signed contracts, but my office would, in the coming months, bring all the cable systems online. The Peoria system had carried everything ESP-TV and ESPN had ever telecast going back to November 17 in 1978.

On September 7th, while all the hoopla was going on in Bristol, I was adding last-minute cable systems to the launch until four o'clock that afternoon. It was Friday, and I had invited my partner in the ownership part of the company, Virgil Newman and his wife Rosalea, to share in viewing the first telecast of ESPN.

After the launch the volume of contracts went up and I was really feeling good about the flow and growth I was experiencing. Not having a secretary made my days longer and longer. I would occasionally have operators request that they return their contracts to the East Peoria office so that I could assure them that they were getting taken care in an efficient manner. I always enjoyed that reaction, because in my mind, they were demonstrating confidence in me that I would take care of them. When those contracts with checks attached arrived, they were immediately dispatched to Connecticut.

In mid-September I attended the Iowa state convention in Des Moines and had an extremely successful trip, bringing some contracts with checks attached back to Peoria with me. Talking with Bill Reilly of Heritage Cable, I received a verbal commitment that as soon as cable systems could be made ready throughout their organization, they would be added to our existing contract. I pointed out to him that it was vital that I be notified when each and every one came on board. He smiled and said, "I wouldn't have it any other way."

Later that fall I again traveled to Iowa to help various communities "turn on" the network. Word was traveling through Iowa that ESPN was working very well for those systems that were getting involved. The big drawback was that so many of them were limited to twelve channels. I knew that time would take us over the top if I just kept grinding it out.

Our Peoria Cable System was having some difficulties with its headquarters in Schenectady, New York, and after months of keeping me from calling the corporate headquarter, the general manager was now pleading with me to call and get his status with ESPN resolved. He briefed me on the contact's peculiarities, which included vulgar language and a generally cantankerous attitude. He was right, except that if you met Paul Schoenwolf head-on, the road smoothed out.

I called and when his secretary answered, I simply said, "Tell Schoenwolf Don Rasmussen is calling to talk with him."

He picked up the phone and asked," Where the hell have you been?"

"I only talk to people with obnoxious names like Schoenwolf and Rasmussen at the end of the day," I replied.

"I'll buy that. What do I have to do to sign a contract with you? They keep sending kids out here from Connecticut, and I keep sending them back."

I laid out what I needed from him and he said, "Okay, put this in the contract and send it to me." It was sent and returned to me within a week. It was the biggest check ever sent to the Peoria office. We now had all of GE Cable Systems under contract. That was a total of close to three hundred thousand subscribers.

I didn't have much of a life away from my basement. One or two evenings a week, I would slough off to hold meetings in the other half of our basement, which held our Shaklee products and had seating for thirty people. Any normal person would just concentrate on his Shaklee business that was earning more money for us than ESPN was. I credited Shaklee for my being able to do everything I was doing, stamina wise, for ESPN. Two years earlier I wouldn't have been able to do it. I was so grateful to have the strength and the ability to concentrate that I needed to enjoy each day of work.

In November I received a call from Bill asking if I could develop a map of the states and lay out a regional affiliate marketing proposal. I didn't hesitate. If I could do anything to help Bill, that was my job. I said, "Sure."

"How long would it take?"

"When do you need it?"

"As soon as possible."

"Would Monday be soon enough?"

"You're kidding! Any time next week would be great."

It was a Friday afternoon, so I shut down the office and headed to the dime store to buy several United States outline maps. I spent the weekend making a list from my trusty old "Broadcast Yearbook" of the number of cable systems and the number of subscribers in each state. Then I began mixing and matching until I came up with a very rough regional balance to work with. I started with five and then seven. Comparing those possibilities, I settled on six regions, which was my initial instinct. After that was settled, I needed to find the proper city to house each regional office.

The offices broke out in the following manner: Northeast, Bristol, Connecticut, Southeast, Atlanta, Georgia, Midwest, East Peoria, Illinois, Southwest, Dallas, Texas, mountain states, Denver, Colorado, Pacific states, Los Angeles, California.

I called Bill Monday morning and told him that I had it put together. He asked some questions and appeared to like the structure until I got to the office location in California. He ordered me to change the city from Los Angeles to San Francisco. I told him that didn't make any sense due to the population structure. He replied, in effect, that he didn't want the office anywhere near Stu Evey. When I objected the second time, he said, "I am the CEO of this company, and I am telling you to change it."

I said okay and changed the city to San Francisco. Then I put it in the mail. Toward the end of the week, I got word that my work had been accepted with one change. The Pacific coast office would be in Los Angeles.

In the first week of December, we were at a major convention in Anaheim at the Disney Hotel. Things got off to a good start on the convention floor as everyone was looking forward to the launch of Satcom III. After the first day on the floor, I went up to the hospitality suite to continue meeting and greeting cable operators. I hadn't been there long when someone pointed me out to Stu Evey. I had not met him when he came up to me and said, "I'd like to know what you have in your basement, so I can replicate it." That led to further conversation in which he made positive comments regarding the volume of contracts and subscribers that I was developing.

In the course of our conversation, he also said something that didn't click right in my head, but I dismissed it as not relevant to the direction I was involved in pursuing.

He said, "We know that you developed the affiliate regional map."

That bounced around in my head, off and on, for years with no specific meaning until the mid- to late eighties when I was beginning to understand Bill's behavior.

None of the shows after that first one in Las Vegas had been nearly as pressure-packed or as busy, but they were all-important in harvesting subscribers.

A pall fell over the convention when it was confirmed that Satcom III had been lost. Some of the activity on the floor was furnished by new cable networks that would be using this dedicated cable satellite.

The discussion on the floor on that day, December 7, 1979, was heavily on the services that were scheduled to commence and were being introduced as the catastrophe occurred.

With a heavy heart, we continued to do our job. Many of the older (three months after our launch, ESPN was an older service) services were circling like vultures seeking to pick up additional subscribers. Personally, I continued my regular routine of visiting with the cable operators that I had already lined up and welcomed those that came by the booth.

After the convention the business seemed to be moving along pretty well. As we turned into 1980, the future looked pretty bright from the

ESPN JOB

viewpoint of East Peoria. I continued to develop new cable systems and some MSOs (Multiple System Operators). It was nothing spectacular, just steady constant business.

In late January I was called to a series of meetings in Bristol. The gist of the meetings was that we were having a difficult time bringing in subscribers. I was surprised to hear this. I had never seen a list of subscribers or cable systems that were a part of the network, but I did have a rough estimate that I scratched out at the end of each day.

With the early contacts from Indianapolis and Las Vegas before I even became an employee, plus my preconceived goal set in my head by Ron Newman that I should have two million subscribers by September 7, 1979, I began working fourteen hours a day from the first day on the job and never let up. When we met in January of 1980, I had produced in excess of one and a half million subscribers, and I felt like a failure that needed to do more.

My business card that I used prior to developing the six-region marketing map looked like this:

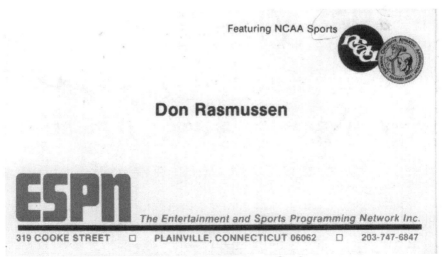

Original ESPN Business Card

JUST A GUY

With the creation of six regional offices, my business card became less flashy and more accurate. The old card provided me with a real kick on the day that is was announced that Chet Simmons was taking over the operation and development of the network as president. I was at a convention in Wisconsin at the end of July 1980 and within minutes of hearing the news, a Wisconsin cable operator approached me and asked me if I would sign the back of my card that is shown above.

I happily signed it for him as he asked me how many cards like this I had signed. When I replied that his was the first, he was ecstatic and having a difficult time containing himself. He said, "I have one signed by Bill and one by Scott and with this, I am the only person with ESPN cards signed by all three Rasmussens. Someday the set will be worth something."

I appreciated his thought and wished him luck, but I thought he was dreaming.

This is a copy of the regional card:

139 E. Washington Street, East Peoria, IL 61611 (309) 694-4413

Donald A. Rasmussen
Midwest Marketing Manager

The Entertainment and Sports Programming Network, Inc.
A subsidiary of Getty Oil Company

Regional business card

:eded to step up my activity to keep things moving for-
tainly felt anxiety about being able to hang on, I needn't
:erned.

, I received a call from Bill advising me that I would be
) come back to Connecticut for more meetings, and he
ring up the subject of meeting our original commitment
...dustry that we were going to be a twenty-four-hour-a-day service. Then he stunned me when he said, "They won't listen to me, but Chet might listen to you."

I didn't give any thought to Bill's statement regarding "they won't listen to me." I was focused on getting twenty-four-hour programming to not only fulfill our promise to the industry, but I also knew that CNN would be coming online on June 1, and we needed to be the first around-the-clock service to maintain our lead in the industry.

We met for a luncheon meeting with Chet at the Farmington Inn. We had five people at the meeting, Chet, me, and three new regional managers, one of whom I knew. Jim Bates was young, ambitious, and obviously the most knowledgeable and brightest of the new managers. After causal conversation over lunch, we got down to business.

Chet's primary concern was, "What do we need to support you in the field to build this network?"

He was very direct and was looking at me when he threw out the question, so I took him at his word, that he wanted direct and honest dialogue.

"Chet, the most important thing that we can do is go twenty-four hours a day, seven days a week." I think he was ready for me.

"Don, the major problem is putting the additional cost on the cable system operators in regard to having additional labor to cover all those hours."

I responded, "Cable systems operate in such a way, by virtue of the technology, that our extending hours will have virtually no effect on labor costs. Most of the hours that we will be adding are hours where the building will be closed and a single engineer is either on duty or on call, and that wouldn't change." I continued," As you know well, broadcast networks are labor-intensive. Cable television is technology-intensive."

ESPN going full time all the time would aid the cable systems in adding subscribers. Let me give you an example. Caterpillar in Peoria has a huge operation with three shifts, six days a week. When we do all day and all night on Friday and Saturday, the late shift workers are ecstatic. I hear about this on a regular basis from the local cable company.

Jim Bates jumped in to verify my statements and expanded on them. A general discussion ensued for over an hour.

Chet had been very involved in the discussion and ultimately conceded that we had given him a lot of food for thought.

I hadn't expected an immediate answer from Chet, and I wasn't disappointed. He had to check out those things that we discussed and then he would make a decision. I figured that it would be a week or two before we heard anything, but I felt that he would agree that this would be a positive move.

It didn't take much time at all after I returned to Illinois from our meetings. I was working the phones a few days in when I received a note in the mail from Chet advising me that he would be making an announcement as soon as his program department could assure him that we not only had the capacity but could also maintain the effort once we started.

I assumed that Bill had been informed, so I just dove back into my work. With more limited area to develop, I enjoyed the closer proximity of all the states to Illinois. I shouldn't have sought comfort so quickly. I got the first of what would be help calls regarding various cable systems outside the Midwest region. That was okay with me; I enjoyed the challenges of solving problems. It was particularly gratifying in that every time I resolved a problem in the field, I would receive a positive comment from the involved department in Bristol.

In April I received a shorthand written note from Chet, simply asking me if there was anything he could do to help me do the job and then he wrote, "Thank you."

The National Cable Show was held in Dallas in May and as usual, I was working the booth on the convention floor and spending my evenings in the hospitality suite, meeting and visiting with cable operators and even some advertising people. The big talk of this show was the introduction of CNN to the cable TV audience coming up on June 1.

For several months prior to this anticipated launch, CNN had an effective spokesman going around the country to the various state and regional conventions. He was a pleasant and enjoyable gentleman who would rather sing the praises of his hometown, Traverse City, Michigan, than anything else.

An aggressive advocate of CNN, he recognized the advantage ESPN had since its inception and launch the previous September. His entire spiel was that "CNN will be so valuable to you, you should do everything possible to get it on your system. The news is so much more important than sports," and on and on. As I caught on to his approach, I did two things to counter his not-so-subtle attacks on ESPN. Number one was always arrange for him to go first when we made our presentations. This was easy to do since everyone wants to beat their opposition to the punch. He would get his digs in and then sing the praises of CNN.

All very good. When I followed the CNN presentation, everyone in the room expected me to counter him with a pitch extolling the virtues of ESPN and blasting CNN. I would start by speaking highly of CNN and the contributions that an all-news network all the time would have on enhancing and growing the industry. After that introduction I would lay out a logical case for including CNN in their channel lineup as soon as possible through expansion. "ESPN will continue to expand your subscriber base, and CNN will be a perfect second service to enhance your cable offerings to your community."

From the time CNN started until I left ESPN, I never lost a cable system to CNN. In fact I am quite sure that I helped expedite the growth of that network. Maybe I should send them a bill?

By this time, we had completed the manning of our last two offices with two gentlemen that I had recommended. Charlie Mills was assigned to the Denver office and Chip Harwood in our Dallas office. Each of these gentlemen brought unique personalities to the table.

Charlie was a colonel in the National Guard and was determined not to leave the guard until he attained a star on his shoulder so that he could retire as "General Mills." His single mindedness impressed me, as I hoped he could do the same with his job.

Chip Harwood brought a level of class to our group. I had observed him at several meetings and conventions and in large groups over dinner. There was just something about him that drew attention.

Both of these gentlemen were receptive when I discussed recommending them for these particular jobs with ESPN.

As we moved through the summer of 1980, one particular happening occurred that will be forever etched in my mind. It was a Las Vegas show, and I was in conversation with Jim Simpson, ESPN's first "name" announcer, when this very large man approached us. He obviously knew Jim and as he approached us, he asked Jim to excuse the interruption. He then looked me in the eye and said, "I just wanted to shake the hand of a Rasmussen." Before I could say anything, we shook hands and he was gone. I looked at Jim and he laughingly told me, "That was Dave DeBusschere."

I looked at Jim, stunned, and said, "Dave DeBusschere was a favorite of mine back in the '60s when he pitched for the White Sox and played for the Knicks. I so respected him to be able to play at such a high level in two major sports. And it didn't hurt that he played for the White Sox."

I hoped that I might have the opportunity to meet him again before the show was over, but it didn't happen.

According to my little informal checks, between new contracts and growth in older systems that I contracted with the previous year, based on monthly reports that we were now getting, I had exceeded two million subscribers.

As the fall convention season approached, I received a request from the Iowa cable convention planning committee to be its keynote speaker. I was pleased to accept. It was a simple opportunity in my view to take a step forward in Iowa for ESPN.

Since the convention always had a vendor's forum, this would give me two shots at putting ESPN in the minds of Iowa cable operators that didn't have ESPN on their systems. This was a clear advantage for ESPN at this important convention.

When I arrived and saw the program, I knew immediately that Bill would have a cat if he ever saw it. On the opening meeting page, there in bold print was the listing for their keynote speaker Don Rasmussen— ESPN founder.

I took full advantage of the situation and had the best convention ever on setting up contracts for new ESPN customers. It was also pretty cool that a number of operators asked me to sign their programs for their kids.

When I returned to East Peoria, there was a message waiting for me to get on a plane and get to Bristol, immediately. I knew what I was walking into when I got that message. Since I was a little kid, to cross Bill meant you were going to get yelled at. I had learned long ago that what Bill thought and wanted couldn't be violated. Disagreeing with Bill was wrong, simply because Bill is right.

When I walked into his office, he went wild. More violent language than I had ever heard came from him. The one thing lacking was any attempt to feign or hint at physical violence.

The first words he said were, "What the hell do you think you're are doing?" After that it would be impossible to reconstruct the dialog, but the message was clear. In specific terms he ranted about being the only "founder of ESPN," and that I had better not ever again allow anyone to even hint that I had anything to do with the start-up. I kind of thought that sounded like a threat.

I pointed out to him that I didn't know of the reference until I arrived at the convention, and frankly, if they wanted to do that and it resulted in substantially more subscribers coming out of the convention, it was okay by me.

That recharged his anger battery pretty good and he yelled something to the effect that he didn't care about the subscribers one way or the other. I knew then something wasn't right, because that was what

I was all about. It was my priority because we needed the numbers to get the advertisers. Generally, all I heard was to get more subscribers.

When he went back to his being the "only founder of ESPN," I couldn't resist, and I mentioned that there was another founder, Scott. Although it didn't settle him down much, the volume level diminished, as he said that he was "just a twenty-two-year-old kid that didn't know anything and was along for the ride."

At that point I knew he was off the reservation; I just didn't know why. With nothing resolved, he dismissed me and told me to get back to Peoria.

I had been amazingly calm throughout the entire ordeal. Thinking back I realized that the 1961 tirade about baseball was purposeful and his physical attack was to maintain his dominance. Since that failed, he had not raised his voice or made an aggressive moves toward me. In light of what followed, I think he was scared and couldn't admit it to anyone.

On Tuesday, September 30, 1980, Bill called to tell me that he was going to submit his letter of resignation effective immediately and he wanted me to hear it directly from him rather than from someone else after he left. I asked, "When are you leaving?"

"As soon as I hang up."

Scott had left the network in the middle of September of 1979 and with Bill leaving at the end of September 1980, I was the last Rasmussen standing.

In October of 1980, I brought in more than three hundred and twenty-five thousand subscribers, and we became the first cable network to accumulate one million subscribers in a month. Jim Bates, in our Northeast region, did three hundred and fifteen thousand, and the other regions made up the rest.

When we completed the year, we had exceeded the six million subscribers that Bill had told me we needed to gain solid access to Madison Avenue and big advertising dollars. From my first foray into harvesting subscribers in April of 1979 through the exhilarating launch at the Las Vegas convention in May before I officially joined the company, I had personally exceeded three million subscribers.

Chapter 20

ENTERPRISE RADIO AND GROUP W

I received word through the grapevine that we had passed the magic six million subscriber count that I had been working to achieve since beginning in July of 1979. During much of the early months of that period, I was receiving little support from Connecticut. The biggest single factor in organizing the affiliate marketing department was the arrival of a lawyer by the name of Andy Brilliant.

When I met him, I didn't like him or his approach. After talking with him for some time, it wasn't difficult to see that, although he was taking some work away from me, he was giving me more time to do what I needed to be doing. The next time I went to Bristol, I was completely on board with what he did for affiliate relations.

Even though I felt I had made a major contribution, after the first six months, Andy provided a structure that went a long way toward reaching the goal line. I had considerably more time to work with cable operators after we had moved the Midwest out of my basement and into a downtown East Peoria office and had been authorized to hire a secretary and an assistant. My assistant was Nancy Janell, a former teacher in District 50 that was seeking a different opportunity. She was a tremendous addition to the operation.

Within days of the good news, Bill called to tell me the bad news. Chet was getting ready to fire me within the next two weeks, "So now that the network has reached six million subscribers and they don't need you any more, it would be wise for you to resign before he drops the hammer. Enterprise Radio will hire you and Jim Bates if you resign before you are fired. Oh, yeah, Enterprise will give you a twelve thousand-dollar raise, and if ESPN doesn't honor your work with the twenty-five hundred-dollar bonus they promised, we'll pay that to."

Talk about incentives; that was the cat's meow. Let's do it.

We resigned and when I went in to see about my earned bonus, Chet hit the ceiling. Nobody, I mean nobody, can hit the ceiling like Chet. He gets loud, abusive, and throws stuff.

I got out with all my body parts intact, but with a sense that I had been had by Bill again. If Chet had been planning on firing me, he certainly wouldn't have gone through all those histrionics just for show.

Jim and I went over to Enterprise Radio to learn marketing, radio style. What we got was a tour of the facility that looked pretty darn impressive. We met some of the talent and officers of the corporation.

Although Scott hired us, just by the locations of the offices, it was clear that Bill was running the show. Scott gave us the necessary material to sign up radio stations and the information regarding travel, paydays, reporting, etc. That was our training.

Back in East Peoria, I began calling radio stations. I called fifteen to twenty Illinois stations without a single favorable response. The second time around I tried to get an education from the negative statements on the viability of our service. This was perceived by the station managers as me trying to learn their industry without putting the time in working in radio to learn all aspects.

Of course, they were right, but I didn't have the time to spend, as the network was waiting to get stations to carry it.

I set up evaluation meetings with a couple of station managers. I wanted them to look at our program, reporting requirements, and most importantly, what reasoning it would take to cause them to become a part of the network.

On the other side of the coin, what would be the reasoning to turn down the network?

The concept was evaluated high in the estimation of both managers. Reporting broadcast history of the network activity on their station was way too complex.

As soon as I reached this point in the discussion, I knew what the main problem was, but I followed through to complete my questions.

All that was left to do was to report my findings to Scott and/or Bill. As I was putting together my findings, I received a call from someone in the Connecticut office, telling me to come to the headquarters for the layout of a project three of us would be doing. I arrived with a plan to turn around our lack of production, which emphasized having experienced radio executive planners study and correct the problem with reporting.

When I arrived, I walked into a meeting that was not heavy on individual input.

We were going to blitz central California, with Scott's right-hand man, Dan Zabel working with Jim and me to improve our skills. With that I was handed a schedule and airplane tickets. All was accomplished efficiently, and I left with my presentation still in hand.

The trip to California was an unmitigated disaster. Following the format, we had zero sales. I had two presentations, with one, maybe, when administrative functions improved at the network. The other two did not have any better results.

No one in the marketing area had any longtime radio experience. Learning of the complexity of radio marketing, as compared to cable marketing, was as different as day and night.

In less than three months after we were hired, I was expecting a discussion with Bill that I would be well served by looking for a different job. The handwriting was on the wall, Enterprise Radio was going to go belly-up. No indication in that direction was ever hinted at.

When I unexpectedly received the dreaded "pink slip" in the mail, I had Beth follow me to the car dealership where Enterprise Radio had leased my car and turned it in. The manager had not heard anything from the company and didn't want to accept the car. I explained to him that the company was about to go under and I didn't want to keep him on the end of a short string as far as our relationship went.

He told me that he would contact the company and if he found anything different than what I told him, he would be in touch with me.

After a few days, my curiosity got the best of me and since I wanted to be sure that I did right by the dealership, I drove out to see the manager.

When he saw me, he came to greet me with a big smile on his face. I knew I wasn't in his doghouse before he said anything to me. The financial man I talked to was very cooperative and a bit surprised that they already had the car back. They told me that a check would be in the mail for the sum still owed. I suggested that he not stay awake until it shows up.

He laughed again and said everything had been turned over to our corporate lawyer, and now we would just wait.

Then he surprised me by saying, "Don, if I can ever do anything for you, don't hesitate in calling on me. You are an honest gentleman, and by doing the things you did, you saved us a lot of time and money." With that we shook hands and I left.

Getting my personal things out of the office was a lot more difficult. The landlord was not nearly as congenial as the car dealership. I had to get a lawyer to write him a letter demanding that I be permitted to retrieve my personal belongings. Then he became cooperative.

WESTINGHOUSE – GROUP W

Jim Bates hooked up with Group W as they were attempting to establish themselves in the cable industry. Jim recommended me to the head of the operation, Lloyd Werner. Lloyd was, as I was to learn, the ultimate corporate animal.

Lloyd was somewhere between Jim's age and mine, which is a great deal of leeway since Jim is almost two decades younger than me. Where Jim was looking for stability to build a solid career, I was attempting to find a company that I could grow with for a couple of decades and find a comfortable retirement. After spending the past few years seeing the country, meeting diverse and interesting characters, the last thing I could imagine myself doing was going back into education.

Lloyd hired me to be the Midwest district affiliate market manager, initially, I think because he thought he could mentor an older guy.

My baptism into the Group W way of doing things was to fly down to Nashville for a large party launching "The Nashville Network." It was quite a party. I arrived and went directly to the Opryland Hotel and Convention Center. As I walked in, I was greeted by Lloyd, Jim, and before long, some cable operators I had worked with earlier at ESPN. I felt like I belonged immediately. After dinner there was a reception and I was looking forward to bed. I was about to head out when I was approached at the doorway and invited (one might more interpret it as a directive) to go to the Grand Old Opry for a show.

After the show as I once again had visions of a comfortable bed and a good night's sleep, a group of old and new friends wanted me to go to a show and dance at one of the clubs featuring country music. Being brand new, and feeling like the old guy anyway, I felt my stamina was being tested, so off we went. It was a good time, and I was able to wrap it up and get into bed shortly after midnight.

It had been a hectic long day, but I was up and at it the next day as I met some of the officials of the Nashville network for breakfast. As we visited, they wanted to get a feel of my interest in country music. I never thought much of my background in the field, but I was able to discuss the Country Music Hall of Fame and talk about some of the talent that I had met at various times and those circumstances. Until I started laying out my experiences, I really didn't realize I had met such a wide variety of Nashville celebrities, which included Dolly Parton, Porter Wagoner, Stonewall Jackson, Farron Young, Joe Stamply, Mother Maybelle Carter, Jean Shepard, Jim Ed Brown, Del Reeves, and others.

Sometimes it is strange how the experience that you have years earlier can be an asset on down the road. Later that summer we had another big event in Nashville, and my staff and I were invited to take a boat ride on Hendersen Lake along with swimming. The network people took great joy in pointing out the backsides of the country music stars' homes as we traversed the lake. We had a grand time and ended up at the Grand Old Opry again. It was on this trip that the head of the Opry told me that any time my wife or I wanted to come to the Opry, just give him a call and he would have VIP tickets waiting at the ticket office.

I mentioned the possibility of going to the Opry to Beth, and sometime later while talking with her sister Irene, Irene got all excited and told Beth that she had always wanted to go to the Grand Old Opry. I told Beth to work out a specific date at least a month down the road and I would make the arrangements.

Irene really enjoyed getting the VIP treatment and loved the show from her prime seat.

Beth had an enjoyable time, but I think being able to treat her sister to something she had never dared dream of doing was special for her.

Another cool event was when Manhattan Cable signed a contract with Group W. We had a great party, and an introduction of the deal was held at Club 21 in New York City.

Now, I'll be the first to tell you, I'm not a very sophisticated guy and I was not very impressed with Club 21, even though I was told that I should be. The highlight of the evening was meeting and spending a lot of time with Tommy Kapra, son of the famous movie director. Tom was an unforgettable character that was more fun to talk with than a barrel of monkeys. I couldn't begin to tell you what we talked about, but we laughed and enjoyed each other's company for over two hours.

After the party, Lloyd Werner took a small group of us out to dinner at this French restaurant within a couple of blocks of Club 21. After a long dinner and discussion, I was still hungry. When the bill came for five or six of us, I about fell out of my chair. The bill came to over six hundred dollars.

Jim Bates explained to me as we were on our way to get the car that it was a famous gourmet restaurant. I suggested that on our way back to Connecticut, we stop and get a non-gourmet burger and fries, because I was starving. Jim told me that he was still really hungry too, so a burger it was.

Those were some of the fun and enjoyable experiences at Group W. The starting up and developing of the marketing effort was far more bizarre, cumbersome, and disjointed.

Upon starting and opening the Chicago office, I was directed to hire twenty-one people. I would have ten marketing representatives, ten marketing representatives assistants, and a secretary.

All of these people would be trained by and through a Group W training program. We would have sophisticated presentation materials on each and every service that we offered. These included: The Satellite News Channel, The Nashville Network, and The Disney Channel.

The middle of the country from the Canadian border to the Gulf of Mexico was my territory. The two other regions were along the East Coast and the West Coast. In all we had thirty marketing representatives and thirty marketing representatives' assistants.

Everything was directed from Stamford, Connecticut. I became more of a scheduler than a manager. And I was also an interpreter of material. In order for me to understand my role, Lloyd had me set up a meeting with a cable company that I had done business with and he would do the presentation, while I observed.

I selected Heritage at their corporate headquarters in Des Moines. I was instructed to observe only. So I sat there and stayed awake through a two and a half-hour chart presentation. When it was over, I could tell that my former clients were more relieved that it was over than they were eager to sign on the dotted line.

When we finished, we were dismissed after a rejection. When I let some time pass before calling them with a follow-up, I was relieved to hear that they wanted to visit with me, if I would be coming alone. I assured them I would be coming alone.

During an afternoon of serious discussion, I walked out with a contract and left some Westinghouse money on the table. Group W was late to the game and was willing to pay cable operators to carry Satellite News Channel.

During this time I was called by Bill to set up a meeting with me to discuss our investment in ESPN. By *our*, he meant *mine* and the discussion would boil down to his playing me to get deeper into my pocket. That always seemed to be his goal. When we agreed on a time, I asked Chet Collins, the advertising manager in our office, to be sure to clear that afternoon so that he could meet Bill.

Chet was a perceptive guy, and I had tremendous respect for him. When Bill first arrived, I took him down the hall to meet Chet. Bill made that introduction period pretty short. He had someone waiting to hear from us. I placed the call and turned on the speakerphone. The call was from one of his lawyers from the group trying to sell our stock. He rambled on for a while and then turned to Bill to finish it up. The call was over, but Bill had some real incentive for me to sign a new agreement.

After he browbeat me for a period of time, I told him that I would have to think about it. So we parted ways.

As soon as he left, I went down to Chet's office. Chet was blunt. "He's a bad guy. How did you two grow up in the same family?"

"When people that know the two of us get a chance to talk with me privately, I get that question a lot. I really don't know how to answer it."

Chet told me that if it ever got to be more than I could deal with, to just give him a call; he knew some folks that could resolve it for me.

The message was clear, but I certainly didn't want to go there.

It turned out that the initial agreement didn't have a closure date on it, so this new one was more complex and intended to replace the first one that we fought over.

I was tired of the constant pressure and decided to just let things sit for a while.

Bill called a couple of days later and I told him to let me mull it over; there was no hurry because he doesn't have a buyer.

Over the period of a year, I was promoted from being a manager to the job of being a director. Now this was a step up the ladder, a corporate kind of thing. It had been made very clear to me that I wasn't a corporate kind of guy.

I wasn't a corporate kind of guy! I knew that. So, why promote me?

That's the easiest question to answer in the world. The thought was that I would quit, but I was asked to continue in my current position until my replacement arrived.

Mr. Pat Grotto was my replacement. He was a very pleasant young man who expressed his amazement that I was so willing to help him get settled in. He asked me what I considered to be the main function of this position.

I answered (paraphrasing), "The function of this office is numbers. We are to get subscribers."

"I was afraid you would say something like that. I have been in this business a long time. Your job is to make upper management look good."

"When subscribers translate into advertising opportunities, upper management will look good."

"When upper management sends you a message telling you how high to jump and get back to them as soon as you come down, a quick response is what they think makes them look good."

"If you're new to the industry and are trying to get three networks up and running at the same time, you better be concentrating on subscribers."

Pat looked very serious and said, "They don't look at numbers until they have to. That simple fact makes my point. Group W has three regional operations: East, Midwest, and West. Each region should be doing thirty-three point three percent of the business in a perfect world. If one region were doing fifty-one percent of the business, and the other two regions were splitting the other forty-nine percent, who would be sitting pretty?"

"That's easy, the one doing fifty-one percent."

"That would be you. But in a short time, you will be gone."

When Lloyd hired me, he pulled up the numbers to show me what a big job I had in front of me in the Midwest. The first thing he said was, "Oh, shit," as he started checking the numbers. "I was already hired, and you had already been kicked up a notch."

He said, "The Midwest is doing fifty-one percent of the business. A corporate guy just looks after his own ego. They all do it. Take the promotion and save as much of your salary as you can until they feel comfortable enough to fire you, then sue the hell out of them and you win."

I said, "It it's not my nature to sue anyone, and I don't want to work anywhere I'm not wanted. I will take the promotion and do the best job I can. When the time comes, I am sure they will ask for a resignation before they fire me, since as you say I have a good case against them."

My new job was working with MSOs only.

Even though I wasn't with ESPN any longer, my name still got me in the right place at the MSO I was calling. We had some frank discussions that were not in the best interest of Group W. It wasn't long before we saw Disney disappear from our line of services, and then it was the Satellite News Channel that was bought by Ted Turner and dismantled.

Sure enough, I was asked to resign. I did, with a specific date listed in my letter.

When I called to find out where my money was, I was told by the financial office that he couldn't talk with me before checking something out. Within five minutes he called back with a short statement, "I still can't talk with you, but the check is in the mail."

I said, "It's been five minutes, don't you mean a check will be sent?"

"No, I showed your letter to my boss, he had a check cut, handed it to me, and said that I needed to get it in the mail before I called you back."

"Thank you, and you can tell your boss that I am not going to sue Group W. I don't want to be where I am not wanted, and I don't want to embarrass your boss for firing the source of over half of the business by obtaining subscribers for our networks."

Corporate leaders that put power and ego above production often do more damage to their company than they do for themselves. Perhaps that was a contributing factor as to why Westinghouse no longer exists.

As Dad engineered, the New Jersey fiasco, on an equal level of duplicity, was the months-long campaign by Bill to get me to resign from ESPN, feigning that he was looking out for me. He used his family power position to get me away from ESPN and destroy a probable good career simply out of envy that I was succeeding in the company. He couldn't, in my opinion, stand the idea of me being the last Rasmussen at ESPN.

Chapter 21

TEXAS – ESPN OWNERSHIP CONCLUSION and MER PROPERTIES

Our move to Texas had come about for two reasons. Having positioned myself over the years, since we provided the funding to secure the Transponder on Satcom I, as being capable of being manipulated by Bill when he and Dad ganged up on me, I felt that the only way I could avoid the loss of any more of our investment was to eliminate the possibility of the three of us ever being in the same room together. The second reason was simply to get out of the Snow Belt, as I had nothing to keep me in Illinois.

Other than sojourns to Texas and Louisiana in the Air Force, Florida, teaching in Utah, and a couple of trips to see Bill in New Jersey and Connecticut, I had spent my life in the Midwest.

ESPN allowed me to see much of the rest of the country and I came to the realization that when the time was right, I would take my family south to a better climate. After the struggles with Enterprise Radio and Group W, I still had a meager income from Shaklee; it was time to leave the Midwest once again.

ESPN had taken me to a small town in central Texas named Brownwood. During the spring of 1983, Beth and I visited Brownwood as well as Waco, which was a larger alternative for us.

I do believe the good Lord guided us to Brownwood, because every time we were in Waco going between the two communities, it rained as if we were on the Gulf Coast prior to a hurricane. We would leave

Waco and drive into complete sunshine before reaching Brownwood. Going back to Waco, the scenario would reverse itself, so the heavens made up our mind.

On Thanksgiving Day of 1983, we moved into a very nice three-bedroom house and looked forward toward a new start away from the corporate world.

In the spring I received another call from Bill advising me that the end was in sight and wanting to do the best for everyone, he would need a power-of-attorney from me to include me in negotiations that he was having with ABC. My first reaction was, "I don't think so."

It wasn't long before Bill called back. Paraphrasing the conversation, he said, "Don, you can do whatever you want, but I want you to be able to make an informed decision, okay?"

"I'm listening."

"These people at ABC don't care about you and me. They are going to conclude this thing, because frankly, we are a pain to them. If you're not here or don't have legal representation present, your little two percent will be forgotten about and just be dropped from the discussion. They really don't care and there wouldn't be a thing you can do about it. After you think about it, give me a call. This will be wrapped up soon so don't take too long."

On an intellectual level, I knew that Bill was lying through his teeth, but that old bugaboo that "Bill is above reproach" in our family couldn't be broken. I struggled with it for a couple of days and finally capitulated.

Bill got his limited power-of-attorney from me along with a statement I made to him on the phone regarding his fiduciary responsibility to represent my best interest.

It was in the middle of the summer that I received a check in the mail for a little over $400,000, which I divided by two and sent half of it to my partner. We had made an agreement, and the only thing I could ethically and honesty do was to do exactly what I did.

At our Chicago meeting, back in 1979, Bill told me that I should give my partner $50,000 and let him sue me. He said, "There isn't a court in the land that wouldn't agree that you gave him a generous payment for the use of his money."

When I tried to explain to him that we had an agreement and I intended to live up to it, he told me to get into the modern world. "Businessmen don't do that, and since you don't have a contract—"

Here I jumped in, since he said the magic word "contract." I said, "He didn't need a contract, he had my word."

We still had some money coming from the ESPN sale as a result of the structure of the sale. This was far larger than the original distribution, and Bill wanted as big a chunk of it as he could possibly get from me. The first thing he came up with was a hot shot CPA from Boston to come out to Texas to meet with me and show me how this thing that Bill had put together was going to work.

Bill told me the day she was going to be in town, so I set up a meeting with Tony Krischke, a CPA, and Darrell Haynes, an attorney, to meet with her and me. I wasn't about to meet her alone without these trusted colleagues. As she came forward to make her presentation, she didn't look real confident. Tony and Darrell were perfect gentleman as they listened to her story.

When she finished, one of them, I think it was Darrell, advised her that they would recommend that I not participate in her proposal as it had numerous questionable components to it. There were parts of the meeting where I felt that she was attempting to get my money in Bill's hands.

At one point she actually proposed that I allow my money to flow directly through to Bill in case Dad passed away before all the money could find its proper place.

They asked her to step out for a minute while they discussed her overall proposal with me. When she left they both broke out laughing. We agreed that I would not give her an answer and that I drive her to the airport for her flight out.

It wasn't long before I got a demand letter from a Naples lawyer demanding $400,000, which came after the second or third phone call from Bill demanding money and if I didn't give it to him, he would sue me for everything I owned and leave me out in the street with nothing. And yes, he could take my house and everything in it. I thought that I had gotten past his intimidation, and I found out once again that you couldn't give in to a bully.

I am quite sure that he felt strongly that if he kept the pressure on, I would eventually capitulate. I was determined to see it through this time. I took the lawyer's letter up to Darrell. After reading it, he said that I needed Dusty Rhodes to handle this

I asked, "Who is Dusty Rhodes?"

He is a top attorney that has a lot of experience dealing with people like your brother. I think he will want to meet with you.

Darrell made an appointment and drove me up to meet Dusty. He had me relate the background and chronology of events that led me to be sitting across the table from him. I'm sure that I didn't include everything, but I did not miss any of the highlights.

"Can you put that in writing and bring me all the documentation you have on this matter?"

"Yes, sir!"

"How much time would you need to put it together?"

"Today is Thursday, how about Monday?"

He didn't respond directly, but flashed his secretary and directed her to make an appointment for me on the following Monday.

I had my work cut out for me that weekend, starting when I returned from Abilene.

On the way home, I was laying out in my mind the formulation I would use to correlate the organization of the documentation for a complete presentation on Monday.

I gathered my material and began preparation of two identical packets, one for Dusty and one for me so that we could discuss any given item with each of us having the paper work in front of us. It worked rather well, as we concluded the entire discussion in about two hours. He then advised me that he would take the case and be happy to represent me and my partner. I was extremely pleased when he made a comment to the affect that I had put together a fine chronological picture of the events pertaining to this situation.

TEXAS – ESPN OWNERSHIP CONCLUSION AND MER PROPERTIES

We concluded the morning with him calling Bill's mouthpiece and advising him that he would be representing us (my partner and I) and advising him that he would send a confirmation letter with a request for documentation on Bill's claim.

When we concluded the morning's activities, Dusty advised me that he would be in touch. He also said, "Now that you have representation, do not talk with Bill if he calls. He shouldn't call since he will know that you have an attorney, but you never know what some people will do."

Bill didn't call, thank goodness.

Dusty called with an appointment time, and I was on my way to Abilene that afternoon. We went over everything, and he indicated that he liked our position, but that we did want to cover that position. "We need to arrange for the possibility that they won't agree to a settlement and will want to go to court," he said. "I will call Larry, Bill's attorney, and suggest two meetings, the first to be held in Dallas and the second in Naples. We have to convince them that we will be negotiating a settlement without raising their suspicion that we are establishing jurisdiction."

"That's easy, Dusty." I responded, "Just invite the attorney. Since Bill has to be here to be served, if he is invited, they could get suspicious, but if he is not, they won't have any reason to be suspicious. I guarantee you that Bill will not allow his lawyer to come and meet with you without Bill being present."

"I'm positive that this will work. By the way, would you like me to describe Bill's lawyer?" I asked.

Laughing, Dusty said, "Tell me."

"He'll be of slight build, have the appearance of a mafia type with slicked-back hair and a black mustache." (This picture of him just popped into my head as we were speaking.) Dusty put everything together. Since Dusty was a pilot and had his own plane, we flew from Abilene to DFW (Dallas-Fort Worth Airport) in his twin engine King Air. It was a quick trip for the three of us. We had a deputy sheriff with us to serve papers on Bill, if necessary. If Dusty was concerned about Bill showing up, it didn't show. We arrived and went to the area where

Dusty had set up a meeting room. While we waited, the deputy drifted away so as not to be seen as a part of our group.

When Bill showed up with his attorney in tow, he was all business. As they walked to the room for the meeting, I stayed behind, having determined that Dusty would do just fine without me. I hired him to do a job; it wasn't my intent to be second-guessing him in what could become a heated exchange.

To appreciate the atmosphere as they walked to the room, picture a calm, relaxed Dusty in a conservative medium-brown business suit; Bill's attorney (see two paragraphs above), both appeared relaxed, and I would have to paint Bill as tight, kind of like a caged tiger.

The meeting seemed to go on forever. We patiently waited and waited, and waited some more. It was getting to the point that the deputy and I had little left to talk about, when in a flash, Dusty stepped out, motioned to the deputy, and they both re-entered the room. Within a minute, Bill, with his man, stormed out of the room and headed in the direction opposite of where I was sitting without even glancing in my direction. I suspected immediately that he was not a happy camper.

When Dusty and the deputy appeared, they were relaxed and not hurried in any way. As we went down toward general aviation to return to Abilene, Dusty simply stated, "The ball is in their court."

I asked, "What are their options?"

"They have really two options, and I think either one they choose will be in your favor. They could choose to negotiate a settlement, or they can choose to go to the courthouse here in Texas."

"They will have to choose to negotiate a settlement, since Bill wouldn't want to go to the courthouse because too much other stuff could come out that would have a steamroller effect," I said.

"It's not that simple, Don, but I think you are right."

We returned to Abilene and although I felt that Bill would try to pull something, just from past experiences, I had a great deal of confidence in Dusty.

This had to be the shortest long wait I had ever experienced. I was pretty sure that Bill and his cohort would examine every possibility to keep this thing going, but they responded immediately and wanted to negotiate a financial settlement sooner rather than later and assured Dusty that as soon as we dropped our suit, they would talk. Dusty, of course, wasn't buying any of that and countered that the suit would be withdrawn only after the agreement was reached.

After a little back and forth, Dusty put it all on the line. "No money for Bill, and we will pull the court action as the only realistic solution." After a short pause, they agreed.

We had to take a trip to Naples to maintain the initial agreement and wrap everything up.

When we were getting ready to leave, Dusty advised me that we would have a second pilot flying with us because of the length of the flight, and we would only make one stop each way for fuel. He and the other pilot would switch off manning the controls. We would be refueling in Alexandria, Louisiana, going, and coming back. We had plenty of time to talk and Dusty avoided discussing any of the details of the first meeting so we talked a while and he napped so that he would be fresh when it was his turn to fly the King Air.

We arrived in Naples in plenty of time to pick up a rental car and head to the Marriott Hotel and get a good meal. Knowing that we were holding all the aces, I got a good night's sleep and had an early breakfast, before heading down to the gorgeous white sand beach for an early morning walk. Afterward, I went in and joined Dusty as he had his breakfast. When he finished it was time to head out for our meeting.

When we arrived Bill was already there and eager for a confrontation. He ordered me into the meeting room. I acknowledged his command and said, "No, thank you!"

I think at that moment he realized his days of dominating me were over as he walked into the meeting room. There must have been a lot of back and forth, because that meeting took over an hour to wrap up.

When they came out, Bill walked by me and said, in what I perceived to be a threatening voice, "Don't you go talking to any reporters about this!"

Such an action had never entered my mind, but he was really surly about it.

When we left, Dusty told me that all the paperwork had been agreed to and for all practical purposes, it was all over. We would have to get together on a couple of occasions, but I could relax, "the money is safely in your hands, and there it will stay." We drove to the hotel, checked out, had lunch, and set out to find a good fruit stand. We found a pick-your-own field and had a fabulous time picking bags of fruit for our wives.

As we headed for the airport for the return trip to Texas, Dusty told me not to be a stranger when we got everything wrapped up. It made me feel good when he said, "In all my years of practicing law, I have had less than a handful of clients that I would want as a friend, and you are in that handful. I didn't know what to say, so I just said, "Thank you."

He then said, "I understand that you would like to have some kind of a positive family relationship with Bill and your dad. I think that as you look back, none has ever existed. For some reason, your dad is totally consumed by Bill and made bad decisions based on information from Bill that negatively affected you and your sister. I know that you will continue to try for a family relationship, but try not to be too disappointed when it doesn't happen. I have seen this scenario play out many times."

He continued, "I have to tell you about a statement that Bill made during our first meeting in Dallas. I had just advised both Bill and his lawyer that if you wrote Bill a check for four hundred thousand dollars, you could be liable for a federal tax fraud charge and a twenty-year prison sentence. His response was, 'I don't care if he goes to prison for twenty years, I want the money.' That is when I came out and got the deputy.

"Don, I have defended nineteen murder cases; I have pleaded before our US Supreme Court, the World Court, and the World Appellate Court, and I have never met anyone as nasty as Bill."

I had been having a very serious wrestling match between my brain and my heart regarding the lies Bill had been telling me for years. I knew that he was lying, but my upbringing wouldn't allow me to believe it. It caused me to make some serious mistakes and bad decisions that I have to take responsibility for.

By the time we took off for Abilene, I was a mixture of relief and sadness. Relief that this ordeal was over, but sad because I knew that Dusty was telling me the truth.

My partner and I had to pay the bill submitted from the Boston CPA to at least give a morsel that Bill could hang his hat on.

I too had something to hang my hat on. After all the physical labor I gave Bill and literally saving ESPN at an early date, all he could apparently think of was some juvenile need to control me by intimidation, and finally, physically.

When he tried it physically, he ended up with three cracked ribs in 1961. His next attempt had been the intimidation that had gone on for years and culminated with his final attempts to take my money. Finally he lost both those battles and I was free, except for that feeling deep in my gut. "If he ever needs me, I will be there for him," I thought , "in spite of myself."

We got on with living and started a project that we found we really enjoyed and turned it into a job that helped a lot of people.

Our daughter Dara had a friend that wanted to come to Texas. She was a lovely young lady who worked as a dog groomer, and Beth and I really liked Kathy Carlson as well. So we made a deal with her. I would buy a house and we would set it up for her as a business with living quarters attached. When she got her business started, she would pay us rent and assume all responsibility for the monthly bills pertaining to the building. We, of course, assumed all responsibility for anything that went wrong with the house and provided appliances.

Don Jr. was going to school, Beth and I were getting used to a new community, and I sure could use some money, as the Shaklee business was not enough to live on at the level that we had become accustomed to.

Dara moved down to Texas when we moved to the country and started college, and Kathy came a couple of months later. About six months after Kathy started her business, Dara got married and left town. Kathy stayed on and has lived in the home and conducted her business, as well as building a fine life and reputation for herself. At the time of this writing, she has been living and working at the same location for thirty years.

Beth and I enjoyed working on Kathy's house so we decided that we would buy some of the old WWII homes that were built during the time that Brownwood was the location of a German POW camp. The US Army had caused the population to double and the ingenuity of the local residents developed hundreds of small houses to be built to house the soldiers. After the war these houses continued to be rented out as the population began to shrink. Soon there was a glut and many of them began to deteriorate. It was from this inventory that we bought and repaired some homes.

We had moved out to the country and thought we had a pretty good set up with a nice home on twenty-five acres about nine miles out of town. As our inventory of homes grew, we spent more time in town and began to think about getting a place for ourselves, but didn't think too much about it until a local banker that owned a small mobile home park approached me about buying his park. He wanted too much money for it for the condition it was in and I turned him down.

As time went on, we continued buying homes, one at a time, and rehabbed them and rented them out. We soon determined that we wanted to help people that were having a difficult time and didn't want to go into government housing. As far back as then, folks were figuring out that government housing was not the best way to go.

I was constantly approached by HUD to open my homes to Section 8 housing. I politely declined.

About eight months after we were really into the homes, my banker buddy asked to speak to me again. We talked about his mobile home park. He had reduced the price twenty-five percent and said that he needed to sell it because he had just accepted a job with a bank in Marfa, Texas, out in West Texas. I told him that earlier I had priced the property considerably less than he was asking for it, and he wasn't low enough for me to even consider it.

After more discussion on potential profitability, he asked me to make him an offer.

I gave him my top-dollar offer, since I wasn't going to pay him for potential that I was going to develop. I was surprised when he agreed. This was in 1985.

Now we had six houses and a mobile home park with thirty-eight spaces including some mobile homes. We continued to live in the country, but with eighteen homes to take care of, we found the desire and necessity to live in town pulling at us stronger and stronger.

In approximately 1987 we bought another mobile home park just around the corner from our first park. This one was slightly larger with eighty mobile home spaces and twenty-five mobile homes. With the purchase of this mobile home park, we created MER Properties to include all of our growing list of properties.

This was a poorly managed mobile home park that had a few years of unpaid taxes. I sat down with the tax appraiser and laid out a plan of action to take control of the property and yet treat the owner with some respect. The owner, Mr. Gene Autry, had no idea that the park was in the shape that it was. When I called him, he laughed and told me that the mobile home park was worth more than that. When I told him that the taxes hadn't been paid for a few years, he was astounded and asked to meet with me.

He came into town on Monday morning and made the rounds, beginning with the tax appraiser, the mayor, and a couple of attorneys, and then several of Brownwood's prominent citizens completely without my knowledge. The next day we met at my CPA's office. Gene and David Krischke had been friends for a long time and when I walked in early, before the scheduled time, Gene was already there, and I walked in on a couple of older gentlemen reminiscing. They welcomed me in as they were talking about their good old days.

In the middle of our visiting, during a lull in the conversation, Gene turned to me and said, "Don, I accept your offer," and that was that. We continued for a while and after a bit, he suggested that I go see Darrell Haynes and lay out our agreement to him. Darrell was my attorney.

After we finished, I swung by Darrell's office. He was aware of what we were doing and I learned that he did some work for Gene as well as the manager that was running the mobile home park in question. He had a pretty good feel of the financial condition of the park. I was talking with his receptionist when he came out and invited me into his office.

I told him that I just came in to set an appointment with him to discuss the mobile home park owned by Gene Autry. That was when I learned that Gene had done some checking on me with several people in town. We set a date and the purchase went very smoothly. Gene had told Darrell to make all the arrangements based on his agreement with me, which is exactly what Darrell did.

We sailed through the deal and took possession of the property in a little over thirty days. After all was said and done, I was talking with Darrell one day and he asked me, "How did you do it?"

"Do what?"

"I have never seen anyone get the best of a deal with Gene, but you did. How did you do it?"

"I told him that I was going to buy this mobile home park and then I laid out my options and his. I was basically just being fair with him because of his reputation."

"Well, you got a good deal and made a friend along the way."

I appreciated his kind words.

I knew that I would have a couple of years' work cut out for me to get this park in good shape. We had drug problems, vandalism, loud parties, and nightly visits from the police.

I met with the police chief and we agreed that any time there was a disturbance in the park that I would be notified immediately, regardless of the time, day or night. Then I would have the facts to act on and get the problems out of the park. I pointed out that there should be no reason for the police to have to be in the mobile home parks every night, and sometimes during the day, dealing with malcontents and other problems.

We had worked together on the first park and he knew that I meant business. My goal was to have a nice, safe place for people to raise a family.

The day-to-day maintenance of the parks and homes made me feel like I was working full time again.

With the acquisition of the second larger park, we moved into a doublewide mobile home and added our country home to our rental inventory.

Within a year or two, I was approached by the Boy Scouts administrator about a piece of property they owned that was adjacent to our biggest park. Their asking price was way out of sight, and I turned them down with the caveat that if they decided to get reasonable, I was open to them coming back and discussing a legitimate and rational price.

As he was leaving, he turned and asked me what I would consider a rational price. I said, "Twenty percent of what you asked for."

"You would pay us twenty percent of what we asked for the property? You just bought yourself a piece of property."

I suggested that he take the information to Darrell Haynes and he and I would get the ball rolling.

I had no idea what we would do with this property, but at less than two hundred dollars an acre, I figured that I would come up with something.

Now I could get back to work cleaning up my properties and providing decent housing for folks while keeping them out of the grasp of the government.

To make these mobile home parks more appealing, I decided to clean up the back of the park that I called Camp Bowie Mobile Home Park #1. At the back of this park, there was a steep hill and a large workshop, with a few acres that were under anywhere from seven- to nine-foot tall weeds.

The weeds were so thick that I would spend a few hours each day with the big sickle hacking and whacking away. After a number of days, I swung the sickle and hit something hard. I backed off and took fewer weeds with each swing until I realized that I had a trailer under the weeds. I carefully cut around the sixteen-foot lowboy hauling trailer until I had a means of hitching it up to my truck. I pulled it over to my storage building, which I have now named "The Barn." After maneuvering the trailer into a retrievable position, I oiled the attached jack and removed it from my truck. I would have to put new tires on the unit and maybe replace some two by eights in the bed, and it would be a very usable trailer.

I went back to hacking and whacking for a couple of more days. Then I discovered, under the weeds, another trailer. This time it was a four by eight stock trailer. Sadly, it needed more work than the lowboy, but it could become more versatile due to the high sides and short wheel base.

Two usable trailers that eventually would have had to have been bought really had me buoyed up. I thought, What else might I find under these weeds?" Now, keep in mind that n that we had chopped all these weeds, we had to rake them and haul them to the dumpster. All this was done with my truck. It would be easier and quicker when I got my lowboy all rehabbed. For now, I would keep after it with the hope of finding something else of use. Then it happened; I hit something that felt like a tire. Sure enough, I had unearthed an early sixties Oldsmobile Vista Cruiser.

"Is it possible, could it be that this old car could be restored?" Possible, but right then it couldn't be moved because my truck wasn't strong enough to move it. I would have to use the tractor's front-end loader just to get it dislodged from the ground. I ultimately decided to let it set there until I cleared the remainder of the area. There would be a couple more surprises before I could clean the area up and begin mowing.

Getting this area cleaned up over a period of a couple of months became a passion to get completed, as it would make the rest of the park look better. We dubbed this pretty much useless land "the back forty," although it comprised just about four acres. Clearing it made it seem like forty acres.

The next discovery was a ten-by-ten storage shed that was so overgrown around it's parameter that even if you knew where it was, you couldn't see it from the top of the hill. The doors were in need of serious repair, and the contents were dozens upon dozens of useless tires that were looked at and then taken to the dump, except those that could be used moving mobile homes.

The most memorable and final discovery lay under a railroad tie in an area of rich black dirt that was home to a gazillion fire ants. We had not run into fire ants until this moment. I got acquainted in a not-too-pleasant fashion. As I grabbed the side of the tie, I was accosted by fire ants. Within seconds I knew I was in trouble, as they were moving up my arms and legs at the same time. I tried squashing them, to no avail. I tried brushing them off, and that didn't work either, so I ran to my truck and headed home. When I hit the drive, I began getting my clothes off as soon as possible. I yelled for Beth and she came out to see what the problem was. As we met near the backdoor, she could see that my body was being taken over by these hungry creatures. She got the hose and started blasting me with a strong stream of water.

That water did the trick, but the damage was done. I was feeling lightheaded and a little weak. When I got in the house, I looked at my arms and saw that they were covered with little whiteheads. I went to bed and started squeezing the pus out one by one. I asked Beth to count the whiteheads as we squeezed them. When we got to two hundred, we stopped counting and kept squeezing.

After we got all of them, I laid back and fell asleep. I didn't wake up until the next day, and I was really sick. I didn't get out of bed for three days. After I recovered, we learned that fire ants don't bite, they sting. Those whiteheads we squeezed weren't filled with pus, it was poison. I guess that without knowing it, we did the right thing in getting rid of the poison.

Back on my feet, I went down to the back forty and evaluated where we were in the cleanup. We had accomplished more than I thought we had. In a couple of days, when I got my strength back, I would complete the rough cleanup and mow the weeds down with one of our riding mowers to allow some of the grass to come through. The place was beginning to look better.

With a stern hand and tremendous, consistent effort and support from the police, we pretty much eliminated the drug dealing, rowdiness, family violence, and vandalism from the parks. From the situation that we found when we took over each of the parks, with the police handling calls nightly in each park, we got to the point that more than once a month was a rarity.

The most difficult activity when you are renting out more than sixty mobile homes is to be consistent in the dealing with each tenant and at the same time maintain a business relationship. If you become too helpful in attempting to help and guide them to a better life, they begin to think you are a friend rather than a landlord. If you have to sit on them to take care of the property that they are contracted to, they sometimes go in the opposite direction and literally tear the place apart before leaving in the middle of the night.

One example of the irrational departure we had to deal with occurred when one young couple didn't pay their electric bill and trashed the mobile home, leaving not only a mess, but a refrigerator with rotting meat. We had to replace the refrigerator, clean the place up, and do other repairs before putting the mobile home on the market again.

After this was accomplished, I received a phone call from the wayward ex-tenant asking, "What did you do with my wife's two ten thousand-dollar fur coats?"

After I assured him that when I declared the home abandoned, there were no wearable clothes of any kind in the home and it had been vacant for over a month after the rent was due, having been totally trashed, he angrily advised me that he would sue me for the value of the fur coats.

I responded, "If you would like the names of a couple of good attorneys, I can provide them for you."

He hung up on me and I never heard from him again. I did file a report on the call with the police department and provided a copy to an attorney that I regularly used and filed a notice with the office of my justice of the peace as well.

I had another eviction situation that had gone on too long. This single mother with one daughter was two months behind on her rent and when I went to her unit, she refused to answer the door. I put a notice on the door and filed the eviction papers. When she received the papers, she was fighting mad and approached me yelling and screaming about me being inconsiderate for not speaking to her before I started to try to get rid of her. Her main argument was, "How could you do this to us so close to Christmas?"

I pointed out to her that she last paid rent in September, which was not anywhere near Christmas.

She then tearfully pleaded that she couldn't pay the rent because she needed to buy her daughter Christmas presents.

You get the picture of the mental capacity I was dealing with here.

Before I got her out of the park, she began hiding her car in different places around the park in an attempt to keep it from being repossessed.

After she had been gone a while, one day she came by the post office in the park and wanted her mail. I looked in the mailbox and advised her that there wasn't any mail there and she really should go to the post office and put in a change of address.

Then she went into a tearful tirade about everyone being against her. I listened and as she calmed down, she asked me, "Why doesn't anyone like me?"

I answered, "Could it be that you are a filthy slob that cheats everyone that tries to help you, you live like a pig, and lie about everything?"

She responded with a straight face, "No—that can't be it."

Moments like this, you just never forget.

One of my fellow mobile home park owners in the town of Early, just next to Brownwood, contacted me about buying his mobile home park. Naturally, he was asking an enormous amount of money for it. He only had seven units with no room to expand, so it wasn't a particularly desirable property.

He then asked me to make an offer. I told him that I would have to check out a few things, which I did and then got back to him.

I laid out all the limitations, costs, and rehabilitation necessary to make it work as a reasonable investment. He agreed with my analysis and asked if I had come up with a price that I would be willing to pay for it.

I told him that I would give him a firm, non-negotiable figure that he could take or leave, but I would not get into a discussion as to value or rationale, simply because I didn't care if I bought this property or not.

I gave him my figure, which was a third of his asking price, and he quietly said, "You just bought yourself another mobile home park."

Oh boy, just what I needed. Well at the price I paid, I should have been in the black in less than two years. With the additional travel, and another set of community-elected officials to work with, I would indeed make this an interesting project.

Right off the bat, I discovered that I had squatters in one of the mobile homes. The tough part of it was that apparently they were not aware that what they were doing was illegal. I called upon the local police, and they informed the couple that they had to move. They didn't.

I talked with the chief of police and he laid out the process of eviction for me. And so it was, although it still took me close to two months to clear them out. They left angrily, stating to me that I had not been very fair to them and that they shouldn't have to pay rent because the man who gave them the key told them they could stay as long as they wanted.

Over the twenty-plus years that we owned the mobile home parks, we had some real-life experiences that certainly taught us some important lessons that I could write a whole book about.

After 2003 we decided that we should sell the motor home parks and retire. It took us a couple of years to get the job done, but without any kind of planning, we sold the parks, packed our belongings, and headed west.

Chapter 22

TEAROOM AND DINER

After running the mobile home parks for some years, Beth began talking about a dream that she had for several years and asked if we could build a tearoom. I responded, in all my wisdom, "What's a tearoom?"

After explaining the concept to me, I reasoned it to be a woman's thing that probably would not have broad appeal and would certainly not be of any interest by men. I was not initially enthusiastic about another project.

Two factors were at work here. The first was her enthusiasm and determination. The second (unspoken) was my inclination to spoil her.

The only thing to do was to visit a few tearooms to educate me as to the possibility of building one. As we began our tour, I soon learned that this really was a woman's thing. With a few exceptions, we didn't see men in tearooms and when we did, they didn't have the enthusiasm that I detected in the ladies.

We were both totally immersed in the concept of healthy eating and supplementation, so when discussing this project, Beth mentioned that everything served in her tearoom would be made from scratch and every meal would be healthy, she sealed the deal with me.

We began looking for a suitable plan and I thought there might be some way of getting the men comfortable in a tearoom setting. Within a couple of weeks, we found an old solid rock house that could be converted into a tearoom. This house had been built in the 1930s and appeared to be an ideal size.

The big hurdle to clear was the fact that it was in a residential area, so we had to submit a petition to all the neighbors to convert that block to commercial.

It turned out that the neighbors included one block in every direction. I drew up a document and the city manager approved it before we began interviewing each and every neighbor that fell into the categorical area. Much to our surprise, everyone signed the document that I would have to present at the next zoning meeting. All were not overly thrilled with the idea, but they all wanted to see progress in their part of town and everyone agreed within a week.

I turned the list of signatures into the city manager and the process began. We had to attend three separate city council and zoning commission meetings before we were able to get our building rezoned. Then we could purchase the building and begin converting it into a tearoom. It's a good thing that work is fun because in addition to managing the mobile home parks daily, I spent a considerable amount of time cleaning up this new property to be in a position to have all the folks in the neighborhood know that we were keeping our word and eliminating an eyesore from their community. The house had been empty for several years. Beth cleaned the interior of the building and began imagining how she wanted to design it. More than with any other property, we worked hand in hand to create a very attractive and appealing facility.

Before getting inside to develop the kitchen and four dining areas, each with its own unique features, I had to clean an area for the off-street parking lot. This was time consuming but very interesting and new planning concepts had to be conquered. First I had to determine the location of the sprinkler system and eliminate all potential leakage areas. After measuring the depth of lines that would be covered over and making sure that we had more than adequate coverage to maintain the system for the hedges that would surround the parking lot. The goal was to prevent the view of parked cars from the two streets that intersected at that corner. I also had to cap all sprinklers that didn't service the trees and plants.

TEAROOM AND DINER

After setting the stage, so to speak, it was time to bring in the contractors. The new street guttering was the first order of business and then we hired a friend who had built roads. I had smoothed out the area as he had instructed so when he came in, it was a matter of laying his base and then the asphalt. From the street it looked like we were getting a good start, but we had one more project to complete before the exterior would be ready to go.

In the grassy front yard, where the two streets crossed, I had a gazebo constructed. This was to become a point of gatherings for picture taking and weddings. The name of Beth's dream would be, "The Gazebo Tea Room."

Now it was time to get busy inside. Even though, or maybe because, the house was built in the thirties, it had a large county kitchen, so I went to a restaurant supply store with a diagram and measurements and bought a stainless-steel table and a commercial dishwasher, a new stove with a built-in microwave oven on top, and a large refrigerator with an extra-large freezer. All would fit comfortably in the space.

We then scraped and sanded all the hardwood floors and refinished them. We did shelves for little nicknacks and painted each room a different color to match the various motifs. One room we called the country room because it had a baby-blue duck wallpaper border at the ceiling level and complementary colors throughout. The former living room and dining room had a combined moniker of the formal room. The back room was designated as the sports room and was filled with sports memorabilia from my playing days, and the hall leading to the room featured a display where there was originally a large closet. A banister made of fourteen baseball bats replaced the doors that had been there. An ESPN banner formed the back wall and crafted tables supported other material. Two particular notes were placed in this area, one was a nice note from April of 1980 from ESPN president Chet Simmons congratulating me on the work I was doing and offering any help he could supply, and the other was from Jim Simpson, our first name sportscaster who had become a good friend during our time together.

When we started this project, I really wanted a room that the men would like to come to in a tearoom. It seemed to work as we developed a pretty loyal following of men who came with their wives. Some couples would come and sit up front in the more formal rooms. The next time they came, the wife would be in the back room with her husband. It was kind of fun to watch.

We had a heart specialist, Dr. Jones, who came to try my wife's fare and after visiting with Beth and learning that everything was prepared every day from scratch without any additives, he began sending his patients to the tearoom. More importantly, he talked to other doctors about the tearoom, and Beth built a fine reputation.

All our neighbors were pleased with the addition to the area, and many of them dined at a tearoom for the first time in their life.

Without a doubt I believe that the time Beth ran The Gazebo Tea Room were among the happiest days of her life.

A CLASSIC CAR DINER

Some years later, after we sold the tearoom, Beth and I took some time from the daily routine of working to drive around central Texas and just enjoy the day. After a long drive that extended as far as Del Rio and through Midland and Odessa, we stopped at one of our favorite coffee shops in Abilene before heading home. The coffee and piece of pie we each had as Beth was looking through a copy of the *Thrifty Nickel* advertising paper became rather expensive. She came upon an ad for an Amtrak stainless-steel railroad car, which I thought was rather expensive, but then I didn't have a clue to what a railroad car would cost!

As she showed it to me, she said, "You have often talked about having a fifties diner, wouldn't this make a great one?"

I really couldn't remember every having said anything about a desire to have a '50s diner, but I immediately said, "That sounds interesting. Why don't you take the paper home with us and I'll check it out."

It would be important to learn a little about the value of this kind of car before we even talked to them about it.

After we returned home and got back into the swing of things, I went up to the Santa Fe Railroad and talked to a couple of railroad people. They were in unison when one of them suggested that I go talk to Mr. Green. When it came to railroad cars, Mr. Green was an expert. What he didn't know about these cars simply wasn't worth knowing.

"Where would I find this Mr. Green?"

"He's in San Angelo."

"San Angelo is pretty good sized city. How would I find him?"

"Just go to San Angelo and ask the first person you see if they could tell you where you could find Mr. Green. Everyone in San Angelo knows Mr. Green."

We thought that sounded a little bit iffy, but we decided to make the trip and see what it might turn up. The next morning we got an early start and headed to San Angelo. As soon as we reached the outskirts of the town, we pulled into a service station and I asked the man behind the counter if he could tell me where I might find a Mr. Green. Much to my surprise, he said, "Sure, drive toward town and when you see some railroad cars on your left, go into that area and ask for the location of the office. There you will find Mr. Green."

I couldn't believe our good fortune, nor the wisdom of the guys in the Santa Fe office back in Brownwood. We drove to the property and before we knew it, we were being introduced to Mr. Green. Mr. Green was over ninety years old and as sharp as a tack. Keep in mind, this trip was strictly research.

After a few minutes of getting acquainted, we got right to the point of our visit. Beth told him of our discovery of the car in Abilene. (The car was actually located in Odessa.)

Without hesitation he blurted out, "You don't want that car, it's a disaster. There were only six of those cars made and as far as I know, there's only two of them still in existence."

He continued, "Over the years I have had a good number of people come by with the idea of building a diner out of a railroad car, but it was always easy to determine they didn't have any idea of what it would take. I do think you two are serious and have the resources to pull it off."

He was beginning to tell us that the only other car was not for sale. He knew this because he had the right of first refusal when they wanted to sell it. Then the phone rang. He excused himself to take the call and I suggested that we wait outside while he finished his call. He responded, "No, stay here."

As we waited we could hear his entire conversation. After some preliminary back and forth, Mr. Green said, "No, I have some people in my office right now that want that car." After some give and take between him and the person on the other end of the line, he said, "They will be right over."

He hung up and shook his head and, smiling, he said, "You know that other car I was telling you about?"

"The one that is not for sale?"

"That was the owner, and they had a buyer for it in Houston. He agreed to accept my verbal exercise of my right of first refusal, and I told him that you would be right over to buy the car."

Although I was anxious to find out where "over" was, I hung on to his every word. Finally he said everything he wanted to say and was waiting for my question.

"Where is 'over?'"

"The car is behind the newspaper office."

I knew that he was having some fun with me by the glint in his eye. I casually asked, "Just out of curiosity, is 'over' here in San Angelo?"

"Oh, didn't I tell you, it's in Lake Charles, Louisiana. Do you know where that is?"

"I have a fairly good idea; Beth and I both graduated from McNeese State College in Lake Charles."

No smile from Mr. Green on that bit of news; instead, he began laughing joyously and then said, "It was meant to be." He told me not to pay more than fifteen thousand for the car.

With that I gave him a business card and told him that we would be in touch, but right then we needed to get back to Brownwood and get packed so we could head for Louisiana the next day.

Our "research" had turned curiosity into either buying a railroad car or disappointing a charismatic, joyful ninety-year-old "kid" in love with railroads and railroad cars.

Before we left, Mr. Green asked me, "Did you notice that fancy 'car' as you came in?"

"You mean the one that looked like a private car?"

"That was President Truman's car."

Without thinking, I responded, "He was Beth's cousin."

"Really?" His bright eyes were flashing and dancing with excitement.

Beth shyly answered, "Yes, our grandfathers generations back were brothers."

Before this could get into a long, projected conversation, I said, "We need to get going if we are going to be in Lake Charles tomorrow."

We went to Lake Charles with thoughts of visiting McNeese as well as examining the railroad crew car. I was pleasantly surprised as we approached the bridge crossing the Calcasieu river how much this seemed like coming home. The growing and learning that occurred in this city as a member of the US Air Force and at McNeese College as well as the sports that were so much a part of my life, all filled my being in a way I never expected. Beth had been with me the entire journey over the years and I could only imagine what she might be thinking. I didn't ask. I was simply enjoying the beautiful view spread out in front of us.

Although we knew that by the time we arrived the newspaper office would be closed, we just had to drive over and look at the car and see how it was set up. A rail bed and tracks had been laid to bring the car to its current location, so I thought it should be easy to move.

With the assurance that the car was indeed at this location, we found a motel that we would stay at and headed out for some good Cajun food for dinner. After a relaxing evening, the following day we were at the newspaper building early to see what we might accomplish. We were greeted as we entered and there was a long conversation between the newspaper executive, Beth, and I. When he learned that we had graduated from McNeese, the dialog became very much a quizzing of us about our time at what was now McNeese State University. He would talk about situations that had occurred while we were there and every time I could identify a student from the late '50s to the early '60s, the price of the car would come down. It turned out that many of the guys I knew had a relationship with the newspaper. He learned that I had played baseball against Frank "Chico" Glenn, who was a basketball icon at McNeese and an outstanding all-around athlete, and Tom Sestak, who went on to play for the Buffalo Bills in the American Football League. The price dropped even more so I thought I would roll the dice and see if my relationships with faculty would do any good. I mentioned Coach Reed Stephens, Dowell Fontenot, and Coach Ratcliff and the price slid a little more.

I was beginning to think that if I could get my memory to dredge up more common friends I might just get the newspaper to pay me for taking the Silver Streak off their hands, but alas it was not to be. After going out and examining the car, we got down to serious negotiation which didn't take long. He gave me a price that was less than half of what Mr. Green had stated was the top dollar I should pay. We agreed that I would pay for the preparation of the car for moving. The newspaper would pay to repair the tracks so that Santa Fe could get a train to the car.

We shook hands and headed for McNeese and lunch. There wasn't much going on and as I was walking around the quad, a big fellow was walking toward me that just looked like he might be an athlete, so I engaged him in conversation about the school. He was a really nice guy and he eventually asked me," When did you graduate?"

"1961."

"Wow! I wasn't even born yet!"

That was the first time I ever felt I was getting old. I'm sure that the look on my face caused him to feel like he insulted me, but he hadn't. We then parted ways. We couldn't visit with any of our former teachers, coaches, or administrators since they had all long ago left the university. We did go to the Ranch for a cup of coffee before heading back to Texas.

TEAROOM AND DINER

A couple of phone calls and I had a Santa Fe brake maintenance man to repair and certify the brake system as "rail ready." Now, as far as the car was concerned, it was just a matter of sitting and waiting. I did go to the Santa Fe office in Brownwood and made arrangements to put the car about a half a mile from its final resting place.

A had the old Boy Scout acreage right next to the largest of our mobile home parks. This would be an ideal location for the diner, with the possibility of unlimited parking and plenty of space left over should we decide to do something else.

I divided my time between working on mobile homes and building a rail bed for the car. Our friends in town provided the ties and rail from Vulcan Materials, and we then purchased several hundred tons of stone and gravel from that company. It was a big job spreading the gravel and getting the stone reasonably solid and level before placing the ties and securing the rail. A good friend, Lloyd Golden, helped me tremendously by practically living on the tractor as he prepared the site to receive the car when it arrived.

As we were waiting for the car I had some unfinished business to take of. I had been taking trips to Chicago every April and September to do something with Dad. Those trips morphed into a dual purpose, keep Dad as active as I could and organize a fortieth high school class reunion.

The morning of April 19, 1993 was just like any other day as I set off to drive to Chicago for yet another Gage Park 1955 Class reunion meeting. First a stop in Fort Worth to see my son and then drive with a goal of being in Illinois before I hit the sack.

As is my norm when driving alone, I was listening to talk radio as I drove through Oklahoma when I heard news of the Waco blaze at the Branch Dividian Complex.

Since I had a TV in the back of the van, I pulled over and picked up an Oklahoma City TV station and saw a video from Waco – it made me sick to my stomach. The rest of the trip was uneventful and all went well with our meeting.

Two years later on the same date headed to our final meeting before the reunion. This time I heard of the Oklahoma City Bombing as I was approaching the Missouri state line. I couldn't pull over until I reached the Springfield area, but when I did get that opportunity I was once again shocked beyond anything I could have imagined. Little did I know that in just a few hours from seeing those horrible scenes I would face the greatest fear that I had ever experienced and for that isolated time have never experienced again.

It was well after dark when I arrived in St Louis and weaved through traffic to position myself for the swooping left curve that wold take me to the bridge and across the Mississippi River. Just after getting into the left lane I saw a motorcycle Policeman in the center lane with lights flashing. I thought oh-oh somebody just got caught. He soon pulled behind and I began to pull over to the left off the highway when I heard him on his speaker; "I will clear the traffic and I want you to pull over to the right." That command was very specific. I looked through my right mirror and saw him stopping traffic as I moved across three travel lanes and stopped off the highway on the right. By this time I was thinking, this is not a normal way for the Officer to be pulling me over for a ticket.

When I stopped, I placed both my hands on top of the steering wheel and waited. Then came the next order. "Exit the vehicle with your hands in clear view!!. I did as I was told and upon stepping out of the van I faced toward the back of the van and saw a bright light and just in front of it I saw that I was staring down the barrel of what I perceived to be a .38 revolver.   Now fear began to curse through veins.

"Step to the rear of the vehicle" was the next order he barked at me, and at that moment I realized that this man is dead serious about something. When I got where he wanted me, with my hands still reaching for the stars, he asked me several questions pertaining to who was I, where was I headed and why? He never asked me for my drivers license; which, I found curious.

After answering his questions, he asked me if I had any proof of those answers?

I responded that I did and if he looked in the back of my van he would find a brief case which contained papers related to our reunion.

At this point he directed me to the rear door of the van and ordered me, while keeping one hand elevated to open the back door and remove the brief case. Which I did.

As he directed me to place the brief case on the ground and then raise both hands again I thought that he was going to open the brief case, but he backed up to behind his motorcycle (all the time keeping the barrel of that gun pointed at me). I thought, this is crazy!

After what seamed like an eternity, he directed me to open the brief case and remove the papers. I detected a little fear in his voice for the first time during our encounter, and that increased my level of fear.

When I opened the case and removed the papers, he lowered his gun and moved toward me again as he said "you can put your hands down." He looked at the papers and smiled.

When he did that I relaxed and asked him, "What is this all about?"

He explained, there was an Arab looking man with McVey shortly before the bomb went off and he was later seen driving a green van with only one screw holding the license plate it in place. I looked down at my license plate and saw that it was cockeyed. I whacked myself on on the forehead and said that I better get fixed. He agreed and thanked me for my cooperation.

The suspect was identified, but got away. Ironically I heard on a radio discussion a long time after this occurred that he was tried and convicted in absentia for the Oklahoma City bombing.

Needless to say – I was really wide awake as I drove to my motel.

* * * *

We had a house mover by the name of Jimmy King move the railroad car to its final destination. The car itself weighed seventy tons. Each set of wheels (called trucks) weighed 17,500 pounds. Two trucks had to be placed on the rails before the car itself could be brought over. It was an awesome sight to see Jimmy maneuver all this large equipment that was required to get the unit in position. When it was in position, it had to be leveled. Jimmy did an amazing job. From corner to opposite corner, over eighty feet in length, the car was level to within less than a quarter of an inch.

When the job was completed, we took a dozen tennis balls and set them throughout the car and not a single one of them had any roll. After the tables were placed in the dining area with glass tops, we went through the procedure again with the same results.

It was now time to begin stripping the interior of the car. This was no easy task and took several weeks. Mr. Green called and asked if he could have some of the material that I had removed from the inside of the car. I so appreciated his contribution, and although he said that he would pay us for it, I preferred to just give it to him.

He drove over by himself and some of the items were quite heavy, so I loaded everything on his truck for him. I told him that when we were ready to open, I would give him a call, as I would like him to see the finished product. He was excited at the prospect. Mr. Green was quite the character. Well into his nineties and when he left with his load, he went motoring out of my drive like he was a teenager experiencing speed for the first time.

With everything cleaned out of the car, it was time to buy a building that would have a dual purpose. It would house the kitchen and the restrooms. I bought a twenty-by-forty metal building with a peaked roof that when reconstructed and placed in position, would form the base for a large sign on top of the car/building.

Due to the size of the kitchen appliances, we decided to procure the equipment needed prior to attaching the building to the car. The appliances would be placed in the building and locked in as we put it in position. Prior to that I needed to cut a twenty-five-foot hole in the back of the car to accommodate a soda fountain counter and access to the car from the kitchen and back.

This was the most harrowing experience in creating the diner. I didn't know, and no one could tell me if the car structure would survive taking out such a large section. Before I started I used a heavy-duty I beam brace in the middle of the intended cut, and prayed. With a stainless-steel cutting blade that cut very well, it still took several hours for me to cut the hole and painfully long minutes as I eased the jack down from its solid position holding the structure in place, we thought. When the brace was removed, the horizontal beam did not move one iota. The car was solid and stable. Now the building could be slid into place.

The process was magnificent. We needed only to weatherproof the connection between the railroad car and the building. We were now ready to receive the "A Classic Car Diner" sign, but that would be down the road a bit, as the interior now had to be completed.

The interior first had to be protected from weather. A moisture barrier was secured to the floor prior to putting sub-flooring in that would eventually be topped with '50s-era black-and-white tile. The ceiling had to be restructured to fit the motif, which then allowed us to begin painting.

We used a high-quality auto body paint and had an experienced painter do the preparation and application. When it was finished, it looked fantastic, and we hit the coloring right on the head. It was exactly what I had envisioned. With the painting completed, I brought in a neon light company and laid out my view as to what the neon inside and outside should look like and gave them the drawing I had made for the whole lighting scheme.

The neon people were very perceptive in interpreting my vision and within a couple of hours, we had it all put together on graph paper with more accurate measurements than I had provided.

I was like a kid waiting for Christmas as time dragged on and on. In less than two weeks, I received the call that they would be coming down the next day to install the lights. This would be a major milestone, leading up to a lot more curiosity from the community. We still had a lot of work to do before we could even begin to think about an opening date.

That evening we tested the lights after dark to get the full impart. WOW! We had done well. The lights were marvelous. On the following day, a pilot that had flown in from the south as the lights were being tested came by to see what we were up to. He told me that the diner lights were the first significant lights he saw as he approached Brownwood and he picked them up about twenty miles out. That sounded good to me. I wondered how much it would cost to put in an airstrip.

Nothing goes as planned. Building something like this, straight from your head to construction, allows you to make more mistakes than you could imagine, but you learn to overcome, improvise, and win battles with city hall to solve problems. The best part of it is that it was fun to create, and Beth and I were having the time of our lives.

As I moved in to check the interior width of the diner, I suddenly realized that the standard booth width was too wide to provide a sufficient aisle for the public, as well as the waiters, to negotiate. This could be a gigantic problem. I made my measurements and then headed out to check the width of the booth of practically every restaurant in town. You will be glad to know that in the town of Brownwood, Texas, the restaurant booth width is forty-two inches wide. To be comfortable with the width and have a legal aisle, I could go with nothing wider than thirty-eight inches for the booths.

Now I had to find out how the difference of four inches narrower for our booths would sit with city hall and the state requirements for the width of restaurant booths. I sat down with the ordinance guru for the city. I asked the question and received an enlightened answer of, "I don't know; I'll look it up and get back with you."

I advised him, as he sat there with a book in his hand, that this was "not a satisfactory answer. I will sit here while you look it up now." I sat back, crossed my legs, folded my arms across my chest, and leaned back.

He glared at me and began studying the book. After about half an hour, I could see him begin to sweat. I maintained my position as he continued to sweat and search. Finally, after only an hour and a half, he said, "I think I found it. A two-person restaurant booth shall be a minimum of forty-two inches. You can't have your booths less than forty-two inches."

It really irked me that he was smiling as he said it. So I said, "Good, that means our booths are 'super singles.' What is the maximum width for a single-person booth?"

The smile disappeared as he indicated that it would be in the same section. It turned out that there was no maximum for a single-person booth, and Joe was none too happy reporting that to me.

I thanked him and advised him that we would not have any two-person booths in the diner; they would all be super single seats. If two people decided to share one side of the super single, that's their business.

Since he was so down by having to give me good news that he thought was bad news, I decided to really make his day. "Joe, you have been a great help today by solving two problems for me."

He asked, "What was the second problem?"

"The fire marshal has been arguing with me over the number of seats allowed in the diner. Now with super single booths, we will be well below his determined maximum, so he'll be happy, I'm happy, and since you solved the problems, you're happy. Thank you again."

Our to-do list was getting shorter every day, but there remained a lot to do. We needed to acquire a jukebox capable of playing forty-five records, after all, this was a '50s diner, and a sound system that allowed the jukebox and portable microphone to be heard comfortably throughout the diner. We also needed to finish off the arch between the car and the kitchen, complete the bathrooms with full-length cut-outs of James Dean and Marilyn Monroe, install all the appliances and the dishwasher, and procure a handicapped lift. There were quite a few steps to get up to the door.

Methodically over the next month, all the work was completed and it was time to have the diner inspected by the county health inspector. I had been forewarned that she had never approved a new restaurant on the first inspection.

We were no different, as the inspector went from station to station in the diner without saying anything. When she finished I received her written report and a verbal explanation as well as a physical demonstration of one item.

I had not had an opportunity to read the report when she began to relay her opinions and instructions. She raved about the amount of stainless steel in the building, and this became the overriding theme of her entire inspection. When she went on and on about the generous use of stainless steel, I knew that her corrections to be made before, what she called her final inspection, would not be significant.

She required that we put in a sink next to the cooking area, to wash hands, and a childproof screen over the large exhaust fan in the smoking area. She asked me when she should schedule her final inspection prior to the opening of "A Classic Car Diner."

I suggested that a week from that day would be perfect. She seemed somewhat startled and responded, "It shouldn't take that long to do those couple of things."

I said, "You are right, but I want enough time to be sure that we get everything totally completed in a top-notch way."

She smiled, shook my hand, and said, "Next week then at the same time."

When she came the following week, she approved everything and handed me my certificate that she had made out before she had left her office. We were able to maintain an outstanding relationship with her from that day forward.

Oh yeah, in one window facing the parking lot was the obligatory neon sign in every '50s diner: EATS.

We opened to a full house with people waiting to get in. That crowd outside was entertained by the speakers that we had mounted on the side of the diner entrance. From late afternoon until well after eleven o'clock, our staff never let up. As the food was served, the jukebox went non-stop. The jukebox was for the ambiance and we didn't want it to sit idle, so we had it set for three plays for a quarter. I would use my experience as a disc jockey and fill any dead spots with stories, jokes, and really bad singing. The people loved it.

I had a pretty hefty debt against the diner and figured that it would take a couple of years to pay it off, but I decided to put all our earnings back into the diner by way of paying off the debt as soon as possible. Beth and I didn't take a dime and in a little over three months, the business was free and clear. Because we had the mobile home parks' income, I had been using some of that money to pay on the diner debt as the diner was under construction. The result was that the amortization on the diner debt was well on its way to being paid when we opened the doors.

It wasn't very long after we opened the diner that we started discussing retirement. We had accrued a lot of property and figured that we could begin selling off some of it and when we decided to make the move, we wouldn't have too much left to get rid of.

We took inventory to determine just where we were. We had three mobile home parks, seventy-five mobile homes, three vacation or possibly retirement properties, the tearoom, and the diner.

The sixty-four-dollar question was, "How long will it take us to sell our twenty-year business growth?"

This reversal in active searching and adding to our inventory to liquidating might take as long to complete as was the journey getting to this point. As we began planning, it was obvious to me that we should begin eliminating the non-money properties first and that which we depend on for our livelihood would be last. I also believed that the most profitable, being the higher prices, would be the most difficult to liberate us from.

As properties were sold, the proceeds were put into our retirement account that at this moment was very small. We embarked on a program that would take eight years to complete.

**Classic Car Diner
1995**

Chapter 23

THE TELEPHONE CALL: ANALYSIS AND CONCLUSION

I had thought that the ESPN money thing was behind me, and I began moving on with my life. Beth and I were raising our son and had a few businesses that were doing okay when our revelry was disrupted by a call from Dad.

He was furious with me because I had the temerity to file a suit against Bill and didn't just give him all the money he wanted. I explained that Bill, through his attorney, had threatened suing me and I made a defensive move because it wasn't logical that I would go to Florida to defend myself against a frivolous lawsuit.

If we were going to go to court, it made more sense to me to have the situation resolve itself here in Texas. That was what it was all about, except for the fact that Bill didn't dare go to court anywhere because of the documentation I had. When he finally realized that he had gone too far and I was finally going to stand up to him, he backed down.

Dad yelled into the phone, "Where in the world did you get that 'crackpot lawyer?'"

I answered that my "crackpot lawyer" was one of the top attorneys in the country and he did a pretty good job; it was Bill and his crackpot lawyer who backed down and sought our cooperation in settling out of court. I pointed out to him that Bill took way too much money from him, and especially Sis, and I wasn't going to let him take any more from me.

He wasn't having any of it and continued to berate me unabated for about five minutes. I knew that arguing with him further would be a waste of time, so I didn't. He finally ran out of steam and concluded the conversation.

As in the past, I had learned when to speak up and when to shut up when Dad was climbing my frame up one side and down the other. However, I really thought that with the passage of time, he had mellowed. He proved me wrong again. Amazingly, after all these years, in Dad's eyes, Bill was honest, truthful, ethical, and had never been wrong. I, on the other hand, was lazy, difficult, not very smart, a liar, untrustworthy, lacked any sense of honesty or integrity, and had never been right.

After an evening of fretting about that call, I couldn't help thinking those old thoughts of not belonging in the family.

The following morning I buried my thoughts in work. I have always enjoyed working since I pushed that concession cart at the drive-in theater before I was sixteen years old.

It bothered me when I allowed myself to think about my family. Sis didn't communicate with anyone, Bill was always angry and I can't budge either one. I would do anything to have a close family and I can't understand why we don't.

A couple of months of not hearing anything from Dad and I was thinking that he may never get in touch with me again. If he did, I knew it would be by phone. We had been in Texas for over five years and he had never considered making the trip south, even though I make sure I get to Illinois once or twice a year to visit with him and take him some place he normally wouldn't go. Once a year I would take him to the new White Sox Park to see a ball game. I took him to see his brother Arnold one year when he told me that he hadn't seen his brother in years.

It always seemed like I was a neighbor that had come by to do something for him. I'm sure a neighbor would at least get a thank you from him. I'd have liked to hear something like that just once.

I was generally in a state of confusion about how family members should act with one another, and why was I so different?

Then it came out of the blue, the reason I felt that I didn't belong and couldn't do anything right in the eyes of my family.

THE TELEPHONE CALL: ANALYSIS AND CONCLUSION

A less than fifteen second telephone call that shook me to my boots and caused me to look at everything differently.

The phone rang while I was sitting at my desk one evening.

"Hello."

"Don, this is Dad, "*You were a mistake when you were born, and you are still a mistake.*" Click. He hung up.

I just sat there holding the phone in my hand and staring at it for how long I don't know.

Beth asked from another room, "Who called?"

"Dad."

Walking toward my desk, she asked, "What did he want? You weren't on the phone very long."

I looked at her and couldn't say anything. Then I began to cry, and I couldn't stop. She came over and gave me a hug. I could tell that she was concerned, but every time I tried to tell her what had just happened, my throat would constrict and the tears kept coming. Finely, I picked up a pen and wrote what Dad had said, even though I couldn't see the paper.

Beth left me alone to deal with my emotions. Slowly, I began to get things under control. I remained at my desk for a long time until I felt like I could talk with her without crying so I could reassure Beth that everything was going to be all right.

Feeling weak and really hungry, I walked into the living room and said, "I'm hungry." I knew that Beth would recognize that statement as a sign that I was beginning to get things sorted out in my head.

I received a big smile in return and she asked, "What can I fix you?"

"A fried egg sandwich with onion." That was my number two favorite comfort food. Number one comfort food, oatmeal, was never eaten this late at night.

As Beth was cooking the eggs, the aroma began to soothe the hurt and anger that I was feeling. As I sat down to eat my sandwich with a glass of milk, I was feeling good enough to talk, but not about the phone call. We talked about nothing in particular and I didn't mention the phone call for a couple of days, but I did do a lot of thinking about it.

I came to the realization that I was selected by Dad, probably before my birth or shortly after my birth when I wasn't a girl, that I would pay for his two big mistakes in life. The first mistake died shortly after her birth on May 26, 1931, and on September 2 1937, I, the second mistake, lived. For that mistake, I would pay the price.

Subliminally, I knew I didn't belong as a part of this family. I didn't know why, but it was always there. From my earliest memories, I couldn't understand why I didn't fit, but I knew I didn't. For one thing I couldn't do anything right no matter how hard I tried.

The phone call seemed to put my entire life into perspective.

The first thing I had to deal with and understand was that none of this was about me. I, as a unique individual, just happened to be there when I was born. My life and the way I was raised was all about Dad's mistake.

Although I had no clue about what was happening as I grew up and began to be recognized, first for my drawing and then later for my writing, it had to be minimalized and discredited.

I realized after the phone call that as long as Dad had the opportunity to control my actions and thinking, I must never eclipse Bill in anything. That got me to thinking about my relationship with Bill.

Although we were taught to look up to and try to emulate Bill, I thought that I really didn't buy into that. Now as I think back, I was a real dunderhead.

I was indoctrinated throughout my life to follow far behind Bill and do nothing that might take the spotlight from him. I was meant to service and honor Bill and never question him. He was the perfect son who never lied, cheated, or took advantage of anyone.

Bob, in a less intense way, was expected to do the same. With Bob's laid-back approach to life, he could easily follow that path.

When Sis was born two and half years after me, she fell right in line and worshiped Bill.

I didn't buy into that concept, even though I didn't know it existed. I just couldn't get any of this through my thick skull. As a result I was always in trouble at home. If Bob threw a ball five feet over my head

THE TELEPHONE CALL: ANALYSIS AND CONCLUSION

and it broke a window, it was my fault because I should have caught it. If I threw a ball five feet over Bob's head and he couldn't reach it, it was my fault for throwing the ball over his head. It didn't make sense to me, but that was the way it was.

After the phone call, I knew that the two most powerful males in my life were Dad and Bill and neither had my best interest at heart. Dad was easy to figure out, simply by the volume of my misdeeds, both real and imagined. The most difficult to understand were accomplishments like making the academic honor roll four consecutive semesters in high school, being elected to a club office and elected as the "Most Obliging Boy" in our senior class, and, of course, being a part of our city championship ROTC Picked Platoon. All of which, as Dad had said, "Bill didn't do that!"

To find a way of quantifying Bill's overall impact on my life was much more difficult to determine. I finally decided that the best way was to follow the pattern of his yelling at me, and if something of a different context should present itself, I would evaluate it.

The number of times that Bill used this tactic was not significant, but their impact was.

In the summer of 1950, Bill came home after a baseball game that we did not attend and in a manner of casual conversation, announced that a scout from the Detroit Tigers had offered him a contract to play professional baseball. He would be assigned to a Class D team. Dad became quite excited, but Bill calmed him down with a statement that he had turned them down.

He couldn't get a military deferment playing baseball and he could get one by going to college. So college it would be for Bill.

The fact that he had turned them down kind of went over my head, but the fact that they would offer Bill a contract amazed me. At the first opportunity during the conversation, I asked, "Why would the Tigers want a player that can't hit a lick?"

He responded that they told him they could teach him that. Then he went off on me about not knowing anything about baseball and I should not be spouting off about things that I didn't know anything

313

about. The minutes-long diatribe was delivered in a loud and angry voice.

Now, I was quite taken aback by his attitude and very much surprised by it. I was smart enough to know that his outburst was not normal, and I interpreted that to mean he was probably lying through his teeth. To myself, I imagined the instructions that the head scout of every major league team gave to their scouts around the country. "Go out and find seventeen-year-old kids that have good speed, a strong throwing arm, and can't hit a lick because we can teach them that."

We had seen enough of Bill's American Legion games, and Bob and I got to go to one of his high school practices, and even participated, to know Bill's strengths and weaknesses. At the practice, Bob went to the outfield and I into the infield because I wanted to get the feel of it with those older guys. My fondest memory of that practice was that one of the batters hit the highest pop fly in the infield that I had ever seen. I called for it and waited and waited for it to come down. Their first baseman was standing next to me when I caught the ball and said something to me that was complimentary. I only hoped that someday I could be as good as he was. He also encouraged me on some ground balls. That was a fun day.

Not quite a year later, I was in eighth grade and the family drove down to DePauw University to see Bill. I had assumed that we would take in a game with Bill playing baseball. He really was a good third baseman, and I respected that.

When we arrived and it became obvious that we weren't going to a game, I asked Bill, "When do you play baseball?"

The Tigers thing of the previous year was child's play compared to the longer and more vociferous lecture I got this time. The particular part that stuck in my head was about the fact that sometimes you have to put things like baseball behind you and move on. He then got specific about me forgetting baseball. I just stood there and took it as the rest of the family witnessed my being berated in silence.

When he finished, I hung my head to show proper shame and thought to myself, "He didn't make the team."

THE TELEPHONE CALL: ANALYSIS AND CONCLUSION

In the ensuing years, I never again brought up baseball and college in the same sentence with Bill. I did, without fail, go immediately to the baseball team's picture in the DePauw yearbook every year when Bill brought it home in the spring.

Either Bill did not play college baseball, or for some inexplicable reason, he was called away by someone for some reason each and every year when the baseball picture was taken for the yearbook.

I was amazed that anyone with any intelligence would tell a boy in the eighth grade to forget about baseball. That is so illogical that it is mind-boggling.

I didn't see much of Bill after his junior year in college, but one game day in the fall of 1954, he showed up for one of my football games. As we finished the pregame warm-ups, I saw him leaving the stadium. I guess he just came by to see if I really was on the team. He did the same thing in 1955 when he was in the Chicago area before his wedding. He stayed until I batted in the bottom of the first. I was hitting in the third spot in the batting order, which is traditionally where a team's strongest or best hitter was placed. I hit a fly ball to the right fielder and as I was heading for the bench, I saw him leaving the park.

I can only assume that he didn't get much joy out of seeing me be successful. Batting third in the lineup would be indicative of that.

In October of 1956, Bill contacted the administrative office at Eastern Illinois University to have them get a message to me. He was on his way to New Jersey after being released from the Air Force and was visiting with a friend in Champaign-Urbana and if I wanted to see him, he would be there for a certain period of time. He left an address, if I was interested.

When I received the message, I picked up Beth and we headed north about forty miles.

There was no rationale other than he was there along with Mickey and my first nephew, Scott. When we arrived I introduced Beth to everyone and then Bill elucidated on the superiority of softball over baseball and really seemed to enjoy relaying his "All Star" status as a catcher at Eglin Air Force Base. That was the only time, other than

Bob's funeral, that I had seen Bill since his wedding until that ill-fated debacle in 1961 discussed earlier in this book (see Chapter 15). I once again was admonished to forget baseball. Surprisingly, I played off and on through 1970.

The next loud, but short and extremely important outburst came on September 14, 1979. Using his position as CEO, he had demanded that I take off work early for an important family meeting in Chicago.

If I had only known about that September 9 breakfast meeting with Bill, Stu Evey, and Chet Simmons, my life would not have gotten as complicated as it was about to.

Beginning in October through the middle of January 1981, I fielded consistent calls from Bill advising me that my being fired by ESPN was eminent, followed with a call advising me that he had stepped in and saved my job.

The day before Ron Newman, our Connecticut leader of affiliate relations, was fired, he called and advised me that I would be fired the next day.

I immediately called Bill and he assured me that he had taken control of the situation and my job was safe for the time being. As time passed I would get signals from Chet that I was respected and in good stead, such as the time he dropped me a handwritten note in April of 1980 letting me know that I could call on him if he could assist me in any way.

While all this was swirling around me, in early August 1980, I was called by the Iowa state cable convention organizers and asked to be their keynote speaker at the upcoming convention. In mid-September this would become the backdrop for Bill's highest decibel, ugliest, nastiest, and longest, most outlandish rant of all time.

Within a couple of weeks, out of the blue, Bill called and announced that he wanted to tell me before I heard it from someone else. He was leaving ESPN effective immediately.

There was no rancor in his voice, just kind of matter-of-fact, without any emotion, followed with, "There are other things I want to do." I didn't know what to say, so I just wished him good luck.

THE TELEPHONE CALL: ANALYSIS AND CONCLUSION

Just like that, I was the last of the Rasmussen clan still working at the network.

In June of 2008 while visiting with Stu and his lovely wife Mary, I learned that for all practical purposes, I had been the last Rasmussen working at ESPN since September 9, 1979.

In late 1980 I received a call from Max Gardner, the Getty lawyer, asking me if I would consider moving to Bristol. I pointed out that the sale of my house would have to happen before I could afford to move anywhere. He said that would not be a problem, Getty would buy my house.

I asked for a couple of days to think about it, and Max said he would get back to me. After all this time, being dumber than a brick, I called Bill for advice.

He told me that this offer was part of their plan to harm the Rasmussens as much as possible. "When they get you out here, they will fire you and leave you in a mess," he said.

For whatever reason, I never heard from Max again.

In early January of 1981, I got word that ESPN had gone over the six million subscriber mark—by how much I didn't know.

Things were happening rapidly, giving me little time to think. Bill called and told me the time was right for me to resign from ESPN. "Simmons will fire you within two weeks. I have a couple of openings at Enterprise Radio, and I will pay you a thousand dollars a month more than ESPN is paying you, but I can't hold the job very long."

What to do?

That base of childhood indoctrination reared its ugly head again, and I submitted my resignation to ESPN. Even though I loved my job, deep down in my gut, a job, money, and virtually everything else in life came in behind that need to be accepted by Dad and Bill. It was subliminal and irrational, but it must be served until the evidence is so substantial that no amount of denial can cover the lifelong meanness that has been imposed and that I submitted to.

After working for just a couple of months at Enterprise Radio, it became evident that the level of naivety regarding the industry was extremely high.

The knowledge and effort put forth by Bill and Scott on the programming was above and beyond excellent. The administration and marketing were far below. Virtually within two months, I knew that I was in over my head, and my attempts to get more knowledge were rebuked; I believe they were because it didn't exist within the framework of the network.

In May of 1981, I received a pink slip in the mail, out of the blue. I immediately called Enterprise, since I thought it inappropriate to be treated in this manner. Bill refused to take my calls. I considered the manner of my demise at ER to be over-the-top rude, if not cowardly.

ANALYSIS AND CONCLUSION

That feeling of not belonging is such a deep-seated feeling that all logic, common sense, intellectual knowledge, and pure gut instinct go out the window when the most remote "kinda maybe" opportunity to change the situation raises its ugly head.

Even after the "phone call," I continued to support Dad in any way possible. In 1998 Dad was ninety years old. I talked to my kids and we decided to throw a big birthday party for him. I rented a banquet room, Edie provided the large cake and balloons, and Alene made a fantastic memory book for Dad. We began a campaign to invite everyone in the family that we could contact, including the entire Oak Lawn Masonic Lodge. I personally called Bill to, number one, see if he would like to participate financially, and number two, request his attendance. He declined both, as he was too busy.

On the day of the event, here he comes with his wife. I had to have the head table rearranged and, of course, ask him to participate in saying a few words during the program. As the oldest I asked him to speak first.

I had hired a photographer, and he took a ton of pictures. ESPN, through the good graces of Rosa Gatti, provided Dad with a banner signed by several announcers, wishing him a happy ninetieth birthday, along with additional memorabilia.

All in all it was a great party. Afterward, when I was alone with Dad, he began to cry. I asked, "What's wrong?"

He said, "Nothing, this is the first birthday party I have ever had."

I felt good.

I had those good feelings rocked a couple of weeks later when Dad called. "I just talked with Bill and I mentioned that the birthday party had to have cost a lot of money. He told me not to worry about it, 'he took care of everything.' Why do you have to lie all the time?"

"Dad, will you ever learn? Bill is the liar."

"Bill would never lie about anything."

Dad lived until just before his ninety-fifth, birthday, dying on December 27, 2002, which was also my daughter Edie's thirty-eighth birthday.

Right after the first of the year, Bill called me to discuss Dad's will and in the process, advised me that he had declared bankruptcy.

I couldn't imagine how he could have blown the millions of dollars he "maneuvered" away from Dad, Sis, and I, plus his own, but apparently he did. I know "maneuvered" is not the right word, but even today I cannot bring myself to use what I know is the proper word.

Over a period of time, he continued to call, asking me to do little things for him regarding his bankruptcy, which I was happy to do, hoping that maybe we could begin to develop a relationship. I should have known better.

In 2004 I was invited to the twenty-fifth ESPN anniversary party. I was well received and enjoyed myself immensely.

I had the opportunity to get reacquainted with Stu and talked with Bill and Scott, as well as Mickey. I also met Laura, the lovely and seemingly vivacious wife of Scott, who turned to Scott and said, "I didn't know you had an uncle!"

Neither Scott nor Bill seemed pleased to see me and five years later, Bill called after the thirtieth anniversary to advise me that he had been there and to let me know that he had "made arrangements for me to be invited to the fiftieth in 2029." He followed this with the biggest horse-laugh I ever heard come from his mouth.

I guess that now, in my mid-seventies, with Dad gone and Bill released from any and all concerns of Dad finding out what Bill is really like, Bill can be more forward in his out and out hatred of me. But why? Why the hatred?

ANALYSIS AND CONCLUSION

I finally understood, that from Dad, it wasn't about me as much as it was about the fact that I was born.

From Bill it was all about me. I was sickly, small, and not very bright. I could easily be dominated. Since he was five years older, by the time I started school, he could count on his position to keep me in line. But, I was always questioning. I don't guess that he liked that much.

When he tried sports, he failed at football, but found a slot as a third baseman that he was darn good at for a few years. According to his statements in a book on ESPN, he always considered himself an athlete. That's good, I never considered myself an athlete, I just was. Making up stories was easy for him.

I didn't make up stories; I learned to be honest. That way you don't have to remember so much. Bill even told me in a derisive way, "You're too honest for your own good."

He followed Dad's lead in keeping me out of professional baseball. I'm not positive whether this was intentional or just a side bar, but with the dressing down I got in 1961 when I arrived in New Jersey, I'm inclined to lean toward intentional.

The constant phone calls I got from him after he had been defrocked by Stu Evey on September 9, 1979 were designed for no other purpose than to get me to stay in a constant state of turmoil. The only purpose could have been to make me ineffective. It didn't work.

Something as simple as me getting elected to a club office in high school showed I had a level of popularity and caused consternation for Dad, and if Bill heard of it, I'm sure for him also. The same could have been said of me being elected the "Most Obliging Boy." That designation for our senior class was a most-appreciated honor because it recognized my penchant for helping others.

Bill, on a couple of occasions, referred to me as a "survivor." This is significant because I survived both him and Dad and their attempts to keep me down.

With the roller coaster ride I lived through, I think that the most important thing I have attained in this life is being, "JUST A GUY."

THE WRAP-UP

Chapter 24

MY ROLLER COASTER HEALTH

My health journey through life's ups and downs as a child, through adolescence, all those working years, and slipping into old age has been somewhat similar to the psychological and emotional roller coaster that I so closely identified my whole being with.

Having been born the third of three boys and the fourth child of five to William A, Rasmussen and Gertrude A. (O'Connor) Rasmussen on September 2, 1937, less than a year after the birth of my brother Bob, set me up for a struggle to gain and retain good health. I didn't know why, I just knew that I was smaller and not as strong as my playmates. I don't know when I became aware, but for as long as I can remember, I was sick and didn't go to school as much as I should have in first and second grade. The one specific comment that I overheard Dr. Schusler tell Dad came after he gave me a good bill of health after getting over my fifth bout of pneumonia. He told him, in effect, "If Don ever catches pneumonia again, he probably won't survive." I really wished that I hadn't heard that.

It was during this time that I developed tonsillitis. The hospital was pretty scary with all these big people walking around wearing white clothes. The best part of having my tonsils taken out was all the ice cream I got to eat when it was over. An older lady, maybe sixteen or so, brought me all the ice cream I wanted, and she wore a different color dress than the much older nurses. It was light blue. With everything considered, I really did not like the hospital.

I was treated, for years, to stories from my parents about some of my diseases, which included virtually every childhood disease known to mankind and I got them all harder than my brothers. I vaguely remember whooping cough, which was horrible. I remember being told that I did not like the doctor when he came to the house. When he came I knew that I was going to get a shot.

In third grade I only missed four and a half days of school due to illness the entire school year. Going into third grade, I knew things were going to be tough since Mom made it known to me on many occasions that she had baby-sat Miss Haleas when she was a child. One of the most exciting things that happened during the school year was a unit Miss Haleas taught on hygiene.

From fourth through eighth grades, I missed no days of school, and I noticed that I had no severe setbacks. In the eighth grade, I did have one setback that was physical, not due to illness.

The guys interested in baseball were setting up a baseball field, and we couldn't find anything to use for first base that was flat, so we used a cinder block.

The first game we played on the field, I was running out a ground ball and could see that it was going to be close at first base, so I turned on the afterburners to beat the throw. My left foot didn't make it to the top of the cinder block. Although I was safe, I fell across the base and felt the toe of my shoe hit my shin. I thought I had broken my foot, but fortunately it was only a severe sprain with pulled ligaments. That was the good news, the bad news was that I couldn't walk for a month and had to keep putting heat on the ankle alternating with ice. Even after I was able to walk, it seemed forever before I could run.

It was in eighth grade that I got my first feeling that I was worth something. Our teacher, Mr. Spizzirri, really took me under his wing and literally made me want to do well and make him proud of me. He really set me up mentally for high school.

In high school I did pretty good health wise, except in my freshman and junior years. As a freshman I had to get glasses. From that point on, which was the beginning of my freshman year through the end of my sophomore year, I felt good and was gaining confidence.

Then in the spring of my sophomore year, I began having pain in my right side. When it seemed to me that it would not go away, I told Dad about it. He poked around awhile and then announced that it looked like I had a bad appendix.

All was well and I played most of our games; my highlight of the summer was when I broke up a no-hitter.

By the time September came, I told Dad that I had been pushing my luck on this appendix thing and we needed to get the doctor to get the removal going.

Dad said, "Not so fast. You iced it from April until now, you can ice it until Christmas break so you don't miss much school."

That was it. I continued to ice my side until the middle of December when I went into the hospital and had the appendix removed. It wasn't so bad, and I had this real pretty nurse's aide that took pretty good care of me. There was something about those freckles.

I didn't miss any school, but when I returned to school in January, I had doctor's orders to wear wool trousers for more than two weeks because the doctor was concerned that I might get an infection due to the cold weather.

In early February of 1955, I was on a Valentine's Day dance committee that met one evening at one of the girls' homes. For some unknown reason, Dad had told me to be in front of the drug store at the corner on Fifty-Ninth and Kedzie at nine o'clock and he would pick me up.

We had freezing weather that night, so I waited inside the drug store until he closed at nine. At that time the owner apologized to me for having me wait for Dad in the cold as he locked his door. I waited and waited and tried to keep as warm as possible as ten o'clock passed, then eleven. By now rubbing my hands together and putting them under my arm pits had no effect in trying to stay warm. At close to eleven thirty, Dad pulled up and I got in the car. He said nothing as we drove home.

As I slowly began to get warm, I felt a tingling in my left ear. By the time we arrived home, the ear was swelling and becoming discolored. Exhausted, I fell asleep and when I got up the next morning, the ear was burning. I looked in the mirror at a Dumbo-like gray ear.

I was afraid that it might fall off. Mom didn't know what to do and since I had a lot to do to get ready for the dance that night, I ignored the appearance of the ear and went to school.

I would occasionally touch the ear throughout the day and one time I noticed that it felt different than it had earlier. I hustled to the bathroom and observed that a piece of gray, dead skin had fallen off. As I touched the ear and rubbed it, about one-sixteenth of an inch of thick, gray matter came loose. Underneath I was left with a fire-engine-red ear lobe.

I realized at that moment that I had a frostbitten ear from my experience the night before. In a short period of time, all the gray fell off and a bright red ear became normal. Nothing was ever said at home about my long wait or the frostbite, but from that time to the present day, exposure to extreme winter weather causes the left ear to burn.

After that all went well health wise until the fall of 1955 when I started college at Northern Illinois University. With baseball out of the picture, I started college and decided to play football. As a new student, we were given a series of shots to prevent various infections. One of those was a tetanus shot and a booster. When I started football, I received another tetanus shot. A couple weeks into our training, I tore my medial collateral ligament. Another tetanus shot and a visit with a surgeon. He gave me two options, since he determined that I had a three-quarter tear. I could quit football and time would heal the ligament tear, or I could have an operation. Since I didn't have a passion for football, I chose time.

I was adrift, so I left school and decided to get a full-time job. Since I made good money as a part-time worker in high school, I expected to find a good-paying job. That didn't happen, so I went back to school and worked part time.

When I enrolled at Eastern Illinois University, I received another tetanus shot and booster. I then met Beth and got married. I left school and joined the Air Force. Another tetanus and booster. After I left basic training and started my training in judo to become an instructor training B47 flight crews in hand-to-hand combat, I got another tetanus shot.

MY ROLLER COASTER HEALTH

From September 1955 through April of 1957, I had been injected with eight tetanus shots plus boosters. Once I put my military obligation behind me, I determined that I had had enough tetanus shots in me to last a lifetime and have not had one since.

While in the Air Force, on a cool, humid Louisiana evening, it hit me like a ton of bricks that I would never play professional baseball. I became depressed and lost control of my emotions. All that worked out pretty well, as I talked with a doctor that night and did not miss any work.

Less than a year later, I was sent to Thule, Greenland. The only physical problem I had while I lived north of the Arctic Circle was a broken hand while training for the All Air Force Handball Championship. Needless to say, with a cast on my arm from the elbow to my knuckles, I didn't go to the tournament. I didn't give up easily; I played a game with the cast on but simply couldn't control the ball and the cast caused me to be able to really blister that handball, making it practically impossible to return. Even with control, I wouldn't be able to compete.

After that I remained pretty healthy until the Utah State Baseball Championship in 1963 when I ended up with a broken leg, which we found out about the day after the game. I had been hit with a pitch flush on my left tibia (the shinbone). I ran to first base, stole second, and then scored the only run of the game as I was brought home by a single.

The next year I broke two bones in my left hand. Foam rubber on the handle of my bat kept me playing without missing a game.

In 1969, while under stress, I had my heart skip a beat or two and I ended up flat on my back in my office. Another trip to the hospital showed my heartbeat all over the place. Late in the afternoon, I was laying there in bed and having negative thoughts when the doctor came in to look at another EKG that had just been taken.

He looked rather stern when he came in. As he looked at the chart in front of him, he began to smile and asked me how I felt.

I said, "Fine."

He actually laughed and directed me to get dressed if I didn't want to wear a hospital gown home. As I was getting dressed, he stayed and gave me instructions to take it easy for a few days. I could work half-days and see how it went. He told me that they initially thought I was going to be involved with this problem for a long time, but through the day the heart slowly got back into rhythm on its own. I have not had a serious heart problem since.

In the next couple of years, it seemed that I had physical problems one after another, including carbon monoxide poisoning, pneumonia, ulcers, leaky heart valve, and I became over weight.

The carbon monoxide poisoning landed me in the hospital for one day, but left me with the most ferocious headaches I had ever experienced. When I talked to the doctor about them, he told me that I would have those for the rest of my life. They began to fall into a pattern of one every seven to ten days. They always hit me at night, and I just wanted to die and get it over with. I would wake Beth up when I moaned, and she knew what it was and what to do for me. I literally couldn't move without intensifying the pain. She would get up and get an ice-cold towel and throw it over my face and head. Within half an hour to an hour, it would begin to subside. This went on for nine years before we solved the problem and I have not had that kind of a headache since.

In April of 1972, I came down with pneumonia. I fought it as long as I could and then gave up and was admitted to the hospital. I received treatment for five days and was released. Well, for the first time in months, I was well rested. That was a good thing, because when I arrived home, the clouds were ominous and threatening.

By nine o'clock, the winds were howling, and then deadly silent, followed by a roar like none I had ever heard before. The house shook, and I heard cracking and breaking.

When the silence had come, Beth and I got the girls out of bed and into the basement. After everything seemed to calm down, I went upstairs and with flashlight in hand, walked outside. Thank God I had the flashlight, since the back porch was gone. I checked the area and all looked fine, except for a lot of debris scattered about.

After checking everything out, I was getting ready for work when I began having severe abdominal pain. By early afternoon it was sufficiently bad enough that I went back to the hospital and was checked in. Tests showed that I had a bleeding ulcer.

After a couple of days of treatment, I was released with a packet of dietary instructions. Having complete faith in the doctors, I followed the directions to a tee. After a month I had ballooned from a 170 pounds to 205 pounds. I really felt the extra weight that caused me to be sluggish and uncomfortable. I contacted the doctor and he said that it was either one or the other. For the ulcer to heal, I had to eat those foods designed to coat the ulcer. It made me wonder about doctors.

Here I was at thirty-four years of age with regular debilitating headaches, a malfunctioning heart valve, bleeding ulcers, and depression building. I was fighting all this while working as a school administrator.

A little over two years later the ulcer started bleeding again while I was attending a superintendents meeting. I knew I was in trouble so I got up and left the meeting and drove to the hospital in Watseka, Illinois. I parked my car and went into the emergency room. I must have looked worse than I felt, which wasn't good. All hell broke out as soon as I entered and before I knew what was up, two attractive young ladies met me and guided me into an examination room and a doctor was there waiting for us. I had never seen such efficiency in any medical facility. I was immediately wheeled down to the x-ray room. On the way I got a shot of something (I was in no condition discuss what they were putting into my body) and by the time they finished the x-rays, I was feeling no pain.

Without knowing what or why, I was booked into a room for the night. I must have been drugged up, and I inquired of one of the nurses as to what was going on. I felt good enough to go home. The registrar came into the room and took my insurance information and said that I might be there for a few days.

The next day I met with a doctor who told me that the bleeding had stopped overnight and I could go home; however, I must go on and stay on an ulcer diet. It was horrible, but I agreed. This diet did nothing for the ulcer and made me fatter.

I had no energy, but I got through the school year. The school board relieved me of my duties. That is a nice way of saying I was fired.

It became apparent that I had additional problems that I had not come to grips with. I was extremely depressed and didn't see any way out of the cycle of physical and mental problems.

"The Fat Guy"
Don 1974 at 205 pounds

While Beth taught school in Villa Grove, I started a country music concert promotion program with the intent of providing Nashville country music acts with local sponsorship. Although it provided me with a diversion, it didn't provide much income. After a couple of months of struggling to get it off the ground, I realized that I didn't have the business background to make a go of it.

I also did a show with Porter Wagoner and Dolly Parton. They were terrific people to work with. I especially enjoyed the time I had visiting with Dolly. She was the happiest, most upbeat positive person I believe that I had ever met.

While I was working on this project, I met a young man in a coffee shop and as we talked, He learned of my physical problems, simply because he asked. When he realized I had serious difficulties, he suggested that I meet a friend of his that could help me return to good health.

The next day at the same coffee shop, I met Herb Price, a master coordinator with Shaklee Corporation. I had never heard of it, but after he offered me a possibility of regaining my health with a guarantee that if I used Shaklee products for one month and didn't feel better in some way that I could tell, with me being the only judge, he would give me a full refund. I knew that Beth would think I was a little crazy, maybe a whole lot crazy, for buying these products when we didn't have much money. I was desperate and willing to try anything and Dr. Shaklee's story of how he overcame cancer with the use of natural foods that led him to develop these natural products, I just had to try them.

I bought just the basic program plus a couple of additional supplements that during our discussion I had deemed would be beneficial—if they worked.

From the depths of depression, within two weeks, I was seeing positive signs in my outlook and energy levels. To make a long story short, within a month and a half, the headaches that doctors said I would have the rest of my life were gone. I started out weighing 205 pounds, and I was down to a 168 pounds without dieting. It was far more than I could have hoped for.

I did two things that I thought I would never do again. First I began looking for a school administrator's job, and second I began talking to people about what Shaklee products was doing for me. It wasn't long before I was lined up to start interviewing for jobs, and I also began selling more product than I thought was possible.

After being interviewed by the superintendent of schools at District 50 just outside of East Peoria, I received a call to come back for a second interview with the board of education. After that interview I was asked to hang around while the board met in executive session. I left the Peoria area with a signed contract in hand for a greater income than I had ever had in education or radio before.

The one stipulation that the contract required was that I have a complete physical examination, paid for by the school board. I was feeling so good that I wasn't concerned about that requirement. The school board selected a doctor in Washington, just east of the school district. He did a complete physical over two days and specifically looked at those areas where I had problems. The results were that I had an ulcer, but it was all pink and "pretty" (his word), there was no leaking heart valve, and everything else looked good.

My physical and related emotional and mental problems seemed to be in the past.

As I started working in the fall of 1975, I entered a period of good health that would extend until the mid-eighties when most of my health problems were self-inflicted. The most serious difficulties occurred after we bought our second mobile home park in Brownwood, Texas.

Shortly after buying the second mobile home park, I was introduced to over two hundred fire ants as you read about in our "Jobs" section of this book. It is mentioned here just to put it into context regarding my health roller coaster.

In 1994 we built a diner out of a stainless-steel railroad car and while gutting it in preparation for construction of the interior, I loaded our flatbed trailer with serious amounts of material that could be sold to a tank car company in San Angelo, Texas. I backed the trailer into our hanger, behind our house. I didn't realize that the concrete floor had been glazed and when I loosened the hitch from the ball on the back of my truck, the trailer rolled backward and I couldn't let go soon enough. I tore several muscles in my back, but not before they dislodged several vertebra in my spine. Fortunately the trailer didn't roll very far and no damage was done to the load or anything in the hanger. I, however, was in a world of hurt.

I yelled for Beth, but had no voice. Nothing to do but walk to the house. I couldn't walk, only shuffle. So I slowly shuffled to the house in a bent over position four to six inches at a time. It took me better than twenty minutes to get to the back door, which would normally be no more than a one or two minute walk. Beth was working in the kitchen and when she saw me, she dropped everything and came to help me.

Without even calling our chiropractor, she got me into the car and to his office in record time. Although Dr. Ehrke had an office full of patients, I was taken to an examining room immediately. Since I couldn't sit or lay down, he examined me standing, bent over maintaining my balance by leaning on the examination table.

Larry (Dr. Ehrke's first name) and Beth maneuvered me to the x-ray room. After he looked at the finished product, he attempted to work my back with little results. When he finished he told me straight up, "You are in for a long recovery period, and for now I will need to see you every day."

He did discuss an option with me and left the decision up to me. You can go to your regular doctor and he will set you up with a surgeon after giving you muscle relaxers and medicine for your pain, which I know is probably intolerable.

I told him that I would rather see his friendly face every day until he determines when I need a break. When we started, I was bent over and used crutches as two forward feet, moving them by the handles in front of me and walking very slowly.

The day we started was June 19 and when he released me on September 9th, I was walking easily, although I did tilt a little to the right side and would for the next eleven years, in spite of the exercises that Larry gave me and I regularly followed.

For the next decade, I maintained good health as we moved toward retirement. We retired to Arizona in 2005, on our forty-ninth wedding anniversary. I began playing golf almost every day. After a couple of months, I noticed that my tilt to the right had been corrected by a really bad golf swing. Now, that was a pretty cool thing.

All went well until the summer of 2009, when I was hit with valley fever, a spore that gets into your system and creates all sorts of havoc. If it gets to your lungs, you are toast. I was fortunate, probably due to my immune system and over all nutritional health after thirty-four-plus years of a consistent Shaklee breakfast. Most people I have talked to that have had it take four to five years to become symptom free. I was able to do it in fourteen months.

Instead of going the medical route with this disease, I had discussions with knowledgeable people and in three steps of using specific topical salves and creams, I was able to minimize prescription drugs. Friends Brad Jarvey, Fred Fosberg, and Shirley Kosikowski all helped me along the way. I believe Brad and Fred moved me in a positive direction and Shirley's formula put me over the top.

A year and a half later, I was diagnosed with psoriatic arthritis followed a couple of months later with two lumbar herniated disks, and the MRI showed at least two cracked vertebra that were mostly healed. Once again I was referred to a specialist, an orthopedic surgeon. Using my assessment of the situation, I turned down the recommendation of the doctor. The MRI the doctor ordered was taken to my chiropractor, Dr. David Shcitelmen, who began working with me. Today I am doing well on our program and am totally pain free.

This was my third serious back injury, and I am pleased that with the help of outstanding chiropractic doctors, my back is still intact and functioning well without being held together with titanium.

A most significant day in my life follows:

THE DAY I DIED

In late July of 1986, we were expecting the birth of our first grandchild and at the same time, Don Jr. was finishing up his third summer baseball camp. Beth headed to Bulverde, Texas, to be with Dara and our newest arrival, and I headed for Chandler, Oklahoma, to watch Don's last game and bring him home. All went well in Texas as I drove to get Don, except that my right side began to hurt a little, not a bad pain, but enough for me to notice. I kept hoping that it would go away as I arrived at the baseball camp, but it lingered.

They had Don playing second base, and he acquitted himself well with a couple of good plays in the field and turned a double play very cleanly. At the plate he had a couple of hits and was really glad that I was able to get there in time for the game. Afterward we gathered up his things and headed out.

We had dinner and I got to listen to his stories of two weeks in camp. It was all nice and enjoyable, except for the pain in my side. I was glad that he had a good time and was really revved upon the trip home. For hours he kept my mind off the increasing pain in my side.

I knew it was a gallbladder flare-up, the worst one that I ever had. After we got home, I got him in bed and tried to sleep. It was hopeless and soon I was on my back writhing on the floor. I wanted Don to get as much sleep as possible, since I knew now that I was incapable of driving and had to get to the hospital.

I waited until six thirty and finally woke him up. I told him that an ambulance was on the way to pick me up and I wanted him to call Mom and let her know what happened. I gave him strict orders to wait until eight o'clock to call her. The ambulance arrived and hauled me off.

Don waited for about five minutes before he couldn't wait any longer. He called his mother and told her that he was scared and an ambulance had taken Dad away. Of course, Beth got in her car and headed to Brownwood.

It was a Saturday morning, so after an initial examination, I was given a shot to bring down the level of pain and put in a room. Every so often I was given an additional shot to knock me out and control the pain. I lay in bed through the weekend and on Monday morning Dr. Locklear came in to examine me. He immediately ordered the operating room to be prepared. My doctor was notified and came quickly to assist in the operation. Even in a state of impairment and barely awake, I felt a sense of urgency in Dr. Locklear's voice, but I couldn't respond in any way.

Before I knew what was going on, I was whisked into the operating room.

While all this was happening, Beth was driving to the hospital. As she made the turn approaching the hospital, she saw a rainbow shining over the hospital and knew that everything was going to be all right. When she arrived, she was directed to an area just outside the operating room where she took out her book to read and settled in comfortably without a worry in the world. She *knew* that I would be okay.

After a period of time, Dr. Humphries, our family doctor, came out and told her "he is going to make it."

She responded, "Was there ever a doubt?"

He told her, "We almost lost him."

Beth then told him about seeing the rainbow, and she knew that I was going to be okay.

I had not been aware of what had been going on all day since I was knocked out the entire time. When I woke up, I was back in my room and Beth was sitting there waiting for me to come around.

What I just had to tell her was fresh on my mind, and to me, it was exciting news.

This apparently happened while I was under anesthesia. I was walking through this large tunnel that was illuminated by a brilliant, yet soothing white light. At the far end of the tunnel, a large figure appeared. He was dressed all in white and even though he was bathed in bright white light, he stood out. As I walked toward him, he raised his hand in front of his body with the palm facing me and said, "Go back, it's not your time." That was it, and the next thing I knew, I was back in my room.

That was my third day in the hospital and I felt like I had just arrived. I told Beth that I was ready to go home. She told me that I would have to wait for a few days. It wasn't long before I agreed with her as the medication began to wear off. I was about to learn that I was under heavy medication when Beth got the nurse and I got a shot of morphine in my butt.

For the next several days, I was in and out of consciousness. When awake, I was generally in pain and needed a shot of morphine. I suspect that it was the pain that woke me, because when I called for a nurse, she would come in ready to give me a shot. One time after I was given the painkiller, I reached down and felt my backside and I was horrified, as it felt like the Appalachian Mountains. I had been given a numerous collection of shots.

Before I had gone into the operating room, a nurse tried to put a tube down my throat. They had to wait until I was unconscious to put it in because my nose was too sensitive for me to allow them to do it when I was awake. Well, this thing had been there for several days and a nurse decided that it was time to take it out and check it. It came out rather easily and she seemed surprised that it was clear and functioning, so she was going to put it back in. I was having none of that, as I remembered how I couldn't stand it the first time they tried.

She told me that I had better just suck it up because it was going to be reinserted whether I liked it or not. I told her in no uncertain terms, "Not in your lifetime!" She left in a huff, stating that she would be back. I immediately called Beth and, almost in a panic, told her to "get out here, quick!"

I don't know how she was able to do it so rapidly, but she was in my room with me explaining to her what had happened before the nurse returned. The nurse told Beth and me that the tube had to be reinserted. I was adamant, and Beth backed me up, that it was not going to be forced through my nose and down to my stomach.

"We will see about that!" the nurse told us.

"I'm going to call the doctor."

I said. "Go ahead, but he is not going to do it either!"

After what I am sure was an eternity for Beth, the nurse came back and said that the doctor advised them that if I wanted to suffer the consequences of not having the tube in my stomach, that was my business and they were not to try to force me.

That was the end of it, and there were no consequences. I got along just fine without it. From that time on, the nurses were easier to get along with and pretty much let me recover on my own terms.

After I had been there for a week, a nurse brought me the usual fare for lunch. The food was soft and pretty much tasteless, very bland. I sent it back and asked for some real food, and much to my surprise, I got it. They can say what they want about hospital food, but that was the best meal I had ever eaten. I don't remember what it was, but it was great.

When Dr. Locklear came in that evening, he gave the nurse that served me holy heck. He came in and saw me and asked, "How are you feeling?" When I told him fine, he seemed surprised.

He told me that the nurse was not supposed to vary my diet without his approval, and so he had to chew her out. I told him that it was my fault, not the nurses and I would apologize to her. He laughed and said that he would put me on a regular diet and at the same time, relay my apology to the nurse. He also told me that I had good instincts as to the condition of my body.

The next day, after just three regular meals, I decided that if I didn't get some exercise, I would have a tough time recovering. So I took my IV pole, sat on the edge of the bed, and when I felt confident, I stood up for the first time in over a week. I didn't go anywhere, as I knew that a little movement was all I could handle. I did that a couple more times without being caught, and the next day I walked around the room. The following day it was time for an adventure. I got up, prepared myself for a confrontation, and walked out into the hall.

I was immediately confronted by a nurse who told me that I was not authorized to be out of bed. I told her that I had been out of bed the past two days and it was time for me to start walking to build up my leg strength. So I walked down and around the nurse's station in a circle and back to my room. The nurse, in the meantime, called Dr. Locklear and told him what I was doing. Dr. Locklear told me of the call the next day after he asked me how I was doing. He then had a serious talk with me. He started out by telling me, "You will never be as sick as you were and live again. That's the honest to goodness truth. Now I want you to come to my office next week for a checkup and see how you are doing in the real world. We have to take an x-ray to be sure that we got everything."

"What do you mean, 'got everything?'" I asked.

"That Saturday morning when you came in, your gall bladder had erupted. By the time I got to you, gangrene had set in and you had gallstones all through your gut. I haven't seen a gut as bad as yours since I left 'Nam. I want to be sure that I got everything."

The next day I was released from the hospital. I had weighed about 165 when I entered the hospital, and I weighed 148 when I walked out. A week later I went back to see the good doctor and he had a series of x-rays taken. He advised me that by the way I looked and felt, he was pretty sure that I didn't have any of that stuff still floating around in there.

He then gave me the bad news. "Beginning now there are two things that you can't eat or drink. No pizza and no carbonated drinks."

I asked him, "For how long?"

"The rest of your life."

"You're kidding!"

"No."

"Can you put the gall stones back in there?" As I said that, I saw him laugh.

"No, relax. You will get used to it."

I went a year without either product before I decided that I had to give it a try. Beth and I went out for a pizza. I wasn't the least bit concerned as I dove into one of my favorite dishes. Nothing happened, except that I ate too much.

A week or so later, I tried a root beer with the same result. I limited myself to one pizza a month for a while and after several good meals, I did the same with a carbonated drink. After all these years later, when I want a pizza, I have one. The same is true regarding carbonated drinks.

Although I continue to enjoy my pizza, I seldom drink root beer anymore. I just don't have a hankering for it.

I know that it seems impossible, but "the day I died" is fact, as well as the fact that I still enjoy pizza and an occasional root beer.

Chapter 25

SPORTS: YEAH, I WAS AN ATHLETE

From my earliest memories, sports were always foremost in my mind. It was pretty easy to think about sports with two older brothers. The three of us shared one bedroom. In those early days, we had a radio that was tuned into the White Sox games almost every day during the season. Back then Bob Elson would do the home games live and when the team went on the road, he would recreate the games off ticker tape from the studio. I would learn later that these were actually made up games simply created from reading the final result of each play. It did make for interesting listening if you didn't know that it was mostly theater.

We were the ultimate Chicago South Side sports fans. Not much football on the radio, but one of the most lingering memories of those days was the 1947 National Football League Championship game. We had this large, rounded top Philco radio in the living room that became the focal point for the entire game. We sat on the floor and "watched" the radio as we hung on every word emanating from that box. I could visualize as Charlie Trippi and Elmer Angsman each scored two touchdowns. It was an exciting game that ended in the Cardinals' only (to date) championship as they defeated the Philadelphia Eagles by a score of 28–21.

The only other time that we gathered around the radio to hear a big sports moment was August 16 1948, the night Babe Ruth died at the age of fifty-three. I was ten years old and totally engrossed in baseball. We sat there on the floor for hour after hour without moving or making any kind of noise, just listening to the reports streaming on the Babe's deteriorating condition.

We played neighborhood baseball every day during the summer, except when we had to take time to mow the grass. With the diamond already put together from early in the spring, the constant wear and tear on the field made the mowing time a lot less during the summer. This was an annual ritual for the summers of our youth.

High school was a different matter. The coach hardly looked at the small kid with a big first baseman's glove. In the week I was there, I was hit two ground balls at first, which I fielded cleanly and never did get a chance to pick up a bat before I was cut. The second year wasn't much better. I got more work in at a single practice shagging fly balls in the outfield and getting batting practice at the end of the work out with Bill's Normal Laundry team.

As a junior I learned from a couple of the guys that the coach had already determined his lineup before practices started. Before the season even began, I was slated as the third-string first baseman for my junior year and second-string in my senior year. Even as a student, I found this to be a bit ludicrous. Sure enough, as a junior, I was hitting in the .280s in the adult league and sitting on the bench on our high school team. It was even worse as a senior, as I sat on the high school bench behind a "slugger" who hit .030 with a ground ball single to left field in thirty-three trips to the plate, but he could occasionally hit a relatively deep fly ball in batting practice. While this was going on, I spent the summer hitting .375 with over forty stolen bases and one error all summer long.

Less than a month removed from sitting on the bench for two years in high school, due to my play with the JC Colts, I was offered an opportunity to play professional baseball in Florida as a member of the Philadelphia Phillies organization that was kaputed by Dad and put me into a yearlong funk.

I don't know how long I might have been going in the wrong direction if it hadn't been for Beth.

* * * *

Football was a game that we played as kids in the neighborhood when it got too cold to play baseball. Our front yard was the neighborhood football field.

It was something to do to burn off energy. In between games, which were not played as often as we played baseball, I would take the football out in our front yard and practice dropkicking, just for something to do. I started doing this in about the sixth grade and continued through high school.

I went out for football in my freshman year, but I felt real negative vibes from the coach when he looked my way. It was like, "Why would a ninety-pound kid with a long, skinny neck even think about playing football?" I didn't go back the second day. I just wasn't that interested.

Although I didn't play the game through my junior year, I continued to enjoy kicking the ball in our front yard all the way through high school. It was simply an enjoyable way of unwinding and sometimes letting out anxiety or frustrations that go along with being a teenager.

Early in September 1954 on a beautiful sunny day, some of the guys had brought a football to school. I noticed them throwing it around and as one of them saw me, he threw the ball in my direction. It hit the ground and skipped past me. I jogged over and picked it up. The bouncing ball had taken me beyond a comfortable range to throw it back, so I nonchalantly dropkicked the ball back to the group.

I had quite unintentionally kicked the ball over their heads. As I walked on, a couple of members of the football team approached me and began discussing my kicking of the football. It was kind of a fun give and take, and they soon went on their way.

The next day, as I stepped outside during the lunch hour, I was confronted by a larger group of football players that wanted to see me kick the ball. With no reason not to, I kicked the ball three or four times. I knew all these guys, so it wasn't anything that I was giving any thought to, other than it was kind of fun. When I finished, one of the guys said that Coach Kane (football coach) wanted to see me.

After school that afternoon, I walked over to the practice field and visited with the coach. He invited me to join the team.

It sounded like fun, so I said sure, and the next day I received three uniforms, pads, and a helmet. Since we had a full team before I became part of it, all the uniforms had been issued, leaving me with an outdated uniform, but what the heck.

My first day at practice was a hoot. Since I had never experienced organized calisthenics in any setting (ROTC was taken in place of physical education), my first day of football was a real eye opener. The opening session of practice taught me my first lesson on resistive exercise when we paired up and did a neck strengthening routine. Ironically, in just seven years, I would be writing a master's thesis on the effects of "resistive exercises."

I hadn't given any thought to the social construction of a football team. I was initiated when coach set up game-like extra point practice. As I took my position in the short punt formation, which would be used for drop kicking extra points, and received the snap, I concentrated on getting off an initial first-practice kick. The offensive line was concentrating on not blocking the defense. The eleven men on the defensive team were concentrating on being the first to get a piece of me. I never saw them coming and suddenly it became very dark, with a pile of eleven players stacked on top of me.

When they very slowly untangled themselves, I got up without saying anything and walked back to the huddle. Then I heard Al Fonseca say, "He's okay," as he looked at the conglomerate of cleat-caused red welts that covered my shins. He wasn't referring to my health, but to my ability to take the punishment and keep on ticking. On the following several snaps, the offensive line had relearned their collective ability to block and I was able to successfully convert several kicks.

I thought that I had survived that pretty well when phase two was put into place. I was to be a defensive back during some passing drills. After being pretty inept as the ends out maneuvered me, I finally intercepted a pass. I was really feeling an adrenaline rush as I headed back up field for maybe two strides before I was hit with a perfect high/low tackle by the intended receiver and another guy, who I had no idea from where he came.

I was beginning to think that maybe this wasn't as much fun as I thought when the practice came to an end and coach called for a couple of laps around the field. I loved running, so this was a piece of cake. I was running with the lead group when, all of a sudden, our running back, Danny Washkevich, cut my legs out from under me. I went down, rolled, got up, and continued running. I ran as hard as I could to catch up with the lead group again and when I accomplished that, I maneuvered myself into position where I was running next to Danny. He knew I was there and when he looked at me, I gave him a big smile. He smiled back and we continued toward the completion of our laps.

I was accepted as part of the club after that.

I learned a lot about the members of the club from this experience and when I moved into a position in high schools later as a teacher, I understood the inclination of football players hanging together during and after school. It wasn't so much that they think they are different and superior to the other students. The time spent together seeking a single tough goal and understanding in each other, a necessary part of reaching that goal, causes athletes, especially football players, to respect and cling to each other. After being a small part of that group, I had a far greater knowledge of what "team" meant. I was disappointed to see the season come to an end, figuring that was probably the only time I would play organized football.

After starting college, with my dream of playing professional baseball blown up, I figured what the heck, I'll just play football and see what happens. I was probably the most inexperienced player going out for the junior varsity team. I reveled in the practices and the team calisthenics. My legs were still in pretty good shape, although I got a lesson on my lung capacity with forty-yard dashes. They really screamed at me that first week. I spent the first weekend just doing sprints two to three times a day for those two days. Our second week of conditioning went much better.

We received a loose-leaf binder with basic play information that we had to learn for the following week. Studying plays and signals was all new to me, but fortunately it wasn't rocket science, and I was prepared when we started the third week with contact drills.

The varsity had been together for a month before school started. The junior varsity began working together after enrollment had been completed, and we had an abbreviated schedule of games. I was looking forward to those.

I had not kicked a ball since we started, as I was determined to play football, not just kick. On our first scrimmage, I took a hand-off and as I made a cut to the right, I got nailed and heard my left knee pop. My college football was over before it started with a torn medial collateral ligament.

Several years later when I was working in radio, I picked up my old habit of kicking a football and running around the track just for the enjoyment I derived from it. The field was behind the junior college in town, and I always thought I was alone. But unknown to me, some of the students saw me kicking and began to watch for me.

I had been kicking for a couple of months when one day a young man came out to talk with me about the Continental Football League. I had heard of it, although I knew nothing of its make-up or structure. He explained quite a bit about the league and said that they would be starting their pre-season workouts in a few weeks and suggested that I go up and work out with one of their teams. To my surprise he had the names and phone numbers of a couple of the teams that he gave to me along with the comment that I was as good at kicking as anyone in the league.

I called the closest team to Moberly, the Omaha Mustangs in Omaha, Nebraska, and after telling him of my pastime and the conversation with a student who was a fan of the league, I received an invitation and a day to report to Creighton University. I had vacation time coming, so I thought it would be fun. While at Creighton, we were housed and had our meals. The amount and quality of our meals was outstanding.

I never worked so hard, ate so much, or slept so soundly in my life. After a week of this and looking toward the end of my vacation time, I decided to call an end to my participation at the camp, which was held at Boys Town. I was pretty tired and I determined that age thirty, it was no time to chase any kind of career in football.

* * * *

My first semester in college, I took a class in gymnastics that was an introduction to all the apparatuses that the school had. The ones that I took to were the parallel bars, the pummel horse, and floor routine. I seemed to do best on the parallel bars, although I found the floor routine most interesting.

After I was injured playing football, I spent most of my available time in the gym working on skills.

As I found myself thinking more and more about getting this semester over with so I could get out of there, except for the time spent in the gym, I was pretty much in a funk. I really didn't understand my negative feelings or relate it to baseball in any way. I wasn't thinking of the future, I was just resenting being locked into this routine of working, studying, and feeling that I didn't want to be there.

After I completed the semester, in which I passed all my courses, I packed my bags and headed for Chicago without looking back. I was done with school.

It wasn't long before I realized that you can't go back home once you leave, so I decided to go to Eastern Illinois University. It was an easy choice to go to the gym and begin working on gymnastics again in my spare time, which wasn't much. I had as my number one goal: making a living.

Eastern had a gymnastics team, and I was encouraged by Dr. Bill Groves to come to the workouts when I could. He told me that I had the build to become a decent gymnast. That was the first encouragement I had received since I started college the previous September.

I adjusted my work schedule to get two workouts a week in the evening work sessions. I seemed to be making the most progress on the parallel bars and concentrated on them.

Dr. Groves asked me to also try the rings to increase my strength, which would benefit my work on the bars. He was right. When I tried the rings, I was as weak as a kitten. As I worked on them, the increase in strength was evident within a couple of weeks. I began hustling from work to get in longer workouts on those nights that I could spend at the gym. I spent more and more time on the parallel bars until one night when I over did it.

As I dipped below the bars with my arms extended to kip up to a straight vertical position, my right hand slipped off the bar and I fell to the mat below. The back of my head struck the metal horizontal base of the apparatus and knocked me out cold.

When I came to, I saw several faces above me that were unrecognizable. I heard some talking, which was originally uncomprehending to me. Slowly I began to hear Dr. Groves's voice as he took charge of the situation. As I tried to get up, he held me down and said, "Don't move yet." Over what seemed to be an eternity, I was allowed to sit up, then stand. I had a woozy feeling, and my head began to pound. I was told to walk it off.

A couple of guys walked with me, initially holding me up and gradually allowing me more and more control until I was walking on my own. I was advised not to go to sleep until at least my regular bedtime or later. I followed the directions and walked over to Larry Mizener's cafe and had a cup of coffee and then walked around the campus until close to midnight. When I went to bed, I only had a slight headache.

The next morning I felt fine and continued with my regular schedule with the addition of checking with the school nurse.

I had planned to go over to Greencastle, Indiana, to see my brother Bob, who was a sophomore at DePauw University, that weekend and I was feeling pretty good, not feeling any side effects of my banging my head. The drive over was uneventful as was our visit. I spent one night at the fraternity house and the next morning I headed back to Illinois. I wasn't ten minutes out of Greencastle when I had some kind of relapse.

I realized something wasn't right and pulled over to the side of the road and zonked out.

I know I had been out for a fairly long time when a police officer banged on my window and woke me up. He inquired if I was okay and then decided on his own that I wasn't. As he and I talked and I explained how I happened to be sleeping on the side of the road, he said I was not in any condition to drive. I agreed that he was probably right. He suggested that I follow him to the Lambda Chi fraternity house and spend another night.

That sounded good to me. When we arrived it caused a little stir as the cop car came to a stop in front of the fraternity house. Bob wasn't there, but a couple of his fraternity brothers recognized my car and me.

They assured the officer that I would get a good meal and a bed for the night and he left.

They did indeed take good care of me and turned me over to Bob when he returned from wherever he had been. We picked up where we left off and squeezed in another day together.

I missed a day's work and a day of classes by the time I returned to Charleston. That was lost money that had to be made up somewhere. The missed classes were not a problem.

I did not return to gymnastics. It was a fun activity, and that is all it would ever have been for me, unlike baseball, for which I had a deep, burning desire inside of me that I apparently couldn't shake.

* * * *

Knowing that I couldn't play baseball, be a full-time student, and work fifty to sixty hours a week in the early summer, I went over to the Mattoon baseball field and had a conversation with Pete Reiser, the old Brooklyn Dodger outfielder. Without ever seeing me on the field, he said that I should concentrate on my studies. Baseball is a tough way of life and anyone with the chance to go to school should. His experience was different from mine and I don't believe he understood that gut feeling that existed in me. The team he was managing was playing in Mattoon that evening.

I think my demeanor off the field caused people who had not seen me play baseball not to recognize the fervor with which I played the game. At that time I could not imagine that it would be four more years before I would get an opportunity to play again.

In the last spring in the Air Force, I was told that I would be playing for the Chennault Air Force baseball team. It was quite a challenge. As a senior in college, I was carrying twenty-two semester hours of credit, working at my Air Force job seven days a week, and playing a full schedule of baseball games along with my commitment to play selected players in handball plus tournaments. Things eased up during the summer with a much smaller class load.

I played probably my worst year of baseball that year, yet hit the longest ball I have ever hit, well over four hundred feet, clearing a light tower more than three hundred feet from home plate.

The real highlight of the year came unexpectedly in Beaumont, Texas. It was a late season game in August and when we arrived, the opposition's coach asked Captain Miller if it would be okay with him if he used a pitcher that had just returned home after a season in the AAA league, assuring Rene that he would only use him in relief. Our coach agreed.

We were playing a close game and trailing by a run when the AAA pitcher entered the game in the top of the seventh inning, and it was just my luck to be leading off. I watched him warming up closely. Other than going to major league games, I had not seen such a smooth delivery. I stepped to the plate batting left-handed. His first pitch was a curve over the inside part of the plate. I pulled it weakly just past our dugout. His second pitch was another curve a little further inside that I took for a ball. With a one and one count, I got a fastball on the outside part of the plate that I hit it fairly well to center field. The center fielder came in a few feet to make an easy catch. I felt good that I caught up with a AAA fastball, but disappointed that I couldn't do more with it.

He struck out the next two batters to end the inning. In the eighth inning, he struck out all three batters he faced. I was extremely disappointed that he struck out all three batters in the eighth inning since I wanted to get another crack at facing him. My hopes were dashed in the ninth as he also struck out the side. We had a good-hitting team, and we just got stuffed. The more I thought about this game, the more I convinced myself that I should give that Phillies scout a call when I got back to Chicago.

Most importantly, as the season wore on, my instincts and awareness on the field improved. I maintained my ability to steal bases, and I went the entire year again without being caught stealing.

1960 Chennault AFB

After I left the service, I talked very briefly with the scout in Chicago. I decided any chance of playing professional baseball had passed me by. I continued playing in 1961 just for the love of the game.

I was having a good year and loving what I was doing. The most fun game was the day "I called my shot."

I call it "My Babe Ruth Moment."

✶ ✶ ✶ ✶

THE BABE AND ME

During his historic baseball career, Babe Ruth is portrayed as having promised a young sick boy that he would hit a home run for him in that day's game, and then proceeded to do it.

In the 1932 World Series with the Yankees playing in Chicago against the Cubs, it is reported that he pointed to the center field bleachers and then he hit the next pitch to that spot for a home run. Whether it actually happened or not has been argued since before I was born to this day. True or not it is a part of baseball lore.

In 1961 our team was playing the Statesville Penitentiary team in Joliet, Illinois (this was a maximum security institution). Just getting in and having lunch there was an eye-opening experience.

We joked on the way to the facility about the fact that they had a real advantage every time they played because they were always the home team.

Playing baseball in front of a couple of thousand convicted felons was an awesome experience. I was playing right field in a rather routine game when the guys in the right field bleachers were getting antsy and engaged me in conversation. I ultimately told them that to make it interesting for them, the next time I went to bat, which was as soon as I went in because I was leading off the next inning, "I will hit a double and have to slide into second to make it."

After the third out of the inning, as I trotted in from right field, I was really chewing myself out. "You idiot! You don't have a brain in your head. You're going to make a fool out of yourself."

As I led off batting left-handed, I hit a Texas leaguer over the shortstop's head on the first pitch. This was an easy single, but I didn't have an option, I had to make it to second.

As I made the turn, I eyed the left fielder and as he was in the motion of lobbing the ball to second, I kicked in the afterburners, causing him to have to reload to fire the ball to second. I beat the throw with my hook slide, aiming my left toe at the right field, first base corner of the bag. All the shortstop had to tag was that left foot. My whole upper body was well to the right side of the base line. The umpire signaled and yelled safe. I had clearly beat the throw, but I think the umpire was as surprised as the left fielder was.

Before the inning was over, a single scored me with what turned out to be the winning run. It was a good thing because after I crossed home, the guards pulled me out of the game because the prisoners down the right field line were really whooping it up.

I told the guards that prisoners in the stands were more likely to behave with me going out there than feel like they were being punished for what I did. The guards were more angry than you could imagine. When I sat down in the dugout, I had a uniformed guard on each side of me. It was kind of surreal.

Out in right field, it had quieted down until they saw that I wasn't playing any longer. Then all heck broke loose until a cadre of guards headed in the direction of the disturbance.

I lost the argument, but we won the game, and "I had called my shot." After the game one of the prisoner ballplayers searched me out and explained that he would be getting out of prison next spring. He said, "Wherever you are playing, I want to play on your team." I gave him Bob Hunt's name and advised him that if anyone would know where I was, it would be Mr. Hunt. He left the field with his team and I never saw him again, but he left a happy man.

* * * *

The following year while I was finishing up my master's degree in physical education, I played with the Mattoon town team, getting in one game playing second base and throwing right-handed as I had learned to do while I was in the Air Force as an offshoot of playing so much handball. I mention it only because hours and hours of learning to throw right-handed was only used in one game.

We played this game at home, and I was back at first base and leading off the bottom of the first when the pitcher froze me with a good fastball on the outside corner of the plate. I should have just turned and walked away since he had me cold, but I heard the umpire call ball two. I naturally acted as if I knew it was a ball all along. I was batting right-handed, and the next pitch was a letter-high curve that I hit a line drive to the right side of second for a single up the middle. Other than that at bat, I don't recall the rest of the game until it was over. The umpire came up behind me and said, "That lefty had you struck out in the first inning, but I wanted to see you swing the bat." I turned around and for the first time, saw that Bob McDowell, my old friend from Miss Guy's education class where I met Beth, was the home plate umpire.

From 1963 through 1965, I played with the Brigham City, Utah Peaches, where in 1963 we won the state championship.

Combining baseball with raising a family, teaching, doing play-by-play, and working on my doctorate had taken its toll on playing baseball and in 1970, I made the determination that my playing days were over. In my last game of that year, a batter decided to take me out as I was catching a throw on a ground ball from our shortstop. The shortstop threw high to first and as I was stretched out making the play, the runner put his shoulder into my midsection without even coming close to the bag. It was pure frustration on his part, but as I got up, it hit me that he could have seriously injured me and the game was no longer worth that risk.

The next week I took a job as superintendent in a small Illinois community.

I didn't pick up a bat again until the summer of 1989. My friend Walt "No Neck" Williams, a ten-year veteran major league baseball player and a pitcher in the short-lived Senior Baseball League made up of former Major League baseball players, called and asked me if I would pitch some batting practice for his son Walt and my son Don so they could practice their switch hitting. Walt would pitch right-handed to the boys, and I would pitch left-handed.

We had worked both boys pretty well and as we finished up Walt asked me to hit a few. He wanted to see my swing. He pitched a couple to me, and to my surprise, I hit them pretty well. Walt turned and yelled to Don, "Watch your dad's swing."

He then pitched a few more times, and I hit the ball solidly. Without telling me, he then threw me a curve that I picked up on and got good wood on. I was getting tired, and he threw me a changeup. That one tied me in knots.

After a good laugh, Walt asked me, "Why didn't you play pro ball?"

I just replied, "That's a long story."

"You have got a good stroke. I can't believe you didn't go pro."

I couldn't go into any details, so I just said, "Thanks." I really felt good that someone with Walt's eye and experience could tell that a fifty-one-year-old man was once a hitter.

In 2005 at age sixty-eight, it became time to retire, so we sold our businesses and moved to Arizona. A large attraction for me was the opportunity to play senior softball. I was about as excited as I could get at the thought of playing competitive sports again.

I played for two years and for the first time in my life, I was overcome with injuries. I spent almost half of my time rehabbing from injuries. Within those two years, I realized, finally, that my body could no longer do what my instincts and head told it to do. I experienced a calf pull, followed by two quadriceps pulls on a sprint to first base. The first one slowed me down for a few strides and with the second one, I was eating dirt. After I recovered it wasn't long before I caught a hard ground ball off my right knee, which knocked me down and broke my left wrist. In my last game, hustling to first, I pulled a groin muscle. That and the fact that this was a recreational league rather than a league based on competition made my decision to walk away easy.

Senior Softball 2007

In the Air Force, after turning down another chance to play football on the Air Force team in Washington, DC, I was assigned as a judo instructor in Lake Charles, Louisiana.

My introduction to the sport was immediate and painful, yet exhilarating. The crash course on becoming an instructor was accompanied by learning and participating in handball to develop quickness.

Over time judo became easier and was the reason for being in the physical conditioning unit. Handball became a passion. Throughout my military career, I played handball at every opportunity. It did provide me with a lot of challenging and interesting situations that I cherish to this day.

I won several tournaments and was able to defeat a colonel who had not lost a game in over fifteen years of consistent play. Colonel Goodman was recognized as one of the best in SAC (Strategic Air Command). He was so devastated by his loss to me that from that day until I left the Air Force, he totally avoided going on the handball court with me. When we played in tournaments, he always requested to be in a bracket other than the one I was in. When it came to the championship game in the tournament, he would forfeit rather than play against me. I beat a captain who had consistently defeated me in regular weekly games. I also cleaned the plow of a young lieutenant who announced that he was the Pacific Coast conference champion in handball at UCLA and wanted to beat the best this base had to offer. After we played he was a little more humble when he lost two games to none.

In my four years in the Air Force, I actually ended up playing, conservatively, well over a thousand games of handball.

Receiving trophy from Base Commander Colonel Bailey

THE BABE AND ME

While I was an undergrad student, I took a course in soccer at Eastern Illinois University. I took to the game like a fish takes to water. My speed, accompanied by endurance, enabled me to score multiple goals in each game that we played. It was shocking to me as to how easy it was. Sometimes in the forty-minute games, I would score all our team's goals. Before the quarter was over, I had scored so many goals that the team I played on won every game and I had scored more goals than the opponent's entire team.

Somebody must have remembered that activity because when I returned to work on my master's degree, I was assigned as an assistant coach on the school's soccer club.

I guess I can say that I really got a kick out of soccer. It was just a fun game.

* * * *

In the neighborhood I grew up in, basketball had never been played during that time in the history of Columbus Manor. It was a completely foreign sport to me, although I did on occasion go to our high school games and found that interesting, but not interesting enough to try the sport that was played indoors.

While in the Air Force, Captain Phillip Young offered me the opportunity to supervise the intramural programs at the base gym, over a cup of coffee at the college union building, as well as work with the weekend activities of the dependents. This would allow me to go to school full time. He was like manna from heaven. I couldn't refuse.

I developed into the overseer of the entire late afternoon and evening programs in the facility.

When I completed my night's work and had time, I introduced myself to basketball. I would shoot hoops to wind down before closing the gym. I got to a point where I hit jump shots, layups, and free throws.

Several years later, in the late '60s, I was a play-by-play announcer at a radio station in Moberly, Missouri. I did several different sports, but generally football and basketball were the mainstays of sports programming. I was also an account executive (fancy name for salesman). One of my advertisers called the station and asked if any of the announcers could play basketball and would be willing to play a game against the prisoners at the Moberly Correctional Center.

Whoever he talked to recommended me as the most athletic member of the staff and "he surely had played a lot of basketball."

Having never played in a basketball game, I turned him down. When my boss got wind of my action, he advised me that if I didn't play, we would likely lose an advertiser. I had little choice but to play.

We had a couple of workouts as a team in preparation, and I guess I did okay because I was selected to open the game and play guard. Nobody had figured out that I had never played the game.

The fun part of the game was going into the prison with all their checkpoints and pat-downs. It sure wasn't Stateville in Joliet, Illinois, but it was effective.

The audience was enthusiastic, and every seat in the gym was filled. I somehow won the prisoners over (I never did figure out how or why). Every time the coach pulled me from the game, a derisive buzz from the crowd let us know they were unhappy. The coach had to put me back in, to the cheers of the crowd. It was really a weird thing. I certainly was not in physical condition to play an entire competitive game, but I had to.

The result was that we won a close game, and I scored twelve points and had one foul. I seemed to have settled in from the top of the key and made most of my jump shots. As the game was coming to a close, the prison team was blocking me out of that area and I quit scoring, but passed it to enough different teammates that we pulled it out.

When the game concluded, we didn't waste any time in getting out of the prison.

The first quarter of the game was my initial appearance in a basketball game, and the final buzzer concluded my career in basketball. I did better than I thought I would do, but certainly had no desire to do it again— except for donkey basketball and faculty/varsity fundraisers.

* * * *

THE BABE AND ME

A most unique sports opportunity presented itself to me while I was stationed at Thule, Greenland. Greenland is owned by and is a province of Denmark, and we periodically had Danish ships come into North Star Bay for extended periods of time. On one such occasion, a group of Danish sailors came to the base gym and inquired as to the possibly of getting some gym time to play "Danish handball."

Our commanding officer turned them over to me as soon as he heard the word handball, with instructions to accommodate them in any way possible. The fact that I had a Danish name was a plus. The sailors and I hit it off immediately as they explained their needs to be able to play the game.

I soon learned that Danish handball was a country pride name for "team handball." They were so into the game that they had nets, which were similar to soccer nets except much smaller.

I got the dimensions from them and called Colonel Bailey, our base commander, and asked for an appointment to see him. I met with him and explained that we needed two of these made and what they would be used for. He agreed and called one of the shops and told them that I would be coming right over and that we needed them as soon as the shop could make them. Talk about walking around red tape. We had the nets in two days.

We cleared the gym for a couple of hours twice a week for Danish handball.

The Danes were thrilled with the nets and excited with the amount of time they had to play. Because my name was Rasmussen, as common as Smith or Jones in Denmark I was told, I was asked to play with them.

Being left-handed proved to be an advantage for me, and after the first week in which I was pretty inept, I soon became a prolific scorer.

Before they concluded their tour at the base, we were drawing pretty good crowds at this different kind of game. After the Danes left, we had sufficient interest and established a couple of teams, and I became a teacher of Danish handball. It was pretty cool.

* * * *

Although I was introduced to weight training in Louisiana, at Thule it was a part of my duties to teach and supervise weightlifting. I endeavored to move the concept to weight training that calls for full extension of the muscle groups with lighter weights. Most GI practitioners of the activity tend to use heavier weights, which cause them to constrict full movement in order to maintain control of the weight.

When practiced properly, weightlifting will build the muscle bigger/quicker; however, the flexibility can be lost. To test this concept, just ask a weightlifter to shoot some basketballs. You will notice that the arm doesn't straighten out completely. On the other hand, people that use weight training may not look like the hunk on Muscle Beach, but he will find that he will maintain his athletic acuity with greater results.

After a year of consistent weight training in Greenland mixed with daily games of handball, I increased strength and weight. During the first year of playing baseball after I came back to the states, I hit the longest drive of my life exceeding four hundred feet. At the same time, I was as fast as I was when I was clocked at three seconds flat from home to first in 1955 by a handheld stopwatch.

My experience in the weight room while in the Air Force led to the research that resulted in my thesis the year following my separation from the military. I had been wondering for some time about weight training activities that might strengthen the muscles of the arm, shoulder, and chest to a point where the act of throwing a baseball could be effectively improved.

In all the formulas I put together to work within the restrictions of the twelve-week quarter system at Eastern Illinois University, I could not come up with a way to teach lower body movement and the structure of hip movement to be included in skills that would be used to measure a complete throwing motion. As a result only the arm motion itself was included in my study.

Apparently, that was enough to stir interest in the topic, since Dr. John Masley, the head of the physical education department, advised me a couple of years after my graduation that my thesis was the most checked-out thesis from the university's Booth Library. In his words, "Don, you really started something."

THE BABE AND ME

Years later I read where my thesis, along with a study done at the University of Wisconsin, were the founding documents that led to the scientific use of weight training in athletics.

* * * *

From my earliest days, the idea of baseball was foremost in my mind. I drove Bob crazy with always wanting to play catch and then to pitch to me. He would pitch tennis balls, mostly worn-out tennis balls, to me by the hour.

Bob had a "live" arm. He couldn't throw a baseball or a tennis ball straight if his life depended on it. From the time we were in grade school through high school, Bob pitched tennis balls to me from approximately forty feet from home plate. Of the thousands of balls Bob pitched to me, fast, slow, and in between, I don't remember seeing a straight ball.

Bob and repetition made me a hitter attuned to the breaking ball. Most young players don't see curves, drop balls, sliders etc. until high school or later. I was blessed having Bob understand where I was headed.

When we got old enough, we always had some kind of game going. In the fall it was football, but when we had an Indian summer, the gloves would come out again.

In my first two years of high school, I was frustrated with the lack of interest from our coach when I went out for the team. My third year was even worse, as I was playing in the adult league from early spring and sitting on the bench at school. I figured I would get my chance in my senior year, but coach was enamored by a big kid that could hit batting practice pitching pretty well, but even high school pitchers owned him. I was thankful when that season was over.

My spirits were lifted as I played within my age group for the first time and was rewarded with a chance to play professional baseball. My first goal had been reached and then pulled from me by my dad.

After that summer I had to earn a living and go to school. I was in such a funk that I wasn't able to play ball again until I was twenty-two and in my last year in the Air Force.

From then until 1970, I played every chance I had and I never lost my zest for the game but I knew that my dream had passed me by.

I had my master's degree and knew that school administration had to be my future, which it was until ESPN came along in 1978.

Although my playing days were over, I have maintained my love of sports to this day, and I expect that will be the case for as long as I live.

Chapter 26

BUILDING A PERSONAL PHILOSOPHY

As a little boy, I didn't think; I just played, ate, and was taken care of by my parents. The one thing that disrupted this joyous time of life was my illnesses. Now, I don't remember any of this and didn't understand what was happening or why.

When I was born, my brother Bob was less than a year old. It was pretty cool that I had a built-in playmate that I got along with, most of the time. I had no way of knowing that the second child born so soon after an older sibling could have physical problems (or worse) due to the depleted condition of the mother's body, having not fully recovered from the birth of the first child.

The psychological condition of the family as I arrived was a disaster. In 1930 a baby girl was still born, which in itself was a horrible shock. Two years later Bill was born. My parents went from the deep depths of depression in 1930 to the ultimate highs when their son entered the world healthy.

Mom and Dad worshiped Bill for simply being alive.

Mom still longed to have the baby girl that eluded her in 1930. Four years later, along came Bob and disappointment that he was not the girl for Mom. Into this world came another boy. Bill was given the job of naming his new little brother and chose to name him James. Before the name became official, Bill was beaten up by a neighborhood boy named James and so along came Don.

Now, with three boys, the last of which was sickly, the family struggled to survive through the remaining years of the Great Depression.

I don't know when I realized that I just didn't fit in the family, but I never remember a time that whatever I did wasn't wrong. I should have been more like Bill, who could do no wrong, or at least like Bob who was quiet.

By the time I reached fourth grade, in my parent's eyes, I was not very bright. It was about this time that I found a book in our living room that I began to read. I don't know why, but I read it through and through and decided that I wanted to be like the subject of that book, not necessarily accomplish what he had accomplished, but be like him. Honest, truthful, courteous, and humble.

Lou Gehrig, Pride of the Yankees, was an example to follow. I would steal a nickel here and there when it was obvious that I wouldn't get caught, and lying was just about an everyday occurrence. I realized I was like everyone else. I didn't like me.

As I began to change, no one noticed, but that was okay. I began to like myself. I wasn't always successful in trying to be like Lou Gehrig, but every time I fell short, I berated myself and determined to do better.

I wasn't old enough or smart enough to understand what I was doing, but these were the first steps to forming my philosophy of life.

I struggled through seventh grade, continuing to be the class cut-up, not doing homework, and without any sense of anything except being a kid. In eighth grade I encountered a new teacher that seemed not to have any idea who I was. It had always been pointed out that this was the year that I had better straighten out, so I always knew that I had to overcome me, but I didn't want to.

Now in eighth grade, I felt that I could be me and try to do well. It worked. Mr. Eugene Spizzirri treated me like everyone else, and I found a level of comfort in that. For the first time, I found that I was being complimented for my work. I later learned that he had turned down the opportunity to go over the records of the students before school started. He had told the principal that he wanted to start out with a clean slate with each and every student. This was the first man that ever earned my respect.

BUILDING A PERSONAL PHILOSOPHY

The next pillar I stumbled onto one day at the library during my years in high school. It was a simple little poem by Grantland Rice that went like this:

> When the Great Scorer comes
> To mark against your name
> He'll write not won or lost
> But how you played the game

The fourth line, "but how you played the game," bounced around in my head for a long time as I realized that I had a long way to go to become the kind of person I wanted to be. There were a lot of hiccups along the way, but eventually I got myself moving in the direction that seemed right to me.

Many of the ideas that caused me to think in these terms came from Dad's words that always seemed to be in response to comments or questions from me, such as, "If someone else pays your bills, you don't care what it costs. If this 'hospital insurance' ever catches on, it will destroy our country."

Another one, "If someone hires you for a job, you owe him the right to make a profit from your labor. If you don't make money for your boss, he doesn't need you."

Thinking about "right" and "wrong," which is vital to establishing a personal philosophy, can sometimes be quite grueling, particularly when you get or receive conflicting messages from those you expect to be reasonable and rational.

An example of this related to education is still puzzling to me.

The Tenth Amendment of the Constitution of the United States says, "The powers not delegated to the United States by the Constitution, nor prohibited by it to the States, are reserved to the States respectively, or to the people.

During WWII Dad, as president of District 122 in Illinois, used his familiarity with Mom's cousin, Congressman Edward Kelly, to get financial help in building an elementary school within the boundaries of District 122. I am quite sure this was not the first time the limits of the Tenth Amendment were very clearly violated. Hardly anyone noticed.

Dad proudly presided over the dedication of the brand new school provided, partially, by the United States government.

In 1965 President Lyndon B. Johnson introduced Title 1 to the country for "the children." Although he repeated, ad nauseum, that this was not a foot in the door to "federal aid to education," it was.

If you don't think so, think of all the "children" that have student loans to pay off.

In the first instance, Dad praised representative Kelly; in the second instance, he condemned LBJ for the same basic infringement.

Today, states are closing in on bankruptcy, paying inflated salaries and pensions to teachers that are beyond the capability of the states to pay.

More importantly the citizen is confused as to what happened. Dad couldn't see anything wrong when he engineered the unconstitutional act of involving the federal government in his local school district, even though it violated his own philosophy of others paying the school district bill.

When I applied this information to my studies in graduate school, the legality of both acts was immediately obvious, except Kelly's action was not noticed and LBJ's blossomed.

If you have principles upon which you establish a philosophy of life and violate them when it is to your advantage to do so, you have no philosophy or principles.

As I grew I added to my philosophy and worked to be consistent in my honesty, integrity, and ethics.

My primary focus today is to treat others as I wish to be treated and respect them as I expect to be respected.

Chapter 27

RETIREMENT:
THE ADVENTURE OF AGING

I had never thought about retirement, or aging for that matter. A few years after turning sixty-five, my always positive and prodding wife made a suggestion one day.

"Don't you think that it's about time for us to begin thinking about retirement?"

My caustic response was, "We're too young!"

"Well, we haven't taken a vacation in years and I want to take one."

"Okay, where would we go?"

"On a 'Getaway weekend' at Sun City Grand."

With that she handed me a general advertisement from Sun City Grand in Arizona that contained a lot of positive statements and a phone number.

"Call them and set a date. Be sure to give us a couple of weeks so we can make arrangements to cover everything here while we're gone."

We had just recently had Beth's brother, Gene High, and his wife Robin move into our Camp Bowie Mobile Home Park #2, which certainly made the thought of taking a trip easier, as they became the focal point of managing the mobile home parks for us.

Beth had included a round of golf in our weekend stay at the adult community, and it was scheduled for the first day of our stay.

It was a pleasant two-day drive, and our accommodations were very comfortable. We spent the first evening driving around and looking the community over. On Saturday morning we had a mandatory meeting and community presentation, and then we were assigned a real estate agent. While looking at homes, I noticed that there appeared to be a similar community on the other side of Grand Avenue. I asked our agent about this place called Sun City West.

He and his wife began to explain to us that "West" was an older, run-down community that didn't have anywhere near the lifestyle of "Grand." The more we learned of that community, the more we wanted to see whatever it was on the other side of the street. After we ditched the realtors, we headed to Sun City West and found it to be anything but run down.

Our time was limited, as I was facing my tee time and later had a dinner engagement with a cousin of Beth's over in Del Webb's first and largest Sun City. Beth was going to prepare a favorite dinner of spare-ribs and prunes with all the trimmings while I was playing golf.

This was my first game of golf in a few years and I was determined to break a hundred. I did, just barely (ninety-nine). It was after the round that I discovered that my knees and back didn't hurt. I was ecstatic. I had been in pain for several years and this revelation had me floating on air as I drove the golf cart to our cottage. Walking in the front door, I couldn't find Beth. The meal was on the counter, ready to go. I finally saw Beth sitting on the patio with her head in her hands. She was crying.

I went out back and forgot all about my lack of pain when she told me that Gene had died shortly after we had left for Arizona. Robin had been frantically trying to call us for two days. Actually, Beth had called her to check on the mobile home parks, only to learn of her brother's death.

We packed the van, stopped by the office to let them know what had happened, took the prepared meal over to Sal and Virginia Guidi's house in Sun City so that they could still have the new taste of my favorite dish, and headed for Texas.

Although we spent much time talking about the fond memories that Beth had growing up with Gene and the time we spent with them in Utah, we finally shared our thoughts of our experience in Arizona. We determined that we would return to the "Valley of the Sun" in about eighteen months and experience the area during the hottest time of the year and see the effect that it would have on my arthritis.

After Gene's funeral, we learned from Robin that the reason they had moved to Texas was that Gene had felt he didn't have very long to live and wanted to spend as much of what was left of his life near Beth. I was so pleased that Beth had been able to have the time she did with her brother, who she adored.

We made the decision to put our parks on the market and retire to either Sun City Texas or Sun City West in Arizona. With no concept as to how long it would take to market the real estate and move in the direction of retirement, we made plans to visit Arizona again in eighteen months, which would be July of 2003. We didn't anticipate a quick sale.

We began looking at property in Texas and at the appointed time, we made another trip to the desert. It went better than we had anticipated. Before we reached Sun City West, my constant companion, arthritis pain, had totally left me. I was ecstatic.

This time we made a tour of some parts of the state, beginning in Tombstone, which we had visited years earlier prior to it becoming such a tourist trap. We went to Tucson's Old Town, Sierra Vista, and a couple of senior communities in between. In all, we were satisfied with the choice of Sun City West, "the jewel in Del Webb's crown." We then spent a few days touring what would turn out to be our retirement home. About a year later, we returned and bought a home.

Now, in addition to a diner, three mobile home parks, a rental home, and dog grooming business, we added an out-of-state residence. It seemed to me that we were going in the wrong direction.

After a discussion with Kathy Carlson, our dog groomer, it wasn't long before Kathy bought the building that housed her business. Within a few months, we sold the smallest and most distant mobile home park, Pecan Valley Mobile Home Park in Early, Texas. The two larger parks and the diner proved to be more difficult to divest ourselves of.

Finally, in November of 2005, we were on our way to Arizona with only one piece of real estate left in Texas that required no maintenance and was for investment purposes. We ended up selling it a couple of years later.

Although it was totally unplanned, we pulled up to our retirement home on our forty-ninth wedding anniversary. That evening I took my bride out to dinner. We celebrated with a scrumptious hamburger at the Dairy Queen. I was sixty-eight, and five days later, Beth caught up with me again.

For the first time since I was fifteen, I was unemployed by design. For the first two months, we simply reveled in the fact that that we had no responsibilities, and we drank in the euphoria of our home and the beautiful blue sky in the desert. We learned the area and tried out way too many new restaurants.

Beginning in January I dove into my kind of activities. There was senior softball played on the awesome Liberty Field in Sun City West, golf at Briarwood Country Club along with amazing meals in the dining room and snacks in the lounge, and Toastmasters that provided me with the opportunity to meet some fantastic people in our neighboring communities. In less than a year, I became the president of the club.

I played softball for two years and learned that I couldn't slow my body down from the pace of baseball. With pulled quad muscles in both legs and my right calf along with a severe leg injury and a broken wrist, I spent about half the time rehabbing. After two years I eagerly decided to concentrate on golf.

I started out really bad and quickly progressed to simply bad with high hopes. As the years piled up, I moved up to mediocre and finally acceptable. My handicap went from a high of thirty to a low of fifteen. It took me forever to break eighty, and I felt that I might be able to continue in the direction I was headed when I contracted "valley fever."

Valley fever is caused by an airborne spore that is common in the West Valley, (thus named because it is west of Phoenix). Valley fever can be fatal if the spores reach the lungs. The medical treatment indicated that it could take four or more years to conquer with the use of prescription drugs.

RETIREMENT: THE ADVENTURE OF AGING

I had developed a respectful disdain regarding the putting of drugs into my body, so after running out of non-drug remedies, I began a search for alternative approaches. Only my hands seemed to be affected, which was fortunate. The most challenging affect was simply eating. My hands and fingers became swollen, curled, and stiff. Many friends from the club offered ideas that, over time, caused improvement. Brad Jarvy, Fred Fosberg, Bob Foreman, and Shirley Kosikowski each provided advice and product that showed positive results. Ed Cavello introduced me to a fellow that had success with a concentrated nutritional approach. Right up my alley, so I listened carefully and rearranged my supplement routine.

With all this help, I couldn't help but bring this fiendish spore under control. Within fourteen months it was under control and with continual application and relentless exercise, I am now doing well. That was quite an adventure.

Over the years I had the benefit of meeting and playing golf with some fantastic people at Briarwood Country Club. The one player and friend that amazed me was Jim Deuel. He and I seemed to parallel each other in playing well and playing mediocre to the point that we would almost always came down to the last one or two holes before the game was determined. As a result we played each other a lot.

In the spring of 2011, I began having severe knee pain in both knees. I figured I could play through pain, but by August I could no longer play golf, so I went to the sawbones to see if we could figure out the cause. He knew better than to simply offer me drugs. During our conversation he asked if I had any psoriasis anywhere on my body. I responded that I had something on my left foot, but it didn't hurt so I hadn't done anything about it. He looked at it and pronounced that I had psoriatic arthritis. The only known treatment is some kind of prescription drug. I suggested that perhaps the cream that he had given me for an earlier skin problem I had might do something for it. He said, "You can give it a try."

I knew that some external treatment would be better than messing around internally with drugs, and I still had quite a bit of it on hand. When I returned home, I measured the size of the rash and applied the cream. The next morning the affected area was much smaller. I continued the applications and within a few days, the rash was gone and my knees no longer hurt. I now have a new game that I play on a regular basis, checking my body for psoriasis.

When my knees begin hurting, I do an inspection of my body to find a breakout of psoriasis and apply the cream. The next day the knee pain is gone. Now when the knee pain (symptom) strikes, I find the psoriasis (the culprit), treat it, and I am fine the next morning. It is a crazy personal game I play, but now I can detect the psoriasis so quickly that it is always smaller than a dime.

Getting old is a hoot.

In October of 2011, Beth and I decided to take a trip to Texas and visit with our son. We had a great time with him showing us around Austin. I really enjoyed watching the bats flying from underneath a bridge. It is a nightly occurrence and always draws a crowd.

Our trip back was uneventful until I pulled into the garage. As I got out of the car, an excruciating and paralyzing pain hit my lower back and practically drove me to the concrete floor. Beth called the chiropractor, and he got me right in.

After examining me he directed me to get an MRI at the hospital. We went to the hospital and after a long and painful wait, I was seen by someone that was less than a doctor, and it showed. He asked me what the problem was and without any hesitation, he announced to me that I had a slight case of sciatica. He had another person come in and take me back to the waiting room after giving me a shot. The shot eased the pain, and I was told to wait and that I would be getting some oral painkiller. The whole time I kept requesting an MRI and had been told several times that I needed a doctor to order one.

I pointed out that I was in extreme pain and when their shot wore off, I would be right back where I was when I came in. All any of them could say was, "We have our procedures."

Isn't modern medicine amazing?

I also heard one of these angels of mercy tell an elderly gentleman in obvious distress that he would be taken care of in short order. When he objected that he had been there for over two hours, she responded, "When you come to the emergency room, you never get out in less than five hours."

Sure enough, a little after five hours from the time we checked in, my name was called and I received the pain pills that I would never use and was allowed to leave.

I called my doctor and asked if he could schedule an MRI for me. He had to see me first. We made an appointment, and a process began that would ultimately get me to an MRI a month after the incident.

Armed with the MRI, I went back to Dr. David Sheitelman, my chiropractor. He said that he would study it and call me.

He called the following morning, and we met that day. "What we are dealing with is two herniated discs, spinal stenosis, and you also have at least two, likely three, cracked vertebrae. The vertebrae are healed. Did you know about them?'

"Is that all? No, I wasn't aware of the cracked vertebrae."

I am relatively sure that the cracked vertebrae occurred in 1994 as a part of the back injury that derailed me for almost three months, but they were so minor that they had to heal on their own.

Getting everything worked out took some time, and I now have to ice that area of the back twice daily, once first thing in the morning and once before going to bed.

Again, isn't getting old a hoot?

Taking a nap is no longer a choice, now it's mandatory.

When you get down on the floor for any reason, it practically takes an act of Congress to get you back on your feet.

Taking a walk used to be an occasional thing, now it's part of the daily exercise routine, at least a mile daily.

Taking supplements daily is now as important as breathing.

Memory exercises are taken daily, or whenever you remember to do them.

You concentrate more on where you are walking to avoid anything that could cause you to fall.

Annual eye exams are accompanied by yearly hearing checkups. We are considered weird because we don't have hearing aids.

In 2007 a good friend, John Gustason, who had an annual physical exam, asked me, "When was the last time you had a physical?"

I said, "About twenty-five years ago." He became unglued and began harassing me until I committed to getting a physical.

I couldn't wait to see him again to "make his day."

I never got to tell him. I received word during a round of golf that on his last physical, he learned that he had pancreatic cancer. He died near the day I committed to taking a physical.

I think I will schedule my next physical for 2032.

I like surprises and aging is one surprise after another.

It is easy to get discouraged instead of enjoying the adventure of keeping going, but this is a part of life, and I prefer to live with a positive attitude.

As Jimmy V (Valvano) while fighting cancer said, "Don't give up. Don't ever give up."

"Getting old is a hoot."
The adventure continues.

Don and Beth 1959 home from Greenland

Fiftieth wedding anniversary, 2006

EPILOGUE

In the fall of 2011, having ceased playing golf due to the accumulated effects of valley fever and psoriatic arthritis, I decided to begin writing this book. Beth had been encouraging me to write my autobiography for some time so that our kids would know about my unusual journey. I didn't think my journey was very unusual, but it sounded like a good idea, so I took a class on the subject and got started. I needed something to do since I couldn't play golf.

I had no idea that it would go in the direction that it has once I delved into my personal history, with Beth's expertise in genealogy giving me the knowledge of my family's background and providing an enlightened base of human behavior with which to begin.

Being the second unwanted child, or if you prefer, accident, my place in the family was established before I was born. The possibility of my overcoming that situation and being accepted was beyond my control, regardless of any and all attempts that I made for the rest of my parents' lives. This situation was a double-edged sword that had a great deal to do with the man I have become. Although I could never do anything right, I applied myself to get prepared for high school, which I had to fight like the dickens to attend, and I worked harder and longer than anyone else to do a job right and to make friends for the first time in my life during high school.

Finally, I began to connect the dots of events, relationships with family members, and decisions by others, as well as myself, that had major and minor effects on the directions my life has taken.

The other edge of the sword was that I couldn't stop trying to be a part of the family. While living in Utah, I convinced Dad that he could go to college by passing a test. He did get in and ultimately received his associate's degree. Many years later, when he was in his nineties,

I drove from Texas to Chicago to attend his Masonic Lodge's annual dinner-dance. It was there that a couple of his lodge brothers asked me if I knew that Dad had graduated from college and that it was the greatest accomplishment in his life. When I told them that I had arranged for and driven him to take the test, and also to get his results, they were stunned. One of them apologized and said that Dad had never mentioned that to anyone they knew of.

For me this was the final nail in the coffin for my attempts to receive his acceptance.

I knew the moment was close after Dad's ninetieth birthday party, in which my daughters and I provided for him nearly one hundred guests. Within a week he talked with Bill and commented that his party had to have cost a lot of money. Bill, who had refused to help with the expenses, told Dad, "Don't worry about it, I took care of everything."

Dad called me and chewed me out for telling him that the girls and I had held the party for him.

When I was stunned by the call, he told me that Bill said that he took care of everything, "and Bill doesn't lie."

While Beth and I lived in Utah, our second and third daughters were born. My parents practically ignored the two youngest and made Alene their favorite. I had to tell Dad that all three children were their granddaughters and if they couldn't accept that fact, they couldn't come to our home. After a short period of awkward attempts with the younger two, I had to banish them again and again. Finally, we moved to Sandy, Utah, and I left the Indian School to force the issue.

It seems as though they couldn't accept having their affection cover more than one child in a family, including their own children.

My relationship with Bill was sporadic and one-sided. In the summer of 1961 after Bob's death, Beth and I worked at his home digging a relief hole in his yard, and in a warehouse for the company in which he was a partner. In 1974 I built a fence around his yard. In the intervening years, we never heard from him. The communications for our visits were set up by Dad. To that point Bill had never crossed our threshold.

EPILOGUE

The biggest and most lasting mental stress that I deal with to this day revolves around the startup of ESPN in 1978.

This book has provided an epiphany. For the first time in my life, I know that the two people I was taught to look up to had their own agendas for me and neither ever had my best interest at heart.

Having missed out on two opportunities to play professional baseball, I have spent my life working more and harder than I should have in what I now realize was a futile, lifelong attempt to forget my dream.

The conspiracy of those two prevented me from playing professional baseball, but they couldn't prevent me from being a ballplayer.

The almost two years I have dedicated to examining my life and writing this book has opened my eyes to so much negativity and outright hatred that existed toward me, that its discovery has freed me. As my attorney and friend A.L. "Dusty" Rhodes said to me years ago, "I understand that you would like to have some kind of a positive family relationship with Bill and your dad. I think as you look back, none has ever existed."

I have looked back, and Dusty sure hit the nail on the head.

On the flip side, I have had a great and loving wife for over fifty-six years that has provided me with so many happy moments, as well as four great kids, that I am happy and content to be JUST A GUY.

ACKNOWLEDGEMENTS

Beth had talked with me over a period of years about writing my autobiography to leave a record of my life for our children and future generations. Nadeen Borders, a teacher at Intermountain Indian School in 1963, had suggested that I undertake organizing an autobiography because, "If you keep going like you are, you will have a lot to write about in a few years."

I kind of brushed her thoughts aside since I hadn't thought I had done all that much. I pointed out to her that I am sure a lot of guys had served four years in the Air Force, completed college, earned a master's degree, played on a state-winning National Baseball Congress-eligible baseball team, and had a year of teaching experience by the time they were twenty-six. She had planted the idea, but I knew that the starting time would be a long time away.

By October of 2011, I was ready and began by taking a class called "Writing your Autobiography" at the Property Owners and Residents Association in Sun City West, Arizona, taught by David Poling, an outstanding teacher and motivator. As I progressed I continued to take advanced classes by Dave. Without his encouragement, advice, and prodding, we wouldn't be at the point we are today.

In addition to Dave, I thank James Andrew Miller, the author of *Those Guys Have All the Fun*, for the inspiration I received by reading his work.

My proofreader and adviser Karen Zach did an outstanding job of correcting my English, as well as giving sound advice on structure.

The greatest contributor to this project was my wife, whose encouragement, dedication, and perseverance kept me on track through all these months. Thanks, sweetheart!

BIBLIOGRAPHY

Birchard, J. (2010). *Jock Around the Clock. Xlibris.*

Evey, S. (2004). *Creating an Empire: ESPN.* Chicago: Triumph books

Freeman, M. (2000). *ESPN: The Uncensored History.* Dallas: Taylor Publishing Company.

Gallico, P. (1942). The Pride of the Yankees. New York: Grosset & Dunlap Publishing Company

Miller, JA & Shales, T (2011). *Those Guys Have All the Fun: Inside the World of ESPN.* New York: Little, Brown & Company

Rasmussen, B. (1983). *Sports Junkies Rejoice! The Birth of ESPN.* Hartsdale, NY: QV Publishing

Rasmussen, S. (2012). *The People's Money,* New York: Threshold Editions.

Rice, G. (1954). *The Tumult and the Shouting.* New York: Dell Publishing Company, Inc.

(Stuart, Evey. Personal Communication, circa 2002)

(Stuart, Evey. Personal Communication, June, 2008)

(James, Bates, Personal Communication, Oct, 2012)

Made in the USA
San Bernardino, CA
28 June 2013